DECLARING INDEPENDENCE IN CYBERSPACE

Information Policy Series

Edited by Sandra Braman

The Information Policy Series publishes research on and analysis of significant problems in the field of information policy, including decisions and practices that enable or constrain information, communication, and culture irrespective of the legal siloes in which they have traditionally been located as well as state-law-society interactions. Defining information policy as all laws, regulations, and decision-making principles that affect any form of information creation, processing, flows, and use, the series includes attention to the formal decisions, decision-making processes, and entities of government; the formal and informal decisions, decision-making processes, and entities of private and public sector agents capable of constitutive effects on the nature of society; and the cultural habits and predispositions of governmentality that support and sustain government and governance. The parametric functions of information policy at the boundaries of social, informational, and technological systems are of global importance because they provide the context for all communications, interactions, and social processes.

A complete list of the books in the Information Policy series appears at the back of this book.

DECLARING INDEPENDENCE IN CYBERSPACE

INTERNET SELF-GOVERNANCE AND THE END OF US CONTROL OF ICANN

MILTON L. MUELLER

The MIT Press
Cambridge, Massachusetts
London, England

The MIT Press
Massachusetts Institute of Technology
77 Massachusetts Avenue, Cambridge, MA 02139
mitpress.mit.edu

The MIT Press would like to thank the anonymous peer reviewers who provided comments on drafts of this book. The generous work of academic experts is essential for establishing the authority and quality of our publications. We acknowledge with gratitude the contributions of these otherwise uncredited readers.

This book was set in Stone Serif and Stone Sans by Westchester Publishing Services. Printed and bound in the United States of America.

Library of Congress Cataloging-in-Publication Data

Names: Mueller, Milton, author.
Title: Declaring independence in cyberspace : Internet self-governance and the end of US control of ICANN / Milton L. Mueller.
Description: Cambridge, Massachusetts : The MIT Press, 2025. | Series: Information policy | Includes bibliographical references and index.
Identifiers: LCCN 2024023044 (print) | LCCN 2024023045 (ebook) | ISBN 9780262552585 (paperback) | ISBN 9780262383462 (pdf) | ISBN 9780262383479 (epub)
Subjects: LCSH: Internet Corporation for Assigned Names and Numbers. | Internet domain names—Law and legislation—United States. | Internet domain names—Government policy—United States. | Digital rights management—United States. | Internet governance—Law and legislation—United States. | Internet Assigned Numbers Authority.
Classification: LCC KF3194 .M84 2025 (print) | LCC KF3194 (ebook) | DDC 384.3/340973—dc23/eng/20240528
LC record available at https://lccn.loc.gov/2024023044
LC ebook record available at https://lccn.loc.gov/2024023045

10 9 8 7 6 5 4 3 2 1

EU product safety and compliance information contact is: mitp-eu-gpsr@mit.edu

CONTENTS

SERIES EDITOR'S INTRODUCTION

SANDRA BRAMAN

No moment in the history of Internet governance has been so dramatic as NETmundial, a 2014 meeting called by the Brazilian government (with the backing of Russia, India, China, and South Africa) and ICANN (Internet Corporation for Assigned Names and Numbers), the global Internet governance body (with the backing of the United States). Discussion of the principles that should guide Internet governance going forward, and just how to better operationalize "multistakeholder governance," had already been underway. Edward Snowden's 2013 revelations of the extent to which the US government was using the Internet for global surveillance of government leaders, including those of Brazil and other countries already pressuring for changes in the extent to which the US dominated the network and its governance, however, turned what had been a cognoscenti issue into a matter of urgent concern and massive public attention.

Often the most important information policy issues are the most obscure, requiring detailed technical knowledge to even appreciate what the problems are, until those matters that are the most human crack them open for public view. NETmundial was attended by 1,480 people from 197 countries. Attendees ranged from vendors to human rights activists, and from government representatives to hackers. The specific policy problem that was the meeting's focus was the "names and numbers" system, the addresses and URLs through which we find each other and what we want to know and do online. The function of assigning names and numbers is handled by IANA, the Internet Assigned Numbers Authority, a corporation registered in California that, in 2014, the US Department of Commerce, via contract, had had nontrivial control over for a number of years. Human rights issues, unsurprisingly given public knowledge of US surveillance, dominated discussions.

As has happened in the past with other then-new information and communication technologies, the emergence of the Internet required—and enabled—new forms of governance. The "global" nature of Internet governance is one dimension of this, breaking from the "international" nature of the history of telecommunications networks, reliant on national representatives in decision-making fora established via treaties among states. Multistakeholderism is the concomitant feature of Internet governance innovations. NETmundial was a global acknowledgment by the United States that full multistakeholderism had not yet been achieved, that it had been playing a disproportionately controlling role, and that it was in full support of the development of processes through which that control could be ceded to others for more genuinely multistakeholder Internet governance.

By the close of NETmundial, there was agreement in principle that the US needed to decrease its role in favor of multistakeholderism that would include a larger effective presence not only for the BRICS and other countries but also for the private sector and civil society. The US lauded the meeting's outcome, but human rights activists felt their concerns had not been adequately addressed and noted that nothing had been said about actual power transfer processes. When, separately, a "NETmundial Initiative" process *was* set up, it soured quickly and died within a few years.

Milton Mueller's history and analysis of the creation of IANA and of what came to be known as "the IANA transition," in *Declaring Independence in Cyberspace: Internet Governance and the End of US Control of ICANN*, does three things. First, it provides insider documentation by a social scientist who was a very active participant observer in the events and processes described, those that preceded them, and those that have followed. The book is, in Milton's words, "a yarn told by someone who was there." As an informant Mueller has been and remains a uniquely keen, intensely present, passionate, and deeply knowledgeable.

Second, Mueller argues that although the United States does still retain significant forms of control, in fact the novel multistakeholder form of governance is still in play, effectively reducing the power of states in general. Third, in an analysis of particular importance to our understanding of the evolution of new forms of governance in this era, he takes the position that US control itself was never as total as imagined. (Other scholars find different types of multistakeholderism across the Internet governance map.) The history Milton tells includes post hoc assertions of authority, political economic tussles among stakeholders, definitional disagreements, all that operational fussing about at ground level referred to as "patching," and more than a few strong personalities. Mueller is among those in the last category, another reason to read this book. It is the third in his trilogy of works on the development of Internet governance, extending his analysis of the tension between what I have termed the network political and the geopolitical—between geopolitically based governance mechanisms and those based in the network—in *Ruling the Root: Internet Governance and the Taming of Cyberspace* (MIT Press, 2004) and *Networks and States: The Global Politics of Internet Governance* (MIT Press, 2013).

The book concludes with three scenarios for possible futures. In the first, ICANN continues outside of the United Nations system, but with sustained US government control, although more restricted than before, via the California-based entity that manages the domain name system. In the second, the United Nations system takes over ICANN, resulting in bloc-based tensions so extreme that the system rather quickly collapses into the third scenario—fragmentation of the addressing system that provides the functional social structure of the global. network of networks. Additional options include abandonment of the system altogether in favor of alternative relational and informational structures, globally or, more likely, in different ways in various kinds of locals.

We shall see.

ACKNOWLEDGMENTS

This book is dedicated to all my colleagues who shared the adventure documented in this book. Special recognition goes to the people who worked with me in the Internet Governance Project. This includes Brenden Kuerbis, who was there from the beginning; Farzaneh Badii, Karim Farhat, and Jyoti Panday: we fought for something meaningful; as well as the early collaborators in Syracuse: Derrick Cogburn, John Mathiason, and my crypto-sovereigntist friend Hans Klein. This also includes fellow travelers in the ICANN regime: Robin Gross, Avri Doria, Rafik Dammak, Konstantinos Komaitis, Tatiana Tropina, Keith Drazek, William Drake, YJ Park, Anriette Esterhuysen, Stephanie Perrin, Malcolm Hutty, Jordan Carter, Kathy Kleiman. Appreciation also to the friendly staff, Adam Peake and Grace Abuhamad; and the numbers people: Peter Thimmesch, Alain Durand, David Huberman, David Conrad, John Curran, Paul Wilson, Nurani Nimpuno, Athina Fragkouli.

1 THE STORY

Fundamentally, this book is a narrative, a story, a yarn spun by someone who was there. The story is about the Internet Assigned Numbers Authority (IANA) transition and the reform of the Internet Corporation for Assigned Names and Numbers (ICANN).

A *story* does not mean *fiction*. My representation of events holds to the highest standards of evidence and logic. Yet it is still a drama in the classical sense. There is a protagonist, antagonists, a plot, and a resolution. The protagonist is a governance regime, an institution-in-the-making, a political vision seeking realization. The antagonists are the politicians, governmental authorities, and interest groups who opposed ICANN's governance model and/or its independence. These conflicts had to be resolved for the regime to function. The problems and conflicts revealed themselves over time, leading in the end to the transition, so the plot has a beginning, a middle, and an end.

The question of *who controls the Internet registries* drove this drama. The Internet registries, also called the IANA functions, are a set of activities and records that enable Internet operators to assign globally unique identifiers to objects on the Internet.

That definition may make control of the Internet registries seem like a very small, narrowly technical problem. In some ways, it is. Yet what seemed small and technical turned out to be very big and political when people started fighting over the policy decisions governing these registries. It got even bigger and more political when a new institution was created to make those decisions, an institution some felt challenged the established international order in communications.

The Internet registries support global compatibility and a distributed, decentralized approach to digital networking—but they also create a point of centralization in the technical system. As central functions that affect all the participants in the system, they must be governed by collectively binding policy. When authority over policy is centralized, political struggles over policy decisions are inevitable. What makes this story unique is that the politics took place within the organizational framework of a private corporation—not the multilateral institutions created by states. That made ICANN a disruption in global governance. This is the story of how that disruption played out. It should be of interest to anyone interested in the digital transformation, because it is about globalization's clash with sovereignty in an increasingly digitized world economy.

Despite the rivers of text that have been generated about "Internet governance," none of it clearly identifies what it is that ICANN actually governs. It is not "the Internet" as a whole. It is certainly not the cables or radio waves that form the physical layer of networks, nor is it the content or the service providers. *ICANN governs the Internet registries.* Chapter 3 explains what the Internet registries are and the role of policy decisions in their governance. Chapter 4 shows how the registries evolved and how a community and a myth—the myth of a unified IANA—formed around them.

The Internet Corporation for Assigned Names and Numbers was the US government's answer to the question of who should control the Internet registries. ICANN was a bold institutional innovation based on policies conceived in 1996, at the peak of liberal globalization. It reflected a thoroughly denationalized vision of Internet governance, a regime rooted not in national governments but in the Internet community itself. This was a radical idea, a notion of popular sovereignty in cyberspace reminiscent of the emergence of the democratic political institutions more than a century ago. Chapter 5 describes where this vision came from and how it had widespread support. Its radicalism is still, in my opinion, insufficiently appreciated—even by many people in the regime.

The story then explains why denationalizing Internet governance proved to be a very hard goal to achieve. The obstacles were both internal and external.

Internally, the US government tried to turn an organically evolved, informal set of authority relationships among the Internet technical community into a hierarchical contractual regime in which many different stakeholders, not just techies, had a say. As chapter 6 explains, policy was supposed to emerge from "consensus" among these contentious stakeholders, but its initial formation was anything but consensual, and ICANN's initial board made many missteps. These startup problems almost destroyed it. While ICANN floundered, the United States kept control, as chapters 7 and 8 recount.

The external problems were as profound as the internal problems. ICANN was supposed to be a substitute for rule by governments. Keeping governments away from the Internet registries, however, proved to be tough in a world organized around sovereign states. Other governments saw ICANN as a threat. It made public policy decisions but was neither a state nor a product of intergovernmental treaties; worse, it was under the contractual control of one state, the United States, which relegated other states to advisory roles. ICANN's disruption of the international communications order was doubled-edged—it was supposed to be a departure from national jurisdictions, but US government sponsorship made it more like a globalization of American sovereignty. The world's sovereign states wanted the US government to share its power over the registries. The Internet community wanted to get the United States out.

There was, in fact, a contradiction between ICANN's claim to be a private-sector-led governance entity and the US government role. For reasons explained in chapter 9, in 2014 the United States recognized the contradiction and kicked off an "IANA stewardship transition" that would end its control. Policy-making power would be turned over to a "global multistakeholder community," just as the original vision had intended.[1] Before stepping down from its supervisory role, however, ICANN had to reform its bylaws to make it accountable to that community. Its liberation from the United States would be conditioned on these reforms. This decision kicked off the remarkable, two-year multistakeholder process documented in chapters 10, 11, and 12.

Finalizing the transition sparked a major political fight in Washington. The power struggle, introduced in chapter 2 and documented in detail in chapter 13, pitted US nationalists against pro-tech globalists. In retrospect, the fight portended broader changes in American politics and geopolitics. The Obama administration, champion and implementer of the transition, succeeded in its goal. The next election, however, brought to power the very politicians that had opposed the transition. Considering what happened next, a successful IANA transition might be considered one of the crowning achievements (or last gasp?) of neoliberal globalization.

The story has a moderately happy ending. The transition could not be reversed. It did not result in the dire consequences predicted by its opponents. The new ICANN realized, to some degree, the radical vision of Internet registry governance via non-state actors. The last chapter argues that that option now seems clearly preferable to the alternatives: continued unilateral US control, a transfer of control to intergovernmental institutions, or fragmentation of Internet governance along geopolitical lines. The bold institutional innovation, however, was battered, frayed, and modified along the way. Chapter 14 examines post-transition ICANN. It dissects three instances in which ICANN has interacted with the system of state sovereignty after the transition, revealing both the successes and limitations of the transition. Chapter 15 assesses the successes and problems of the so-called multistakeholder model, the legitimizing claim of Internet community self-governance. It argues that multistakeholderism, in fact, is not the critical feature of the regime. Multistakeholder governance is a derivative of *governance by non-state actors*, and thus a move away from state sovereignty. While the story is not over, we have achieved enough perspective to assess what was a truly consequential experiment in global governance.

WHY TELL THE STORY?

Did the experiment succeed or fail? Latent in this question is a bigger one: Is a world system based on territorial state sovereignty immutable, or is it changing as globe-straddling technologies and overlapping jurisdictional boundaries become a more prominent part of our lives? What does it mean to "govern" the global interactions of digital technologies? The answers to those questions are likely to be relevant not only to Internet infrastructures like DNS but to the governance of cybersecurity, artificial intelligence, cryptocurrencies, social media content, and other transnational communication services and infrastructures. There is a need for an independent scholarly account and evaluation of the ICANN experiment.[2]

For this reason, the book chronicles the transition not as something that started in March 2014 (when the US Department of Commerce announced its intent to pursue a transition) and ended in October 2016 (when the IANA contract expired), but as the resolution of an issue that went back to the origins of the Internet and its identifier registries. To function as a public medium, the Internet and Web protocols required globally unique identifiers to be allocated and assigned to network administrators and users. These resources had to be managed by registries. The sudden worldwide convergence on the Internet protocols in the early 1990s made it necessary to institutionalize the governance of these registries. In making these changes, US policy makers, the Internet technical community, and civil society advocates opted to create a global order based on non-state actors and private contracting. That experiment, however, was not complete until the United States ended its control. How and why did that transition take place? Why did it take so long? What political and economic interests impeded the transition, and what pressures led to its ultimate realization? It is also important to assess, eight years on, what difference the transition seems to have made.

A book-length analysis of the ICANN experiment is further justified because Internet governance has taken a sharp right turn since the transition concluded. As noted in chapter 16, public policy has become anti-global and protectionist ("protectionist" in both the economic and social sense). Technological nationalism, digital industrial policy, and concepts of digital sovereignty are ascendant in the United States, Europe, China, and Russia. Yet ICANN, which contradicts all those principles, still exists. How does the empowered Internet community navigate the tension between resurgent state sovereignty and open, global, self-governed Internet registries?

An analysis of the transition also provides an opportunity to set the record straight about the so-called multistakeholder model. ICANN and its transition have proudly embraced "multistakeholder" as the preferred label for the governance model that it represents. Indeed, the US government imposed on the transition a requirement that it must uphold this multistakeholder model. The transition process itself scrupulously strove to adhere to that ideal of a participatory, bottom-up, consensus-based processes. This account provides the first real breakdown and analysis of the multistakeholder process used, and derives from that a balanced assessment of the strengths and limitations of Internet community self-governance.

POSITION AND PERSPECTIVE

As the beginning of this chapter hinted, I was a participant in this drama. As a scholar focused on telecommunication policy, I first got wind of the conflicts over Internet governance in 1995 as a visiting scholar at the Hong

Kong University of Science and Technology. I recognized, as many others did at the time, that the Internet was a revolutionary departure from the old world of national telephone monopolies. I saw this as a historic change and was eager to observe and participate in it. The more open, informal governance arrangements emerging around the Internet made it possible for experts and advocates like me to jump into the processes.

And jump in I did. I joined email lists in the 1995–1996 period where I witnessed raucous but fascinating debates about control of the root of the domain name system and attempts to reform IANA. On these lists, I saw Internet Engineering Task Force (IETF) elders, domain administrators, network operators, and Internet entrepreneurs engaged in uproarious discussions. I began to attend meetings about these clashes in Europe and the United States, and I began to write both scholarly papers and policy briefs on the issues. When the US government began to intervene, I submitted comments to one of the Department of Commerce's earliest proceedings.[3] When it became clear that this community of actors was going to be forming a new global governance institution, the promise, frustrations, and intellectual challenge of that project sucked me in and kept me heavily engaged for the next twenty years.

As ICANN's policy development mechanisms first came into being, I helped to create the Noncommercial Stakeholders Group, initially a quixotic, heavily repressed constituency in ICANN but ultimately a successful attempt to gain representation and voice for civil society in the new regime. With that foothold, I participated in many policy development processes and internal organizational reforms, including the new top-level domain proceedings, the divestiture of the .ORG top-level domain, and several attempts to reconcile Whois with privacy rights. I met, talked with, debated, attended meetings all over the world, drank beers, and ate dinners with many of the decision makers and participants in this community. As governments reacted to the ICANN regime, I also became an active participant in a United Nations process, the World Summit on the Information Society (WSIS). After 2001, WSIS became yet another, even more expansive venue in which the Internet, ICANN, and change in global governance institutions were on the agenda. As part of a transnational network of civil society advocacy groups mobilized to insert their voices into the process, I attended WSIS preparatory meetings, the final summit in Tunisia, and witnessed firsthand the intense debates over the roles of state sovereignty and the US government in Internet governance.[4] Starting in 2004, when we formed the Internet Governance Project at Syracuse University, several colleagues and I engaged in running commentary and analysis of all these processes and the policy issues they raised. During the transition proper, I was elected to serve on the IANA stewardship coordination group, which worked out the transition plans for each of the three registries: names, numbers, and protocol parameters. I was also an active participant in the accountability reforms working group. In 2015, IGP moved along with me to the Georgia Institute of Technology, where we held an event in October 2016 celebrating the successful conclusion of the transition and wryly awarded Larry Strickling, of the National Telecommunications and Information Administration (NTIA), a "Certificate of Completion."

Throughout it all, my colleagues and I had a very clear policy agenda: a globalist, liberal-democratic approach to information and communications policy. We favored the permissionless innovation fostered by the Web, the erosion or elimination of national borders on information flows and digital services, the promotion of globally competitive markets, and the support of creativity and free expression against overreaching intellectual property lawyers or cultural protectionists. We considered ourselves advocates for a global Internet community, not a community divided into territorial states. Those attitudes led to an eager embrace of the opportunity for innovation in Internet registry governance. If we were going to build new institutions around the Internet, moreover, we thought they should be open, representative, and accountable.

It may be considered "unscientific" for a social scientist to produce a book about events he not only participated in firsthand but actively tried to shape. I do not agree. Participating in social processes produces superior knowledge of them. And if participation is a prerequisite for understanding, how does one participate meaningfully without having a stake in the outcomes or a position on what decisions *should* be made? If one learns about a social system by going inside it, one will learn even more if one tries to make it change, see how far it reflects one's preferences, see where the resistance comes from, see whose preferences matter and whose don't. While it is important to acknowledge it openly, I make no apologies for the fact that I was part of the story being told here. I believe that makes me better able to interpret the records and artifacts than a detached "scientist" building some contrived equilibrium model or feeding transcripts into a machine and blindly spitting out quantitative analytics of textual artifacts. I also think that the participant-shaper role does not necessarily conflict with the desire to be scientifically accurate and objective in one's analysis. Honest people advancing norms may have slanted preferences, but in the end, they also have a vested interest in accurately assessing the effects of their actions and the feasibility of their dreams for reform.

METHOD

My method was to construct an accurate and detailed narrative of how the relationship between sovereign states and the governance of the Internet registries evolved. The narrative is founded on two theoretical constructs: *state sovereignty* and *institutions*. Both constructs rest on notions of self-governance, as sovereignty is a way of institutionalizing the relations among states, and states are ways of institutionalizing the self-governance of nations. Chapters 2 and 6, respectively, define and explain these concepts. Drawing upon the rich primary sources described below, I focus on the role of states in the governance of the Internet registries and the degree to which a new community, not defined by territorial nation-states, institutionalized its governance responsibilities.

There is abundant documentary evidence for tracking these processes. The early development of the Internet registries, from 1971, is recorded in the IETF's Requests for Comment (RFC) series. All RFCs are available online. The US government's role in the formation and oversight of ICANN is publicly documented in executive branch policy announcements and in formal US Department of Commerce proceedings, notices, and public comments. The NTIA—the Commerce Department agency responsible for supervising ICANN and Verisign—publishes all of its contracts and amendments online as well as maintaining links to key policy pronouncements related to DNS, Verisign, ICANN, and the transition. Between 1999 and 2016, there were also numerous congressional hearings on topics relevant to the book's theme, including testimony from stakeholders. Congress also passed resolutions or proposed bills related to Internet governance, ICANN supervision, and the transition.

ICANN itself provides the richest source of information. There are extensive records of ICANN meetings and the deliberations of its subgroups. This includes recorded transcripts of plenary sessions at in-person meetings, long trails of documentary records of policy development processes, schedules, board resolutions, policies, and proposals put up for public comment, all online or buried somewhere on ICANN's website. The comments and position papers of various stakeholders in the proceedings can also be found. One of the richest sources of information about the transition process is the archive of the email lists of the working groups, a vast compendium of discourse about the transition and evolving drafts of agreements. My participation in the process, as explained above, made it much easier to navigate this mountain of documentation; indeed, it is hard to imagine how anyone not involved could make sense of it all. In addition, ICANN's public relations department has made video recordings of many participants in the process, including former CEOs, nearly all members of the IANA Stewardship Coordination Group, and some favored stakeholder representatives. Contemporary news reports and some scholarly papers—which are cited in endnotes or included in the list of references, respectively—round out the list of sources.

An additional source of evidence supplements the fixed documents: interviews with a few prominent actors in the transition processes. I conducted thirteen open-ended interviews between November 2021 and August 2023. These one-on-one interviews filled in certain gaps in the record by getting insider perspectives and allowed me to see how the interviewee interpreted events and test my own interpretation against theirs. A list of interviewees is in an appendix, along with a list of actors who refused to be interviewed or did not respond to requests. All interviews but one were recorded; in some cases, they are quoted in the text. None of us, however, wanted the recordings to be published, as this would have made the discussions more guarded.

All these evidence sources were used to construct a narrative explaining how this governance innovation came to be, why the US government held on so long, why it finally let go, and how the global Internet community inherited the responsibility to govern a critical Internet infrastructure—the registries.

With all the preliminaries in place, let us now turn to Washington, DC, in 2016 for a preliminary peek at the conflict over the transition and the issues it raised.

2 THE SHOWDOWN

On September 14, 2016, in a packed room in Washington, DC, Senator Ted Cruz presided over a Senate hearing titled "Protecting Internet Freedom: Implications of Ending U.S. Oversight of the Internet."[1] The hearing was the Republican senator's last-ditch attempt to prevent the Obama administration from ending the US government's supervisory control over ICANN.

Cruz's opening statement was a carefully prepared act of oratory, full of pauses for dramatic effect. The Internet, he began, "was invented by the incredible ingenuity of the American people, with the financial support of American taxpayers." "In the spirit of freedom and generosity," he said, "the American people didn't try to keep the Internet just to themselves but made it available for the benefit of all humanity." The Internet's origin in this country, according to Senator Cruz, justified a special role for the American government. "Since the Internet's inception," he claimed, "the US government has stood guard over critical Internet functions." This guardianship, which he said was based on "the First Amendment," has made the Internet "truly an oasis of freedom."

That oasis of freedom was now at risk, according to the senator. "In 16 days, without seeking the consent of the American people, without seeking the consent of Congress, the Obama administration has stated that it intends to relinquish the [US] government's historic guardianship and give it instead to an international body known as ICANN." He went on to describe ICANN—an organization ushered into existence by the US government itself—in unflattering terms. "It is not a democratic body. It is a corporation with byzantine governing structure designed to blur the lines of accountability; [it is] run by global bureaucrats, who are supposedly accountable to technocrats, to multinational corporations, to governments, including some of the most oppressive regimes in the world, like China, Iran and Russia." He went on to claim, "Once the [US] government is out of the picture, ICANN escapes from having to worry about the first amendment, having to worry about protecting your rights or my rights." America's enemies would come to dominate Internet governance. The Internet, he mused, might then be run "like many Middle Eastern countries that punish what they deem to be blasphemy," or it "might look like Russia or China, where speakers are punished or incarcerated when they engage in political dissent."

"Why risk it?" he asked. "The Internet right now works, it's not broken. What is the problem that is trying to be solved here?"

Opposite Cruz's position on the dais sat one of the key witnesses: Lawrence Strickling, the assistant secretary of commerce who headed the National Telecommunications and Information Administration. The NTIA had been the lead federal agency supervising ICANN for the past eighteen years; it was now prepared to end that role. In his testimony, Strickling expressed confidence in what he called "the multistakeholder model" of governance. He told the subcommittee that ending US control was necessary to realize that model. It would put the "global Internet community" in control. Maintaining the privileged position of the US government would discredit multistakeholder governance and play into the hands of America's rivals, who wanted intergovernmental organizations such as the United Nations' International Telecommunication Union (ITU) to take over ICANN's role. "I urge you," he said, "do not give a gift to Russia and other authoritarian nations by blocking this transition."

That September 2016 Senate hearing was one of the closing acts in the drama chronicled in this book. Nevertheless, it makes for a good beginning. The confrontation between advocates and opponents of ICANN's "transition" brought out, in the most colorful manner, all the key problems posed by ending US control of ICANN, while at the same time illustrating many of the ironies and misconceptions associated with it.

WHO CONTROLLED WHAT?

Senator Cruz repeatedly equated control of ICANN with control of "the Internet." This was a rhetorically powerful but distorted picture of the situation. ICANN does not rule the entire Internet. It only governs the *Internet registries*—the ability to coordinate unique identifiers. Its control of the domain name system's root registry, for example, gives it the power to develop policy for the domain name industry and to license organizations to operate top-level domain names like .COM or .ORG, or companies who sell registrations under those top-level domains, like GoDaddy or NameCheap. Conflating governance of the Internet registries with control of "the Internet" has been a common trope in debates over Internet governance for a long time. We will explore the relationship between ICANN's functions, the domain name system (DNS), and control of the Internet in some detail in chapter 3. For now, we can say that it is an exaggeration to equate control of ICANN, or even of the DNS, with control of the Internet.

Senator Cruz and many other opponents of the transition also asserted that the United States supervised ICANN to protect free speech on the Internet. This was untrue. The First Amendment protects US citizens from US government censorship. By vesting governance of the Internet's identifier registries in a private, nonprofit corporation, the creators of ICANN had placed them *outside* of First Amendment law. ICANN was not a state actor, either before or after the transition.[2] Thus, eliminating US contractual control of ICANN had no direct impact on individual free expression rights on the Internet.

That should have been obvious. Even with US supervision of ICANN from 1998 to 2016, governments around the world had been blocking and filtering domains, censoring websites, arresting dissidents for online speech, spying on Internet users, and regulating Internet service providers. Neither ICANN nor the US government was in a position to prevent this. In fact, the United States never applied and *never intended* to apply its own constitutional free speech protections to registry governance via ICANN. On the contrary, as chapters 6, 7, and 8 describe, the United States sometimes encouraged or facilitated deviations from those principles.

Domain name policies, however, can intersect with free expression issues. It is possible to disrupt or temporarily suppress websites by blocking their domain names. It is possible to regulate content indirectly by holding the power to grant or withhold domains from websites. Even the names themselves can raise issues of content regulation and permissible speech. Should there be top-level domains of obscene words, or a .GOD or .NAZI top-level domain, for example? ICANN had been embroiled in such debates since its inception. If control of the Internet registries fell into the hands of an authoritarian government, it would be possible for it to assert more control over speech on the Internet.

STATE SOVEREIGNTY VS. GOVERNANCE BY NON-STATE ACTORS

If the congressional showdown was not a clash between US-guaranteed Internet freedom and authoritarian states, what was it about? The real choice was between two forms of governance, two types of institutionalization. On one side was globalized governance by non-state actors, based on private contracts. On the other side was governance by a sovereignty-based regime, involving national governments, intergovernmental organizations, and formal treaties. This was a choice of historic significance in global communications and in international relations. It had, and still has, important implications for the evolution of the digital ecosystem.

Sovereignty refers to a state's power to make independent decisions binding on its own population.[3] It also implies the power of a state to regulate what comes in and goes out of its territorial boundaries. Sovereignty refers to an order based on mutually recognized territorial borders, "the territorial limits within which state authority may be exercised on an exclusive basis"[4] The absence of overlap preserves a state's supremacy and avoids competition and conflict with other political entities, a cooperative win-win for all states (except those who think they can grab additional territory at another state's expense).

That definition of sovereignty describes an ideal type, of course. Meticulous political scientists will rush to inform you that a state's supremacy is never absolute and that all kinds of external constraints and pressures limit its autonomy.[5] This is correct but misses the bigger point: state actors *value* autonomy and power, and thus will use sovereignty claims to gain them. States reliably prefer more sovereignty to less and resist anything that limits their autonomy and power without getting something in exchange. Moreover, states are engaged in constant disputes with other states about what is and is not a compromise of their sovereignty, which means that the ideal type plays an important role in structuring international relations.

With autonomy and borders at stake, it is not surprising that sovereignty claims played a big role in world reactions to ICANN, and in the transition. The Internet's rise was already eroding states' control of communications by altering the conditions needed to control information coming into or going out of their borders. ICANN's formation further challenged their autonomy and power, by placing formal governance of the Internet registries in private-sector hands and removing it from multilateral institutions. Add to that the unilateral control the US government held over ICANN and IANA, a blatant violation of the principle of sovereign equality in the United Nations charter, and it should be clear that the directions taken by Internet governance posed major challenges to a model of global governance rooted in state sovereignty. The first scholarly papers to raise the issue of sovereignty in cyberspace, in fact, were not attempts to apply traditional forms of state sovereignty to the Internet but claims that the "cyberspace" created by Internet connectivity was its *own sovereign space*.[6] Legal scholars argued that the Internet needed new "emergent law" because of the way it "cut across territorial borders, creating a new realm of human activity and undermining the feasibility—and legitimacy—of applying laws based on geographic boundaries."[7]

Even international law scholars paradigmatically committed to notions of state sovereignty have recognized that it is severely constrained in cyberspace.[8] This is because the Internet's technical standards are uniform globally, and the world has already gotten locked into the valuable global interoperability enabled by mutual adoption of the Internet protocols and joint reliance on compatible identifier registries.[9] Further, any attempts by states to assert sovereignty in cyberspace risk creating certain types of jurisdictional and technical fragmentation and threaten to undermine the open, liberalized, globalized information and communications order created in the 1990s.[10]

As chapter 5 will show, ICANN was supposed to be a radically new form of governance. It would be independent of national governments. It would be global, not territorial—like Internet connectivity itself. It would be open to participation by anyone, not just official representatives of national governments. The community of Internet users and suppliers would govern themselves. By pursuing the transition, the Obama administration was trying to finalize this new mode of governance. The congressional dramas enacted over ICANN and Internet governance were about this clash between sovereignty-based and global, private-sector-based governance principles.

Senator Cruz and his allies did not like what they saw of this new governance model. Cruz's opening statement could not have done a better job of expressing the nationalist, sovereigntist viewpoint. The Internet, in his view, was not a globally shared protocol, a software lingua franca that enabled the interconnection of tens of thousands of private networks built and operated by organizations of any type, anywhere in the world. It was, rather, a creation of *our own* nation-state. US supervision of ICANN expressed and promoted US power, in his view, and should stay in US hands. While Cruz was wrong that US control projected its constitutional values into the entire global Internet, he was correct that eliminating US supervision would give up a privileged role for the American state. Viewed from that nationalistic mindset, the transition was inexplicable. It would cede control of what they thought was a strategic asset—policy authority over the DNS root—to a global group, a form of unilateral disarmament that could only reduce America's power relative to that of its adversaries. Like Donald Trump, Cruz's erstwhile competitor in the 2016 Republican presidential primaries, the senator was upholding an approach to Internet governance based on America First.

Ironically, but with perfectly symmetrical logic, the Russian and Chinese governments saw Internet governance in much the same way. Although Senator Cruz excoriated them as enemies of the Internet, they, too, wanted sovereignty over cyberspace. Russian nationalists had been promoting a "sovereign RUnet," a nationally bordered Internet that eliminated Russia's dependence on a domain name system administered by a corporation headquartered in the United States and supervised by the US government.[11] Likewise, the virulent nationalists of the Chinese Communist Party had been implementing and promoting a sovereignty-based model for Internet governance since the early 2000s.[12] Although they found working with ICANN on DNS policy unavoidable and participated in the regime with their typical pragmatism, China's preference for governing the Internet through the ITU was well-known.[13] These countries hated the idea of an independent ICANN precisely because it was not under the control of governments. They differed from Cruz only because they were on the other side of the power equation. They wanted Internet identifiers to be controlled by their nation-state or, if that was not possible, by the ITU, a multilateral, United Nations agency where all nations had equal power in a one-country, one-vote system. Like the populist Republicans, the Russians and Chinese—as well as various African and Middle Eastern states—viewed the political oversight of ICANN by the United States as an expression of the preeminence of one state.

The debate over the transition revived themes from the late John Perry Barlow's famous "Declaration of the Independence of Cyberspace."[14] In that 1996 manifesto, Barlow had warned the world's governments that in cyberspace, "you have no sovereignty where we gather." Regardless of how narrow or imperfect its regime of governance was, ICANN represented an attempt to depart from the sovereignty-based system. When asked to whom ICANN would be accountable after the US government was no longer supervising it, the answer given by ICANN, the US Commerce Department, and supporters of the transition was: *to the global Internet community*. This appeal to a transnational community echoed Barlow's claim that he was a citizen of a new, sovereign political community. In the ICANN transition, this new, transnational polity was claiming ultimate authority over the Internet registries. Who constituted this community? Whoever or whatever it was, the *global Internet community* was founded not on sovereign nation-states but on the communicative and operational ties created by the Internet itself.

One could assert that this global Internet community was a myth, an invention, a dream, and in some sense, it was. Yet so are *all* nationalities— French, German, Chinese, Venezuelan, European. At one time they were all new forms of collective solidarity created and promoted by kings, rulers, or political movements seeking to assert and legitimize their power to govern. Their boundaries were once just as ill-defined and unreal as cyberspace's. The plasticity and constant conflict among these national identities throughout history reflects the demands of various communities for self-determination.[15] The attempt to make ICANN accountable to a new, transnational global Internet community was similar.

In the end, the populist-nationalist revolt against the ICANN transition failed. On October 1, 2016, the United States government terminated its contract with the Internet Corporation for Assigned Names and Numbers, ending its formal supervision of the organization and its control over the DNS root. The original vision of ICANN was enacted. The story of how that happened is worth telling.

3 POLITICAL OR TECHNICAL? THE INTERNET REGISTRIES

During the entire history and prehistory of Internet governance, there has been debate about whether decisions were political or technical in nature. Nowhere is this debate sharper than in discussions of the so-called "IANA functions." IANA stands for the Internet Assigned Numbers Authority, a term invented by the developers of the Internet protocols in 1988. The US government's control of ICANN (and Verisign, which operated the DNS root zone) came from awarding them contracts to perform a set of activities. Eventually these functions came to be bundled together under the label "IANA functions."

Senator Cruz and his allies equated US control of the IANA functions with control of the Internet. So did many foreign critics of the United States. ICANN and its defenders, on the other hand, often downplayed their policy and political significance, representing them as clerical forms of technical coordination performed by apolitical experts. At the same time, it became evident during the transition that ICANN considered it very important to remain the organizational home of the IANA functions, revealing that there may be important powers or benefits to be had by holding on to them. Further, from 2010 to 2013 it was not uncommon to hear claims that Internet freedom would be lost if these functions were taken over by the ITU or some other intergovernmental institution.

So, are the IANA functions a source of great power? To answer that question, we must first identify these functions and describe the activities included under the label. Only then can we understand what was actually being "given up" or "transitioned" on October 1, 2016, and only then can its implications for global governance of the Internet be assessed.

THE REGISTRY TRINITY

The IANA functions consist of the management of a collection of authoritative global registries. *The Cambridge Dictionary* defines a registry as "a collection of all the official records relating to something, or the place where they are kept." They derive their importance from their status as "official" records, ones that the public can reference for an authoritative answer to questions about who owns or controls something. The *Internet* registries are official records. They keep track of unique technical identifiers: top-level domain names, Internet Protocol (IP) addresses, network numbers, port numbers, and other numerical or alphanumeric values that a protocol running on the public Internet might use.

An IETF document from March 2014, "Framework for Describing the IANA," states that these registries are "critical to the operation of the Internet, since they provide a definitive record of the value and meaning of identifiers that protocols use when communicating with each other."[1] Put more simply, the Internet is a software-defined world, and registries coordinate the use of specific numerical values within that software ecosystem so that they can be *globally unique*. Global uniqueness fosters compatibility among networks and applications. It allows software developers and network operators to assume that the values they will encounter when interacting with certain protocols will be consistent everywhere. Without a registry to maintain consistency and uniqueness, the interoperability of the Internet will suffer; the execution of code will break.[2]

The registries encompassed by the IANA functions are often summarized as a trinity: names, numbers, and protocol parameters. *Names* refer to the authoritative registry of top-level domain names, also known as the DNS root registry. Post-transition, this registry is run by ICANN, which contracts with Verisign to maintain and publish information about what names exist in the root. *Numbers* refer to two types of numbers: autonomous system numbers (ASNs), which assign unique values to network operators to aid in the routing of packets, and IP addresses, the numerical values that identify the origin and destination of packets. Registries keeping track of the assignment of ASNs and IP addresses are now maintained by Regional Internet Registries (RIRs), though they were originally assigned their number blocks by IANA.

A *protocol parameter* is not a registry per se, but a category that can refer to many registries. Whenever an IETF standard defines a protocol that requires setting aside certain ranges of unique values, the standard creates the need for a new registry. If a protocol requires the use of a defined port number, for example, a registry will record which applications are using which ports. The IETF-defined standard for ASNs created a 2-byte space, which allowed for 65,536 unique numbers that could be assigned as network identifiers.[3] These acts of standard setting define the *parameters* or ranges within which registries must work. So, the protocol parameter function refers more to the *power to define* registries than to their operation. For that reason, the function is closely associated with the IETF's standardization activities. Any new protocol or application developed in the IETF might create a new one. Thus, the concept of a registry trinity, while useful as a description of the division of labor between IETF, the RIRs, and ICANN/Verisign, is a potentially misleading simplification. The third leg of the trinity, protocol parameters, is a higher-level concept that encompasses the other two.

Once Internet protocols go into operation, someone must *maintain* a registry to keep track of which values are being used and to whom they have been assigned. Uncoordinated assignments can produce operational conflicts (e.g., two networks with the same ASN will confuse routers and misdirect data packets). In some cases, the IANA itself maintains the registry; in other cases, it delegates operation and maintenance of the registry to other organizations.

REGISTRIES AND GOVERNANCE

It would be hard to come up with a set of activities apparently more technical and less political (and more boring!) than these. Yet they do pose problems of policy and governance. The maintainer of a registry will inevitably face choices: Who gets the exclusive right to own or use a specific identifier? For how long? What conditions are attached to its use? Is registration free, or is it a paid service? Can an assignment be taken away? What procedures must be followed to make a registration, to modify one, or to take it away? These choices must be guided by policy.

The Internet standards development community directly acknowledges a role for "policy" and "policy development" in the management of Internet registries. The Internet Architecture Board's "Framework for Describing the IANA" defined decisions to "make updates or additions" to a registry as a "policy role." As part of that policy role, changes to a registry must define "what sort of review (if any) is needed, the conditions under which update requests would normally be granted or when they might not, the security requirements of these interactions, etc."[4]

Registry policies can have a strong influence on the governance of technical systems and their users. Across a wide variety of social systems, records in registries signify and enable ownership and control of physical and virtual resources. Consider what would happen if someone could enter a local government's information system and arbitrarily change the lot number in land ownership records. How would anyone know what they own? How would taxes be assessed? Alternatively, consider phone numbers. These virtual resources are assigned exclusively to one's device as unique values in a registry maintained by mobile network operators. What would happen if an unauthorized person could change the registry so that data sent to your phone went to someone else's mobile device? When it comes to virtual resources, registries are not just records of occupation; they can determine control. Nearly all digital assets—including cryptocurrency tokens as well as domain names and IP addresses—owe their existence to registries of one kind or another.

As official records of ownership, occupation, or control, registries also become centers of *identification* and *accountability*. They allow third parties to determine who owns or controls a resource and to hold them accountable for actions or problems associated with its use. This is true of both physical and virtual assets. The registration of a corporation in a government's records, for example, not only signifies its existence but (depending on policy) may also make it publicly identifiable and subject to scrutiny. A bitcoin address or a domain name registration both coordinate uniqueness and mark ownership and some level of responsibility for how those assets are used. How much information about the owner of a registration is available to the public is another policy choice latent in the operation of a registry— one that became a major issue in ICANN.

REGISTRY POLICIES AND INTERNET GOVERNANCE

If it is to be globally interoperable, the Internet requires several central-ized, authoritative registries. The ongoing maintenance of these registries requires rules and governance: well-defined procedures and some kind of transparency and accountability on the part of the person or organization making or changing entries in the registry. There may also be debates about what is a good policy or a bad policy—that is, about who gains and who loses from decisions to make changes or additions to a registry. How intense these policy debates become depends on the economic and political stakes. This introduces a political-economy element into what appears to be mere technical coordination.

The international community confronted this fact shortly after Russia invaded Ukraine. As a punitive measure, the Ukrainian government pro-posed to ICANN that it should remove the top-level domains for Russia (.RU, рф) from the DNS root registry. ICANN's board flatly refused to do this, but if it had, it would have disrupted Internet connectivity both inside and outside Russia. Anyone using a Russian domain might not be able to communicate with people on an ICANN-supported domain. ICANN's refusal to follow the Ukrainian request evinced a clear policy choice: global Internet compatibility is more important than the foreign policy goals of any one government.

ICANN's creation in 1998 was provoked by a crisis over a seemingly sim-ple registry policy decision: Should new names be added to the list of top-level domain names? This was consequential because the proliferation of websites after 1993 made selling second-level domain name registrations under a top-level domain (such as *example.com*) a profitable, explosively growing business. Adding new top-level names to the root zone created val-uable virtual real estate, enabling new businesses to enter the domain name market. In the mid-1990s, this led to a chorus of demands for new top-level domains. There was also strong opposition to those demands. This was a policy choice, not just a technical decision.

The question of new top-level domains thrust onto the manager of the DNS root registry many choices. Should there be new top-level domains at all, and if so, how many? What is the application process? What if there were competing applications for the same name—how to decide who gets it? Because domain names were semantically meaningful, an additional set of policy questions arose over rights to use names. How would trademark owners be affected by new top-level domains? Could obscene or sacrilegious words be awarded as top-level domains? What geographical territories should be recognized as countries and given DNS labels? Should country codes be assigned only to governments, or could non-state actors operate them? All these choices had to be guided by policy. This in turn posed new governance issues. Who would make these policies? Who would be represented in the decision-making process?

Though deeply embedded in the technical system of DNS, none of these questions could be answered on purely technical grounds. They were matters of global Internet policy. Yet there was no global institution to make such policy decisions for the DNS. That explains why ICANN was formed.

PROTOCOLS AND POLITICS: A FRESH LOOK

The analysis of the IANA functions here illuminates the way a seemingly technical function is linked to politics, policy, and institutions. If a networking protocol such as IP is to be globally compatible, it requires globally centralized registries for IP addresses, domain names, and network numbers. This is a technical requirement, but even something as abstract and technical as coordinating unique identifiers requires humans to make policy choices.

This does not, however, mean that "protocols have politics," if by that we mean specific power relations or institutional configurations are "built in" to the design of the protocol. No. There is an interdependent and far less deterministic relationship between human society and technical systems. The operations of the technical system itself will require certain choices to be made, but humans will make them. What policy decisions are made is contingent on social factors, many of which are external to the technical system. Which organizations or persons have been vested with decision-making authority over the registry's policies? How visible and publicly contested are the choices? How high or low are the economic stakes? Sometimes the choices have distributional consequences and high stakes; sometimes they do not. Further, the societal effects of the choices are limited by the system's influence over society. Protocols "have" politics only in this limited, contingent, and interactive way.

In the case of the IANA functions, the political "power" achieved by whoever performs them comes down to two critical questions: (1) What *normative values* will guide the policy choices governing the Internet regis-tries? and (2) To whom are the people making the choices *accountable*? For most of the Internet's history, the primary value governing the Internet reg-istries has been *global compatibility*. The Internet's developers were deeply devoted to that goal. The people making the policy choices were account-able primarily to the technical community and the operators of top-level domains and Internet services, all of whom benefited from global compat-ibility, though they gradually became more accountable to a broader set of stakeholders, including trademark holders and governments.

If optimized for global compatibility, the IANA functions *are* largely cler-ical. A neutral administration of the Internet registries does not try to dic-tate the normative values or purposes for which the resources are used but establishes nondiscriminatory procedures for distributing them to appli-cants. It attaches conditions on registrants only to prevent interference externalities with other registrants. This largely clerical operation of the Internet registries, however, has major political implications. It reflects a policy that favors user choice and decentralized, private decisions. Global compatibility reduces the power of national authorities and facilitates the autonomy of Internet consumers and producers. The neutral administra-tion of a registry enables actors on the Net to do what they want, regardless of the wishes of their sovereigns or other authorities. This is not the absence of politics but a very powerful and dynamic politics of liberal enablement.[5]

The same registry functions, however, could be governed by other val-ues. They could be used, or abused, to regulate Web content. They could be used to tilt the playing field to privilege some economic actors over others, for example, by redistributing wealth or creating political or cultural advantages for favored groups. As the Internet matures, pressures to move in these directions have increased. How society institutionalizes the registry functions, therefore, is important. This is why a detailed analysis of the fate of the IANA functions and their intersection with arguments for governing or controlling global communications is needed. It contributes to an under-standing of how the administration of global technical systems by social institutions accomplishes, or departs from, the goal of liberal enablement.

4 CONSTRUCTING "THE IANA"

The IANA is a construct created by the Internet technical community. It was invented as that community began to formally organize itself into the standards development organization we now call the Internet Engineering Task Force (IETF). Starting in 1988, that community pushed forward an operation run by Jon Postel at the University of Southern California's Information Sciences Institute (USC ISI) as the policy authority for the protocol parameter registries.[1] They gave it a name: Internet Assigned Numbers Authority (IANA).

The authority of this IANA, however, was never formalized legally or contractually. Postel's status was based on informal cooperative relationships among a set of colleagues who were funding, experimenting with, building, and operating what became the Internet. In that distributed system of trust- and reputation-based authority, we find both the source of the ICANN regime's challenge to national sovereignty and the seed of the idea of a "global Internet community."

This chapter traces the historical development of the IANA functions. The narrative makes little sense unless one bears in mind that the Internet was an *emergent* phenomenon. That is, it was an unanticipated product of an open-ended evolutionary developmental process. The original inter-networking project funded by the US Defense Department's Advanced Research Projects Agency (ARPA) did not anticipate becoming the administrator of the protocol standards and identifier registries of a public, global, commercialized system connecting billions of homes, organizations, and businesses; it spilled over into that spontaneously.

ASSIGNED NUMBERS

Before there was an Internet protocol or an Internet, the small community of networking researchers funded by ARPA perceived the need to keep track of network identifiers. The earliest documentation of a somewhat primitive registry they maintained was RFC 349, dated May 1972.[2] In it, Postel published a small set of "Standardized Socket Numbers" to aid the networking activity of ARPA researchers.[3] SRI International, a Menlo Park, California–based Defense Department contractor, served in a complementary function as the network information center of the ARPANET. It had served in that capacity since 1971. SRI maintained a primitive registry of the names of computers on the ARPA network.[4] There was no Internet address registry at that time, because there was no such thing as Internet addresses yet.

From May 1972 (RFC 349) to May 1987 (RFC 1010), Postel and/or his colleague Joyce Reynolds updated the Assigned Numbers RFC nineteen times, on average about once every nine months.[5] Reynolds was a computer scientist from USC who started working with Postel in 1983. The early Internet developers recognized that protocol parameter assignment was an ongoing process, so they stuck in a disclaimer: "If you are developing a protocol or application that will require the use of a link, socket, etc. please contact Jon to receive a number assignment." In effect, Jon Postel was the registry personified. In 1983, Reynolds began authoring the Assigned Numbers RFCs with Postel and eventually became their primary author. There were no references to an IANA at any time during these years.

ENTER THE INTERNET

In September 1981, the ARPA researchers passed an important milestone. The foundational protocols of what we now call the Internet—that is, Internet Protocol version 4 (IPv4) and Transmission Control Protocol (TCP/IP)—were defined and formally specified in RFCs 791 and 793, respectively. The change was reflected in the title of RFC 997, a March 1987 update to the Assigned Numbers series. It was now titled "Internet Numbers," not just "Assigned Numbers." RFC 997 documents the IP addresses and autonomous system numbers (ASNs) that had been assigned to 100 or so universities, research institutes, military agencies, government agencies, and corporations.

The Domain Name System (DNS) came along shortly after; it was formally specified from 1984 to 1987.[6] Thus, the contemporary registry trinity of names, numbers, and protocol parameters was not fully in place until the end of 1987.

Responsibility for the new Internet system of names and numbers was divided between Postel and Reynolds at USC ISI and the Defense Data Network's Network Information Center (DDN-NIC), which was operated by defense contractor SRI International. In RFC 997, Reynolds and Postel indicate that the DDN-NIC played the lead role in maintaining the registry for ASNs and IP addresses. Just as the older Assigned Numbers RFCs pointed readers to Postel for "current information" about protocol parameters, RFC 997 pointed readers to SRI for "current information" about number assignments.[7]

DNS responsibilities were also divided. Postel played a leading role in defining the original top-level domains (.MIL, .GOV, .EDU, .ORG, .NET, .COM) and thus seemed to have policy authority, but SRI maintained the primary DNS root and served as the registry for domains under those TLDs.[8] There was no evidence back then of an explicit conceptual distinction between the policy role and the operational/maintenance role in the DNS.[9]

With the protocols completed and documented, the military considered TCP/IP to be an operational tool and not an R&D project, so civilian agencies started to take over funding for the Internet technical community. Starting in 1986, the US National Science Foundation (NSF) funded the Internet backbone and began providing support to connect regional education and research networks to it. Soon a transnational community of education and research networkers grew up using the Internet protocols. A Coordinating Committee for Intercontinental Research Networks (CCIRN) formed in 1987 and met annually until 1994.[10] Using NSF and NASA funds, the University of Hawai'i connected education/research networks in Japan, Korea, Australia, New Zealand, and Hong Kong to the NSFNet using the Internet protocols and identifiers. The Internet community was seen as a cooperative venture—"US led, but not US-owned," according to David Conrad, who worked at the University of Hawai'i at the time and later became the manager of IANA under ICANN.[11]

From 1988 on, the spread of TCP/IP networking into civilian society was becoming evident. As personal computers and office networking began to take off, the Internet protocols seemed to be the best way to meet a growing need for compatible data communications. The economic value of services based on these capabilities was also becoming clear. Discussions and debates about privatization and commercialization of parts of the Internet began.[12] And that is when the Internet standards development community started to assert itself and "the IANA" construct first surfaced.

BIRTH OF THE IANA CONSTRUCT

RFC 1083 (December 1988) contains the first documented appearance of the label "Internet Assigned Numbers Authority" and its acronym "IANA." RFC 1083 was not a standard or a list of assigned numbers. It was an attempt to describe and formalize the way the Internet Activities Board (IAB) and its collection of working groups developed standards and managed registries. The IAB was an informal governing board for the growing technical community; the working groups became the IETF. The IETF was literally inventing itself, explicitly defining roles, responsibilities, and procedures as an open public institution rather than a closed military research project. In that effort, the IAB created a label for its protocol parameter function, saying, "The protocol standards are managed for the IAB by the Internet Assigned Numbers Authority." It listed Reynolds, not Postel, as the IANA contact. Postel was listed as the RFC editor, a function that nevertheless required close cooperation with the IANA because (as noted in chapter 2) new standards can create new registries that need to be coordinated.[13] Since both Postel and Reynolds were housed at USC ISI, it was clear that the IAB considered USC ISI to be The IANA.

In its self-conscious act of self-organization, the Internet technical community recognized the IANA as the coordinator of its protocol parameters. This probably meant all protocols, including names and numbers, but that was not stated explicitly. Who created this IANA? Not a government contract. In RFC 1083, the authority for the IANA is said to come from the aforementioned IAB, itself an unincorporated committee selected by "the community." The community so described was the small one clustered around network engineering and Internet standards development. While it was centered in US research centers, universities, and technology companies, it did include people from the United Kingdom, the Netherlands, France, Japan, and Australia as well as the United States. Although it had gestated in the womb of the military-industrial complex, this community

considered itself to be autonomous. They began to define their own institutional structures and began to assert control over their own destiny. The
next step in this evolution made their policy-making role explicit and initiated a departure from nation-state authority.

RFC 1174 (1990)

The publication of RFC 1174 (August 1990) was another important milestone.[14] RFC 1174 described itself as "recommendations from the IAB to
the FNC [Federal Networking Council]."[15] Written by Vint Cerf, one of the
designers of TCP/IP and a leader of the Internet technical community, it
reflected a recognition that internetworking was going global, and therefore the authority to manage IP addresses and address registries needed to
be distributed to entities outside the United States. By making the case for
delegating IP address registries to foreign entities, RFC 1174 paved the way
for the establishment, in 1991, of the first truly independent (i.e., not a US
federal contractor) Internet address registry: RIPE-NCC in the Netherlands.
RFC 1174 also opened the door to additional foreign delegations in the
future. It designated an informal international organization, the CCIRN, to
decide which organizations would be eligible to receive IP address blocks. IP
address resources, in other words, were being treated as public goods in the
service of education and research networking, not as exclusive government
property. In short, the power to run an Internet registry was being given
to foreign entities, and key forms of policy making regarding an Internet
registry were being delegated to nonstate actors. Indeed, in RFC 1174 the
Internet technical community seemed to be giving policy guidance to US
government agencies—not the other way around!

RFC 1174 was thus a major advance in the globalization and privatization
of the Internet. It also contained a bold set of assertions about the locus of
authority over Internet number registries. Its introductory summary states:

> Throughout its entire history, the Internet system has employed a central Internet
> Assigned Numbers Authority (IANA) for the allocation and assignment of various
> numeric identifiers needed for the operation of the Internet. The IANA function is
> performed by USC Information Sciences Institute. The IANA has the discretionary
> authority to delegate portions of this responsibility and, with respect to numeric
> network and autonomous system identifiers, has lodged this responsibility with
> an Internet Registry (IR). This function is performed by SRI International at its
> Network Information Center (DDN-NIC).[16]

There are two truly remarkable claims here. First, it projects the IANA's existence backward into the "entire history" of "the Internet system," when in fact its formal documentation as an element of the Internet standards development process dated back only eighteen months. It was really the technical community itself, not "the IANA," that was continuous over that time. Second, it advances the claim that the IANA had "discretionary authority" over the IP address registry and had "delegated" operations to SRI. This was a breathtaking reconfiguration of the lines of authority. The IAB was asserting that it was empowered to designate SRI to act as the registry for numbers, when in fact SRI performed that function under a Defense Department contract and had contracted with DoD since 1971. In fact, Postel, Reynolds, and ISI did not have any enforceable "discretionary authority" over SRI. Or did they? No records indicate that SRI, or anyone in the US federal government, objected to these assertions in RFC 1174. Indeed, the US National Science Foundation (NSF) incorporated its recommendations regarding the provision of number registry services into its 1993 contract with the successor to SRI's DDN-NIC, Network Solutions, Inc. (NSI).[17]

By following IAB recommendations, the US government was recognizing the Internet technical community as legitimate shapers of Internet policy and relinquishing power to nonstate actors. In the assertion that "the IANA" had existed from the beginning and held policy authority over address registries, we see the *myth of the IANA* taking shape right before our eyes. As the myth gathered momentum, it began to claim that policy authority over *all* the Internet registries was unified around a single apex at USC ISI.[18]

What is often lost in accounts of this history is that, prior to the creation of ICANN, there is no evidence of any federal contract to perform something called "the IANA functions."[19] Postel's DARPA-funded research was for generic "Internet Research" and did not designate funding to anything identified as the IANA functions. In a 2015 report to Congress, researchers from the General Accounting Office were unable to find copies of any DARPA contract for the IANA functions. They only found references to a 1995–1999 contract titled "Tera-node Network Technology," which covered multiple tasks, one of which was "Network Infrastructure Activities," but did not mention IANA. That contract started in 1995, well after the IETF had invented the IANA and well into the beginning of the domain name wars. No text from government contracts has ever been cited that specifically mentions IANA or defines IANA functions prior to the creation of ICANN.

In reality, the IANA was an informal construct endemic to the Internet community. In an interview, David Conrad described how it worked in the mid-1990s:

> Number stuff was handled by Kim [Hubbard] at Network Solutions, Daniel [Karrenberg at RIPE-NCC], and myself at APNIC. We always viewed SRI as a parallel set of functions, the operational side, which was overseen by Jon [Postel]. So Jon would go and tell SRI, here, allocate this /8 to Ford [Motor Company]. Jon would write it down in his notebooks, and SRI would go and do whatever magic was necessary within their databases [to make the addresses functional on the Internet]. You could make the argument that it [the IANA] was an informal reality. It was an accepted convention: the functions that are now called the IANA functions were performed by Postel, or people under Postel.[20]

A contract? No. A formal, government-delegated authority? No. An "accepted convention" among the Internet technical community? Yes.

By describing the IANA as a myth, I do not mean to imply that the Internet technical community was being deceptive, nor that they consciously and deliberately misrepresented the situation. Rather, they were creating a construct that reflected their own organically developed institution. The IANA construct surfaced in a liminal sociotechnical environment where "accepted conventions" among the Internet community could effectively govern the system. Myths, in this sense, are not lies; they are lodestars. The Internet protocols were clearly on the cusp of global success. The intention of federal policy makers to turn the Internet loose into the private sector was evident. The Internet technical community contained the architects of the system, who naturally felt a sense of ownership over their creation. In their view, it made perfect sense for them to manage the critical identifier registries that kept the system unified and interoperable. They believed that technical governance of the Internet required an independent, unitary registry authority embedded in their own standards development organization. They believed that these functions should be performed by an experienced person known and trusted by their community. The Internet needed *The IANA*.

THE IANA FAILS TO LAUNCH

Informal authority can be very effective—until it is contested, its legitimacy is challenged, or its commands are ignored. From 1995 to 1998, Postel and the technical community's policy authority was challenged. The challenge came as a by-product of the opening of the Internet to the public and the NSF's decision to commercialize domain name registrations in September 1995. A public Internet that allowed commercial services raised the stakes of DNS registry policy. Money could now be made, or lost, based on registry policy decisions—especially the issue of creating new top-level domains. During that critical period, Postel made three distinct efforts to settle policy conflicts over how many new top-level domain names should be added to the DNS root. Each one was unsuccessful.[21] This happened because Postel did not, in fact, have policy authority over the DNS root. And it was not clear who did.

The crisis of authority prompted the stakeholders involved, including the US government, to institutionalize the registry policy authorities by delegating them to a new, transnational private sector institution. In the minds of many, that new organization was supposed to be a "new IANA." The point of this chapter, however, is that prior to ICANN, there *was no single, integrated authority* over the Internet's names, numbers, and protocol parameter registries. If the IANA of the myth had really existed, none of the turmoil around domain name policy would have occurred in 1995–1997. In creating ICANN, the US government was not building an organizational structure around an existing unitary IANA; it was rectifying a power vacuum. The creation of ICANN was an attempt to formalize the lines of authority among the Internet registries and consolidate them under a single corporation—while also trying to graft onto it entirely new, more broadly representative mechanisms for policy making. The US government's plan to *privatize* IANA, ironically, required *nationalizing* it first. This created the global conundrum that the IANA transition finally resolved: US government control of a global multistakeholder institution designed to keep governments away from the Internet.

The next chapter explains how and why that governance experiment took shape.

5 A GLOBAL INTERNET COMMUNITY

As conservative nationalists mobilized to stop the ICANN/IANA transition in September 2016, transition supporters had a surprisingly tough time explaining to a US audience why it needed to happen. Why should the United States "give up" something that seemed to be a source of power?

The simplest answer was that a transition to the private sector was already settled policy. The 1998 Commerce Department "Statement of Policy" authorizing the creation of ICANN, known as the White Paper, had made its full privatization an explicit goal: "The U.S. Government would prefer that this transition be complete before the year 2000. To the extent that the new corporation is established and operationally stable, September 30, 2000, is intended to be, and remains, an 'outside' date."[1]

As this passage shows, the White Paper had envisioned a very quick transfer. The US government expected the "privatization" to be over and done with before the 2000 elections.

By 2016, however, that goal had been articulated four presidential terms ago. Not only had the transition not happened, but the vision and momentum behind it had dissipated, leaving it vulnerable to challenge. The delay poses three questions:

1. What *was* the original vision that motivated the creation of ICANN?

2. If quick independence was one of the original policy objectives, why did US oversight last so long?

3. Why did the Obama administration abruptly return to that objective in 2014?

The answers to those questions are the key to understanding the transition and its significance for global political economy. This chapter answers the first question. Chapters 6, 7, and 8 answer the second question. Chapter 9 answers the third question.

THE VISION: A SELF-GOVERNING INTERNET COMMUNITY

The idea of an independent global governance institution had its roots in the evolution of the Internet itself. The Internet's developers, what we now call the technical community, developed and implemented Internet standards and protocols during the 1980s. From 1990, the entire world of computer networking began to converge on their protocols. As this happened, Internet- and Web-based industries and applications gradually came to dominate all forms of media and communications. The Internet's success followed and depended upon the liberalization of telecommunications in nearly all the world's leading economies. A globalized, privatized, and commercialized economy grew on top of that infrastructure. Its economic success was largely due to the creative interaction of private business and open, nonproprietary standards and registries. This new economy was regulated primarily by the market, not by international cooperation among state actors. Two momentous historical coincidences amplified the trend: the fall of the Soviet Union and China's turn to a market economy open to foreign capital and trade. There were now few barriers to the advance of a global digital ecosystem.

The United States became the undisputed center of the global market economy during the 1990s, with all that implies for structural power, technological leadership, and flows of information, capital, goods, and people. Under the leadership of a single global hegemon, which American politicians and diplomats loved to refer to as the "rules-based international order," the United States ushered in a system of globalized trade, transport, communication, and capital investment.[2]

While the Internet facilitated and thrived on this multinational integration, it only *reflected* and *expressed* US centrality; it was not by itself the cause of it. The Internet did, however, bring something new and vital to the table: an open, transnational system of software development and standardization— primarily the IETF, but supplemented by several other new standards and industry bodies, such as the World Wide Web Consortium. All were situated in the private sector and global in outlook, with no hard political ties to specific nations. The Internet technical community thus provided an essential meeting ground for fusing together a global digital ecosystem.

This liberalized environment made the idea of a self-governing global community both plausible and desirable. A new governance form, global like the Internet itself, was the logical extension of the policy development problems generated by the IANA registries. ICANN's formation reflected a belief that the governance conflicts over the Internet registries could be resolved by delegating that authority to "the global Internet community as a whole."[3]

Support for this vision could be found in three distinct stakeholder groups: the Internet technical community itself; the telecom and computer business community (and their advocates in the Clinton-Gore administration); and rights-oriented civil society groups. There were significant differences in the values and objectives of these communities, but their concerns converged in a solution space that included the governance model that eventually became ICANN.

THE INTERNET TECHNICAL COMMUNITY

The Internet technical community was a transnational network of computer scientists, network and software engineers, and education/research network administrators. Their power was derived not from their numbers or their wealth but from their knowledge of how the system worked. As was shown in the previous chapter, this small community coalesced around the IETF and education and research networks, and it began growing and self-organizing as the Internet opened to civil society and commerce.

The technical community explicitly identified itself as a *community* and infused its work with a combination of communitarian and individualistic/ meritocratic values. It was communitarian because it had distinct group norms and made decisions based on consensus. It was individualistic and meritocratic as well, however, because it did not care much about participants' nationality and organizational affiliation; its processes encouraged results based on technical merit, not on corporate affiliation, governmental sponsorship, or stakeholder group representation. The technical community was also based on voluntary consent and resistant to hierarchical, top-down orders. The holy scripture of this order was not a bible with sacred teachings but its common RFCs, which reflected a shared commitment to openly developed, voluntary, nonproprietary standards. Members of the technical community believed in the goodness of the Internet, the technical merit of its protocols, and the social benefits of universal compatibility. They thought of themselves as *stewards* of that system and were fiercely devoted to remaining in that role.

Though centered in the United States, the technical community was transnational. Europe, Australia, Hong Kong, South Korea, and Japan had similar education and research networks actively cooperating with the American academics. The Internet community spread worldwide as students from Latin America, Africa, China, and elsewhere returned from computer science departments in the United States or the United Kingdom or began working for Western companies.

The Internet Society, founded in 1992, was the first (rather shaky) attempt to give the technical community an incorporated organizational form.[4] While its efforts at formal organization were weak, interest in its activities burgeoned as the Internet gained momentum. From 1993 to 1999, the number of attendees at IETF meetings, held three times per year, went from about 600 to 2,300. A larger online network of perhaps ten thousand people actively followed its doings and participated in its activities. In addition to face-to-face meetings, they relied on email lists and open documents available online.

The technical community did not think in terms of nation-states. When tussling over new top-level domain names, a working group formed by Jon Postel changed the term "International TLDs" to "generic TLDs," because *international* implied that the domain name system was organized around national governments. Postel and his cohort wanted to consciously distance the Internet from that.[5] The full extent to which this emerging community resisted external state authority over their creations became clear in 1997–1998, when Postel and his community tried to create a new global policy-making institution on their own, independent of the US government.[6] When they failed, however, it became unmistakably clear to them that the Internet technical community was not in itself sufficient to inherit the governance authorities it sought.

BUSINESS AND THE CLINTON ADMINISTRATION

The second key community feeding into the vision was composed of business interests and policy makers in the US government.[7] The business interests included participants in the burgeoning computer networking industry, NSFNet contractors such as MCI and IBM, and commercial information service providers. It also included representatives from the recently liberalized telecommunications industry, software developers, and web-based businesses. The Clinton–Gore administration was enthusiastically aligned with this group.[8] Their main concern was e-commerce. They were interested in how the business potential of the new technology could be realized.

Since the late 1980s, information technology advocates had been anticipating the possibilities of e-commerce on what was sometimes called an "information superhighway" or a "Global Information Infrastructure."[9] When Bill Clinton won the presidency in 1992, these tech policy advocates, led by the new vice president, Al Gore, came into power.[10] The policy agenda of this community came together around the Clinton administration's 1997 Framework for Global Electronic Commerce (FGEC). The task force that produced the FGEC was formed in December 1995, with Ira Magaziner at its head. Its product laid out a comprehensive vision for what we would now call Internet governance. It was a vision that prevailed for the next twenty years.[11]

The FGEC expressed a growing belief "that an increasing amount of the world economy was going to be connected to the Internet," according to Becky Burr, a member of the Magaziner task force.[12] The FGEC described the Internet as "an appliance of everyday life, accessible from almost every point on the planet" and asserted that it would "revolutionize retail and direct marketing"; have "a profound effect on the global trade in services"; and dramatically "lower transaction costs and facilitate new types of commercial transactions." All these projections turned out to be true.

The FGEC coupled this appreciation for the potential of Internet-based e-commerce with a concern that uncoordinated and intrusive attempts by governments to regulate Internet commerce would stifle its promise. They saw different jurisdictions going off in different directions; Germany, for example, had adopted a distinct technology for electronic signatures that, they felt, would be obsolete in a short time. Their attitude was "Don't jump in and regulate before we all understand what's going on and identify globally acceptable norms."[13]

The framework articulated five principles to guide public policy:

- *The private sector should lead.* "Innovation, expanded services, broader participation, and lower prices will arise in a market-driven arena, not in an environment that operates as a regulated industry."

- *Governments should avoid undue restrictions on electronic commerce.* "Parties should be able to enter into legitimate agreements to buy and sell products and services across the Internet with minimal government involvement or intervention."
- *Minimalist role for government.* "Governments should establish a predictable and simple legal environment based on a decentralized, contractual model of law rather than one based on top-down regulation."
- *The Internet is different.* The regulatory frameworks established over the past sixty years for telecommunications, radio and television do not fit the Internet, due to its decentralized nature and to its tradition of bottom-up governance.
- *Globalized e-commerce.* "The Internet is emerging as a global marketplace," so the legal framework supporting commercial transactions should span "state, national, and international borders [and] lead to predictable results regardless of the jurisdiction in which a particular buyer or seller resides."[14]

All these principles were consistent with a turn away from national sovereignty in communications. Markets and globalized self-governance would take the place of territorial governments.

In the FGEC, we see not only a reliance on private ordering but also a notion of a global policy community. The Clinton-Gore administration published a draft of the framework on the Web and circulated links to it via email lists, making it accessible to a world audience.[15] While we now take that type of dissemination for granted, Magaziner was one of the first to set that precedent.[16] Burr says there was a "desire to have a global conversation about how to deal with governance of the Internet that would deal with its implications for the global economy. It wasn't about projecting American legal systems, but about understanding how you could create global systems."[17] There was a great deal of discussion of the Internet, e-commerce, and its implications for taxation and security in Europe, Canada, and Australia as well. But none of those countries had issued a statement or policy so boldly global in scope.

The FGEC recognized that policy decisions would affect stakeholders outside of the United States, people who had a right to be heard and to have their interests taken into account. US hegemony had put the nation in a position to see itself as a producer of global public goods such as new

Internet governance institutions. Some elements of this vision, such as the references to "bottom-up governance," had been learned from the technical community, whose leaders had acquired substantial prestige among American government officials. But the business and political community's vision focused more on legal and economic policy objectives; they saw cyberspace as a global space for commerce and believed that jurisdictional boundaries should not be allowed to hamper its development.

The DNS wars, which reflected novel conflicts of interest among registry operators, trademark holders, and free expression advocates, were raging during the publication of the FGEC. The FGEC acknowledged the DNS wars directly and cited the Clinton-Gore administration's decision to form an interagency working group under the leadership of the Department of Commerce to address the problem. In forming ICANN, the administration followed the policy framework set by the FGEC: private-sector leadership, contractual governance, globalization.[18]

RIGHTS-ORIENTED CIVIL SOCIETY

The third community consisted of civil society groups concerned with individual rights on the Internet. This included organizations such as the Electronic Frontier Foundation (EFF), the Domain Name Rights Coalition, Computer Professionals for Social Responsibility, the American Civil Liberties Union, consumer protection advocates led by Ralph Nader, and a variety of law and policy scholars from academia (including myself). They were initially drawn into the DNS wars by the freedom of expression issues raised by domain name–trademark conflicts. They became more deeply engaged when the formation of a new governance institution raised questions about representation, accountability, and the distribution of power. Despite their critical perspective they, too, supported institutional innovation.

As noted earlier, the EFF's John Perry Barlow had articulated the most radical and stirring version of the civil society governance in his famous "Declaration of the Independence of Cyberspace," which presented cyberspace as an independent, self-governing domain.[19] He told the assembled representatives of governments and corporations at the Davos World Economic Forum in February 1996, "You are not welcome among us. You have no sovereignty where we gather."

Perry's manifesto is routinely mischaracterized in ways intended to make it easy to dismiss. Sometimes it is framed as a naive claim that it would be impossible for states to control cyberspace, but this charge is obviously off target. Why would Barlow feel the need to assert independence from states so aggressively if he felt that it was impossible for states to control cyberspace? In fact, it was the threat of impending government interventions—primarily the Communications Decency Act of 1996—that had provoked his manifesto. Others interpreted it as an assertion that the Internet was a Wild West that was ungoverned or ungovernable,[20] but this is also a serious misinterpretation of his message. Barlow was advocating *self-governance* by a new, autonomous community, not an absence of governance. His declaration was clear about this:

> You claim there are problems among us that you need to solve. You use this claim as an excuse to invade our precincts. Many of these problems don't exist. Where there are real conflicts, where there are wrongs, we will identify them and address them by our means. We are forming our own Social Contract. This governance will arise according to the conditions of our world, not yours.

While much more sweeping and philosophical-political than the self-governance ethos of the Internet technical community, Barlow's vision was fully consistent with it. He simply gave a more grandiose, political spin on what they already believed.[21] The Internet was built from the bottom up by autonomous actors who were not motivated by national loyalties. Hierarchical power was out; cooperation was in. Intervention by traditional states was not likely to be helpful and was not welcome. The civil society groups, too, were enthusiastic about the current uses and future potential of the Internet and strongly opposed governmental intrusions into it. The intervention of states, they believed, would just bring surveillance and censorship. Civil society groups and academics had resisted the Clinton administration's attempt to undermine encryption technologies.[22] They had mobilized against the administration's attempt to subordinate internetworking to trademark and copyright interests.[23] They had been unified in opposition to the Communications Decency Act of 1996.[24] This was the civil society grouping that converged around the formation of ICANN.

While supportive of Internet autonomy, the civil society groups often sounded a discordant note in the deliberations around ICANN's formation. They understood more than the other two communities that decisions regarding the DNS root registry constituted *policy making*, not technical management. Registry governance was not for techies only: it could affect user rights and freedoms. This in turn made them quite sensitive to negotiations about process and representation: how policy decisions would be made, who would be represented, how decision makers would be selected and to whom they would be accountable. They knew that business stakeholders would go along with or even support restrictive controls on internetworking in response to the interests of law enforcement and intellectual property protection. Civil society groups saw that the technical community was often unaware of the ways their policy decisions affected individual rights, and that the technical community was sometimes too eager to accommodate the demands of business or political players in exchange for retaining control of the Internet registries.

Nevertheless, on the question of globalized self-governance, civil society had much in common with the technical community and business interests. All three, for example, supported globalized compatibility and connectivity in ways that challenged territorial sovereignty. The technical community valued global compatibility and thought national borders were "not relevant" to naming and numbering.[25] The push for globalized markets made businesses see jurisdictional boundaries as inefficient and harmful.[26] Similarly, civil society groups pushed for norms and principles regarding Internet freedom that were universal and transcended state authority. All three communities chafed at restrictions on the inclusion of non-state actors in formal intergovernmental institutions and sought opportunities for direct participation. All three relied on the easy transnational flow of money (which the civil society groups did not fully appreciate until authoritarian governments started attacking their access to foreign funding sources).

THE PROBLEM OF ACCOUNTABILITY

The crisis over DNS policy brought these three communities together and made it necessary for them to accept a common governance structure, with the US Commerce Department acting as broker. Despite some different ideas about Internet policy, there were key areas of agreement recorded in the June 1998 NTIA White Paper.

A new institution. There was agreement among all three communities that a new institution should be created. The White Paper said the United States would "enter into an agreement to establish a process to transfer

current U.S. government management of DNS to . . . a new entity." While
the technical community would have preferred to keep the contentious
policy decisions within the framework of the IETF, by 1998 they were forced
to accept the fact that a wider circle of stakeholders needed to be included
in DNS policy making.[27] For the technical community, the optimal solution
was for the new institution to be built around Postel and hew as close as
possible to their IANA construct. Business and civil society, on the other
hand, favored a new institution precisely because they were dissatisfied
with the way the technical community was handling the policy debates.
They wanted a more open process and believed that negotiating the design
of a new institution would allow them more direct channels for policy
influence and better accountability mechanisms.

Nongovernmental. All three communities rejected the idea that governments should set policy or control the DNS. They did not want a legal or
regulatory framework established by a single country, nor did they want an
intergovernmental treaty. There were several different motivating factors
for this. Some feared governments would bring in stifling, repressive rules.
Others felt that established state bureaucracies did not understand the
Internet functions well enough to regulate them. To the business communities, the most common and important reason was that governments were
territorially fragmented, and they did not want the Internet to be subjected
to a jurisdictional tangle. Similarly, for the technical community, universal
compatibility was the raison d'être of the Internet and a major cause of its
success; ergo, the Internet should be ordered on a seamless, global basis.
The technical community was also allergic to state hierarchy and saw their
consensus-based open standards process as superior to the state-sponsored
standards and bureaucracies of governments. As far as I know, no organized
stakeholder group, and certainly not the US government itself, was pushing
for retaining governmental authority over the Internet registries in 1998.[28]

Global representation, participation, and accountability. A third point of
(partial) consensus was that the new institution should be internationally
representative. It should listen to input from and facilitate participation
by all affected parties. As the White Paper put it, "The new corporation
should operate as a private entity for the benefit of the Internet community as a whole. . . . Management structures should reflect the functional
and geographic diversity of the Internet and its users. Mechanisms should
be established to ensure international participation in decision making."

Although all three communities agreed on this, they turned out to have deeply divided notions of how that principle should be implemented, and the breaking point of consensus turned on the problem of accountability.

The technical community was a small, trust-based community forged around standards development. The narrower technical nature of the outputs and the shared norms and social conventions developed over many years among a relatively homogeneous group of experts made consensus decision-making feasible. Adoption of IETF standards was always voluntary, so if there was no consensus, there was simply no standard. The technical community never had to resolve public policy issues that involved hierarchical regulation of business, nor did they need to choose sides in economic conflicts of interest. They were especially allergic to democratic methods such as voting and majority rule. Their accountability method was based on trust—trust in a self-selecting network of expert elders. Business interests were accustomed to relying on law and litigation for accountability or political lobbying. Civil society, in contrast, tended to support open deliberation and inclusive democratic methods to resolve conflicts.

In the formation of ICANN, these different ideas swirled together into an organizational structure that was neither the IETF-like creature that the technical community wanted nor the industry self-regulatory entity that the business interests and US Commerce Department expected it to be nor the democratic, participatory body favored by civil society. It was, in fact, an ill-formed hybrid of all three models that (as the next chapter will show) left the issue of accountability unresolved.[29] There was a global Internet community, and it had indeed been empowered by the FGEC and the White Paper, but getting it coalesced around specific rules, procedures, and policies proved to be horribly complex and slow.

6 "ICANN IS NOT FINISHED YET"

In July 1999, only a year after the publication of the White Paper, a US House subcommittee held a hearing with the ominous title "Domain Name System Privatization: Is ICANN out of Control?"[1] A powerful Republican Senator, Thomas Bliley of Virginia, was making an issue of ICANN.[2]

The chair of the subcommittee, Fred Upton, opened by noting, "Problems have developed in the transfer of the domain name system from the public sector to the private sector. . . . This impasse needs to be addressed before the administration's transfer plan can go much further."[3] Many in Congress were criticizing the Clinton administration's handling of the "transfer." They cited delays in the attempt to introduce competing registrars. They noted NSI's and ICANN's unresolved fight over ICANN's attempt to reduce NSI's market power.[4] They echoed widespread criticism of ICANN's choice of an unelected interim board of directors and attacked that board's early decisions. Holding meetings in private and an attempt to impose a $1 fee on all registered domain names were two of its most commonly cited missteps, but there were others.

In her testimony, J. Beckwith (Becky) Burr, the Commerce Department's lead advisor on Internet governance, came to the defense of ICANN and the White Paper plan. The delays and problems, she explained, were understandable by-products of the ambitious plan the Internet community had set for itself:

> ICANN agreed to do something that was literally unprecedented; create a private sector organization that encompasses all of the many and varied Internet constituencies, to do that on a global basis, and to create a process that would allow

for consensus-based decision making with respect to domain name management issues. Given that tall order, it is not at all surprising that ICANN is not finished yet.[5]

Burr's last sentence provides the key to understanding why the transition did not take place by September 30, 2000, as planned. A transition did not take place because *ICANN was not finished yet.* As this chapter demonstrates, ICANN was not finished when Burr testified in 1999; it was not finished by September 30, 2000, as the White Paper mandated; it was not finished in 2005; it was not finished in 2012.

THEORIES OF INSTITUTIONAL FORMATION

Why wasn't it finished? ICANN provides a laboratory experiment in the formation of governance institutions. In social science, institutions are defined as a set of humanly devised rules that structure social interactions in particular ways, with the proviso that knowledge of these rules must be shared by the relevant actors.[6] In the words of one political scientist, they are "sets of implicit or explicit principles, norms, rules and decision-making procedures around which actors' expectations converge" in a specific governance domain.[7] Institutions create a dynamic equilibrium among human actors on recognized rules and procedures. The theoretical literature notes that institutions arise from social conflict but sublimate it. They create order out of conflict by providing diverse, contentious actors with a set of mutually known guidelines for their interactions, facilitating more efficient cooperation and stronger social development and growth.[8] Game-theoretic conceptions of institutions also emphasize that these convergence processes are path-dependent and can have different equilibria depending on the sequence of actions and various other contingencies, which is why a historical analysis of their evolution is required to understand them.

ICANN was a radical institutional innovation. At a time when most established policy-making institutions were rooted in national states, its responsibilities were global, not national. The communities thrown together by its formation were diverse and had serious conflicts of interest to negotiate. This contentious community deliberately chose not to avail themselves of existing national-government institutions (and if they had, it might have made things even more contentious).[9] It was a bold attempt to start from scratch.

To form a new governance institution, competing actors must agree on what it is they are governing and develop compatible expectations about how decisions will be made. This process takes time, and the more diverse and contentious the collectivity is, the more time it is likely to take. The actors must negotiate new ways of resolving conflicts of interest, develop common expectations, make credible commitments to abide by the decisions, and—perhaps most importantly in this case—confer trust and legitimacy upon the agreed rules and processes. They must also have a strong enough interest in collective or cooperative action to overcome the tendency to pursue their own interests unilaterally or in other forums.

In its first five years, ICANN failed to institutionalize much of anything. There was one notable exception—the 1999 Uniform Domain Name Dispute Resolution Policy (UDRP), which provided a more efficient way to resolve domain name–trademark disputes by obligating registrants to participate in a globalized arbitration process governed by agreed rules.[10] UDRP was the first—and the last—time ICANN ever made a policy decision as quickly and decisively as everyone had expected it to. Everything else about ICANN was contested, unsettled, and subject to drastic criticisms and major revisions. As a result, Internet registry governance still needed to be anchored in and accountable to an established authority structure. That default authority was the US government.

An alternative explanation for the delay sometimes surfaces. Some have attributed the failure to privatize ICANN by September 30, 2000 (the date the US government had projected) to the September 11, 2001, terrorist attacks. While that traumatic event did have a major impact on US foreign and domestic policy, there is no evidence that 9/11 had anything to do with the delay in ICANN's independence. Indeed, the explanation does not work at the most basic level of causal sequence: the Al Qaeda terrorist attacks took place one year after the September 30, 2000, "outside date" in the White Paper. In other words, ICANN *had already missed the deadline.* Further, the records of ICANN, the Commerce Department, Congress, and the White House provide not a single statement linking a refusal to complete the transfer to the 9/11 attacks. On the contrary, they show that, while the goal of privatization remained, the US government surveyed the political contention and organizational chaos around ICANN and concluded that it was not ready to stand on its own.

The Bush administration's first head of the NTIA, Nancy Victory, made this clear in her July 31, 2003, congressional testimony. "The Department of Commerce, which currently serves as the steward of critical elements of the DNS," she stated, "believes that the stability and security of this important global resource can best be achieved through privatization of the technical management of the DNS."[11] To achieve that goal, she said, Commerce was issuing one-year memorandums of understanding to ICANN to make it "focus on improvements in 5 major areas."[12] Those improvements included some rather fundamental things, like "clarifying ICANN's mission and responsibilities" and improved accountability and transparency. Nothing in her statement mentioned the war on terror or provided any indication that 9/11 had affected the privatization policy or its schedule.[13] The US government was retaining its supervisory powers in order to push ICANN to improve. In other words, ICANN remained under US control because *ICANN was not finished yet.*

Why did it take so long? What would be required to "finish" ICANN?

Two challenging problems had to be solved. I will call them the *internal* problem—the need to institutionalize policy-making processes and some form of accountability to its global community—and the *external* problem—the need to reconcile ICANN's global policy-making mandate with the powers of sovereign states.

Both problems were so profound that they remained unresolved for nearly two decades. Central to the thesis of this book is that neither problem could find a lasting, stable equilibrium without the surrender of US government control. As long as the US government was the real source of accountability, ICANN's internal policy development processes lacked acceptance and credibility; as long as one government—the United States—controlled the Internet registries, ICANN's relationship to state sovereignty was contradictory and unstable. By relinquishing control, the United States resolved the internal and external problems *at the same time.*

THE INTERNAL PROBLEM

All new governance institutions face bootstrapping problems—that is, the problem of putting into place authority structures and procedures when there are no existing authority structures and procedures to use.[14] An organization must be incorporated, but who would run it? The organization's board must be constituted, but who would select the people on it? Bylaws must be created, and rules and procedures for policy making developed, but where would they come from in the absence of defined procedures and decision-making authorities? Eventually, the procedures must be used and their results accepted by the contending parties. Difficult under the best of circumstances, ICANN's bootstrapping process faced intense factional disagreements over policy outcomes and power struggles over representation of the involved communities.

After the White Paper, Jon Postel and his allies in the technical community had come up with an organizational proposal for what they liked to call the "New IANA." There would be three supporting organizations (SOs), one for each part of the Internet registry trinity: a Protocols Supporting Organization (PSO), an Address Supporting Organization (the ASO), and a Domain Name Supporting Organization (DNSO). Each of these would be relatively autonomous entities that would develop registry policy in a bottom-up manner, but each had to be recognized and approved by the new IANA's board of directors. A nonprofit corporation established under California's Nonprofit Public Benefit Corporation law would recognize and supervise the SOs. IANA was still conceived as the apex of the trinity, but its process was meant to be bottom-up like the IETF's.

It sounded straightforward. Yet the attempt to implement this blueprint unraveled from 1999 to 2003. The reason why is clear in retrospect. The Internet technical community had created an informal, distributed system for the governance of Internet registries. It had evolved organically, and its actors were accustomed to working as peers in a nonhierarchical environment.[15] The US government's "privatization" plan, in contrast, tried to centralize these functions in the hands of a single, formal corporate entity, ICANN, which would take over an IANA that, as we have seen, was not really a single organizational entity. This misconception made the government think of its task as "privatizing IANA"—that is, pushing this centralized entity out of the government and into a private sector receptacle. Complicating things further, the Commerce Department, in deference to the Internet community's bottom-up ethos, asked this corporation to be created and accepted by "community consensus." Yet the community from which it demanded consensus was no longer just the techies in the IETF who had worked together for twenty years but also competing business interests, trademark lawyers, civil society organizations from all over the world, and a few foreign governments. Consensus among these groups was much harder to find.

By formally delegating the IANA functions to this corporation, moreover, the US government was creating a hierarchy, a formal legal entity that was supposed to control the IANA functions in a top-down manner. Because of the need for a single centralized DNS root, it would have no competitors, no members to which it would be accountable, and (eventually) no governments supervising it.

Suddenly, there was hierarchical power to be had. A small group of people connected to Postel, his lawyer, the US government, and its consultative partners then appointed themselves the controllers of this hierarchy. This was the ICANN initial board, which was announced on October 26, 1998.

In my book *Ruling the Root*, I documented Postel's and the Internet Society's aggressive assertions of authority over the DNS root and their willingness to challenge even the US government to maintain their control.[16] After the NTIA shot down these efforts, the faction backing Postel succeeded in pushing the United States to abandon a direct, government-mediated privatization process and instead issue an open call for a "new IANA" generated by the Internet community. Because Postel and his allies firmly believed that they *were* the Internet community, they saw the White Paper's call for a new corporation as an opportunity to reclaim the initiative they had lost in 1996–1997. The composition of the initial board, however, reflected government pressure to include business interests in IANA governance.

One could argue that the need for bootstrapping made a unilateral move to incorporate under a self-selected board inevitable, even justified. The fact remains, however, that as soon as the initial board was announced, it alienated almost everyone who was not privy to the secret negotiations that led to its selection. Who were these people and to whom were they accountable? Sadly, the one person everyone respected, the only one who could lend this gang of strangers legitimacy—Jon Postel—died ten days before the move was made public.

Shorn of its main claim to legitimacy, the initial board then worsened their situation by making a series of unpopular decisions based on an arrogant belief that their selection by Postel and his advisors in a closed process had given them some kind of mandate from the global Internet community.[17] The board tried to force country code top-level domains (ccTLDs), which had been delegated their domains by Postel years earlier, to sign contracts, the contents of which were dictated by ICANN. They also tried to assert more authority over IP address registries, which predated ICANN and had formed their own communities of interest. David Conrad, an insider in the number registry community at the time, stated:

there were so many missteps by the original staff of ICANN, Louis [Touton], Mike [Roberts] and Esther [Dyson]. So many assertions of control, so many efforts that were not appreciated by the existing communities. I was in meetings with ARIN and ICANN [in 2002–2003] and was annoyed at the way ICANN . . . attempted to assert control over the address space, just like the way they had attempted to assert control over the ccTLD space: you have to bow down to us, and we will give you what you need. That didn't go over very well.[18]

This was the first manifestation of the accountability problem that would haunt ICANN until the transition.

Nevertheless, while nominally in possession of hierarchical power over a globally distributed system, ICANN quickly discovered that they could not assert much real authority over it. NSI, which held operational control of the DNS root and controlled almost all of the domain name registration market, had become an enemy and was not volunteering to subject itself to ICANN's proposed regulatory regime. ICANN's attempts to assert contractual control over ccTLDs were resisted or ignored, but ICANN was in no position to knock entire countries off the Internet by taking the delegations away.

As for the numbers registries (RIRs), large swaths of the IPv4 address space had already been privatized—either given to private organizations without any contractual obligations or delegated to private, nonprofit regional registries in Europe, Asia, and North America. All the regional number registries were supporters of IETF and Postel and considered IANA to be the source of their number allocations. The new ICANN, however, rejected their first attempt to form the Address Supporting Organization. The RIRs interpreted this as an attempt by ICANN to centralize power over number allocation at their expense. Two years of tough negotiations ensued.[19] In 2003, the RIRs formed the Number Resource Organization, an independent consortium.[20] A November 2003 letter from the NRO to ICANN made it clear that the RIRs could operate the number registries without ICANN if they had to. It also shows that more than three years after the White Paper's "outside date" to make ICANN independent, the RIRs thought it reasonable to prepare for the possibility of ICANN's failure.

Another IANA function listed by the White Paper was the operation of root servers. Thirteen servers around the world provided redundancy and geographic diversity in the resolution of top-level domain names.[21] The White Paper had authorized ICANN to institutionalize the root server operators (RSOs). An agreement between the NTIA and ICANN set September 30, 2000—that date again—as the deadline for the completion of the task.[22] Yet ICANN never accomplished that task. Postel's relationship to the RSOs had been based entirely on informal delegation decisions. There were no written, binding contracts with *any* RSO, nothing defining their rights and obligations, and no formal process in place to eliminate an existing RSO or select a new one. The root server "system" was just hanging together based on voluntary cooperation and common DNS software utilization. (By 2024, ICANN still had not taken over and formalized RSO administration.)

Even the RFC editor functions and protocol parameter registry, which Postel and USC ISI really had controlled, did not move smoothly into ICANN. The IETF's leaders believed that Postel's operation at USC ISI had been delegated the IANA functions by the Internet Architecture Board (IAB).[23] The US government, on the other hand, saw the IANA functions as a contract from the Commerce Department. Hence, the IETF was blindsided by a February 1999 announcement in *Commerce Business Daily* that the NTIA planned to issue a sole-source contract to ICANN to perform the IANA functions. The IETF leaders wrote a shocked letter to ICANN's board chair indicating that they had no idea there was an "IANA contract" that could be taken over by the NTIA. "What is the relationship between the IETF and ICANN in general?" they asked.[24] Eventually, the IETF and ICANN clarified their relationship, signing a memorandum of understanding in June 2000 that became RFC 2860.[25] It recognized that "the IANA technical team is now part of ICANN" but required ICANN's IANA to manage protocol parameter assignments "according to criteria and procedures specified in IETF RFCs."[26]

ACCOUNTABILITY AND MEMBERSHIP

In reviewing the responses to its call for a new corporation to come forward and take over the IANA functions, the NTIA was warned repeatedly that whoever or whatever this corporation would be had to be accountable the broader community. The NTIA agreed, but the group incorporating ICANN left accountability mechanisms unspecified. Suspicious of the initial board, the engaged community advocated for a voting membership as a way to keep the new entity accountable, and the NTIA agreed. Responding to pressure from the community and from the Commerce Department, ICANN's initial board and staff grudgingly agreed to create a voting membership, even though they hated the idea. Membership was to be open to the global Internet community, regardless of nationality. It promised to allow those members to elect half of the board. (The other half would be selected by the supporting organizations, ASO, GNSO, and ccNSO.) ICANN created a membership advisory committee that attracted foundation support and enthusiastic civil society activists excited at the prospect of global democracy.[27]

After making that promise, ICANN tried for two years to break it. ICANN's lawyers were unrelentingly hostile to any form of membership, as it would give power to participants at the expense of the corporation. It took more than a year for the board to define what membership would look like, and it did not hold elections until 2000. Even then, ICANN drastically changed the idea of a global voting membership. Now, members would elect only five board members, and instead of global voting the electorate would be segregated into five world regions. This meant that the initial self-selected board would still be in control, regardless of the election outcome.

Despite successfully holding an election, and despite the severe limits on membership and elections, ICANN's managers still deemed a voting membership a threat.[28] The board modified the bylaws to abolish membership and replaced it with a new At Large Advisory Committee (ALAC) based on a complicated organizational and regional hierarchy intended to bring in participants without giving them any power.[29] The corporation would fund people to represent "individual Internet users" at their meetings. ALAC would be entirely a creature of ICANN, Inc. It took another five years for the ALAC to be fully in place.

In essence, ICANN evaded true accountability for years. As a substitute, it offered endless forms of participation: open working groups, review committees, comment periods, advisory committees.[30] ICANN considered itself accountable because people could participate in its processes and express their views. Its board and staff, however, still held all the decision-making authority. The board could modify the bylaws at will. They could disregard what the participants and the supporting organizations said. ICANN had no shareholders, no members, and no market competition. Only the US government held any external disciplinary authority over it.

THE SPECIAL CASE OF THE NAMES SUPPORTING ORGANIZATION
The attempt to create a domain name supporting organization turned into the biggest mess of all. We must begin by noting that until October 1998,

it was NSI, not Postel or ICANN, that was really in operational control of the domain names registry. And NSI was no longer an obscure government contractor; it was now a commercial registry making millions of dollars from the sale of domain name registrations in .COM, .NET, and .ORG. These domains constituted about 90 percent of the market, making NSI effectively a monopoly in the registration of generic (non–country code) names. The emerging community wanted to introduce competition in the domain name market by allowing competing registrars to sell domains in .COM, .NET and .ORG and by adding new top-level domains. NSI naturally resisted this, as it would be a major reduction of its market power.

Yet a California nonprofit benefit corporation like ICANN had no authority to force NSI into its regime. Only the US government had any formal control over NSI. It came from a 1993 Cooperative Agreement with the National Science Foundation that had been taken over by the Commerce Department.[31] The Commerce Department proceeded to use amendments to the Cooperative Agreement as a means of regulating the prices and performance of NSI. Its goal was to subject the company "to rules emerging from the consensus based, bottom-up process spelled out in the White Paper."[32] This, too, took time (and litigation). From 1998 to 2004, all the key policy decisions regarding competition in the domain name registration market were made by the NTIA, not by ICANN's putative policy development organization, the Domain Name Supporting Organization (DNSO).[33]

The NTIA's attempt to regulate NSI led to the October 1998 amendment to the Cooperative Agreement that gave the US government control of any changes to the DNS root zone.[34] This action mooted an antitrust lawsuit against NSI,[35] but it also made the US government the de facto policy authority over the DNS root registry, setting in motion the geopolitical conflicts that would dog ICANN for the next fifteen years.

While the NTIA eventually succeeded in roping NSI into the ICANN regime, ICANN in its first ten years never succeeded in creating an efficient, widely accepted policy-making process for domain names. ICANN did not have a preexisting, organized Names community to draw upon. All it had was a bunch of interest groups from business, civil society, and aspiring domain name registration companies that had converged around the making of ICANN itself. The protocols and numbers supporting organizations were rooted in more homogeneous technical community entities that predated ICANN. The names supporting organization, on the other hand, took the form of an ICANN-designed and funded legislative body. In other words, it was not the type of bottom-up supporting organization Postel had envisioned; it was a part of ICANN itself. ICANN took it upon itself to define and recognize "constituencies" representing different stakeholder groups: businesses, intellectual property interests, connectivity providers, registrars, registries, country code registries, and noncommercial domain name holders.

As ICANN tried to create a policy-making organ for domain names out of nothing, its representational structure, procedures, and authority were in constant turmoil. Although it tried to model the names policy development process on IETF-style working groups, decisions based on bottom-up consensus simply did not work when domain name policy making was involved. The differences were readily apparent to policy experts but ignored by ICANN's founders, who were intent on imitating the prestigious technical community. One obvious difference is that compliance with IETF standards is voluntary. No one who disagreed with an IETF standard had to follow it. ICANN policies, on the other hand, would be imposed upon all domain name registries, registrars, and registrants whether they liked them or not. Another key difference: IETF standards aimed at ensuring technical compatibility, not economic regulation. Most of the time, compatibility is a positive sum game for all players. Trademark protection policies or industry regulations, in contrast, involved choices with clear winners and losers. Broader protection for trademark holders means less freedom for registrants, for example. This also made agreement on procedures more difficult. Open working groups could be stacked. The power to "declare consensus" could be abused by working group chairs representing a special interest. Moreover, the DNSO's original representational structure was tilted, overweighting business interests whose main goal was to maximize protection for trademark holders. Further, if standards developers in IETF cannot agree—if there is no consensus—the IETF simply does not produce a standard. In ICANN, in contrast, interest groups and governments often demanded that policies solve problems whether or not a consensus could be found, and dissenting opinions would be ignored. All of these factors made ICANN policy development radically different from IETF working groups.

In 2002, in the wake of ICANN's battles to rope them into its contractual regime, the country code top-level domain managers seceded from the

DNSO and formed their own supporting organization, the Country Code Names Supporting Organization (ccNSO).[36] The DNSO became the GNSO (Generic Names Supporting Organization) That was only the first of many restructurings and changes in the domain name supporting organization. The core goal of institutionalization—a settled set of norms, rules, and procedures around which "actor expectations converge"—remained out of reach for a long time. ICANN overhauled the representational structure of the GNSO from 2007–2009 to rectify representational imbalances—a good move in terms of fairness. It infuriated the business interests, however, who mounted a counterattack that kept representational arrangements in flux for another two years.[37] In the meantime, no one really accepted the results of GNSO processes, anyway. With enough lobbying and backroom pressure, they could be bypassed or reversed. During the implementation phase, it was common for the staff and the various interest groups to relitigate issues that participants thought had been settled by the policy development process. For years, ICANN participants debated what was "policy" and what was "implementation."[38] Laborious, contentious meetings of working groups and the council would produce an outcome, but the board or the Governmental Advisory Committee might not like it. Additionally, any time ICANN tried to make a policy decision that had major consequences, lobbyists descended upon the Commerce Department or Congress in an attempt to get them to steer decisions in a certain direction.

THE EXTERNAL PROBLEM: SOVEREIGNTY

The *external problem* pertains to how ICANN's private-sector-based global governance regime would fit into a world of sovereign states. Sovereignty, too, is an institution, and whatever its ambiguities in meaning, it forms one of the major principles and norms underpinning the international order.

Despite all its protestations to the contrary, ICANN was assuming a global public policy-making function for the DNS root registry. Domain names had become a prominent part of Internet policy. They posed questions and conflicts over the proper scope of intellectual property rights online, competition policy, the accreditation or regulation of registries and registrars, the privacy of registrant data, and decisions about what names or meanings to permit in new top-level domains—an issue that bled into controversies around website content. All of these are undeniably *public policy* issues.

By privatizing and globalizing policy making for Internet identifier registries, the ICANN regime was clearly taking an important part of Internet policy out of the hands of sovereign governments and international treaty organizations and putting it in the hands of a private corporation. Official US policy sanctioned that bold posture, but would other governments accept it? Resolving the external problem triggered an adjustment process that, like the internal problems, would play out over many years.

GAC AND THE ROLE OF GOVERNMENTS

ICANN's founders were aware of their intersection with states. Its original November 6, 1998, bylaws created a Governmental Advisory Committee (GAC) that would be "composed of representatives of national governments," to "consider and provide advice on [ICANN] activities . . . as they relate to concerns of governments." The bylaws instructed the ICANN board to "consider any [GAC] response prior to taking action" on any proposal it published for public comment.[39]

The GAC was a strange creature: an intergovernmental organization encapsulated in the bylaws of a private corporation. ICANN's founders thought it was a clever move. States could express their concerns but were not fully part of the private-sector-led policy development process. Though the bylaws barred governments from seats on the board and gave them no direct representation in the supporting organizations, they were not shut out. They could offer advice collectively, developed in their own little cul de sac. Governments were stakeholders, but they were quarantined— confined to a separate room and not directly part of the policy-making or final decision-making process. Ultimate decision-making authority would remain with ICANN's board.

That idea worked in some ways. As we shall see, governmental representatives active in GAC developed some loyalty to the "multistakeholder model." Maintaining governments as quarantined stakeholders, however, was not a stable equilibrium. The boundary between states and Internet community allowed "infection" (influence) to spread in both directions. The problem was that governments and the ICANN regime represented *competing, potentially incompatible* policy-making authorities. National governments are not "stakeholders" in the same way that businesses or civil society groups are; they purport to represent the interests of *all* stakeholders in their jurisdiction (though the publics so represented are fragmented into different territorial publics). While it is true that states qua states can have their own distinct stake in Internet policies—for example, those related to cybersecurity and surveillance—those stakes are supposed to be representative of a collective public interest. ICANN was supposed to provide a vehicle for private interests, non-state actors, to negotiate their own definition of a global public interest. The GAC brought the conflict between private-sector-led governance and state-led governance right into the heart of ICANN's processes. Inevitably, as time passed and GAC became more populated, active, and empowered, it began to compete with the GNSO and even the board for policy-making authority within ICANN.[40] The GNSO and the GAC became alternative, unintegrated policy development forums, introducing delay and uncertainty and forcing the board to act as a broker between the two, further blurring lines of accountability.

THE WORLD SUMMIT ON THE INFORMATION SOCIETY

Despite the GAC, the relationship between states and ICANN was unsettled—and unsettling. The World Summit on the Information Society (WSIS), a United Nations process that took place from 2002 to 2005, brought this tension out into the open. WSIS became the vehicle by which foreign states challenged the entire rationale for ICANN and the US role in it. Brazil, Russia, China, South Africa, and many Arab states did not welcome the idea of a US-led nongovernmental global governance institution. They saw ICANN as an encroachment on their sovereignty and wanted to replace it with an intergovernmental organization. Nearly all governments in this process claimed that public policy making for the Internet should be reserved to sovereigns. The pro-sovereignty camp included both democratic and nondemocratic governments.

The clash with sovereignty was complicated by the unilateral control of the DNS root held by the United States—which was, after all, a government. Not only was the unique US role a clear departure from the principle of sovereign equality, but it also was inconsistent with ICANN's underlying principle of self-governance by the Internet community.[41] If governments should stay out of Internet governance, why did one government, the United States, approve all additions, deletions, or modifications to the DNS root zone? Why did the United States alone have life or death power over who would perform the IANA functions?[42]

The WSIS process played out over three years. In some ways, it ended up as a victory for ICANN. An early (March 2003) draft of the WSIS Declaration of Principles had called for ICANN's responsibilities to be moved to "a suitable international, intergovernmental organization."[43] But that declaration did not survive the end of the process. Civil society, business, and the technical community (as well as the US government and a few other liberal democratic states) lobbied for what was now called a "multistakeholder model" of governance. The final document, the Tunis Agenda, called for the involvement of all stakeholders in "the international management of the Internet," thus endorsing multistakeholder governance to a limited degree.[44]

This shift occurred because the global Internet community, however fractious it was within ICANN, was still unified in its preference for self-governance. Even those who hated the way ICANN was working out believed that direct participation by business, civil society, and the technical community was preferable to policy making by nation-states in the ITU or some new intergovernmental entity. It was also apparent that some of the strongest advocates of sovereignty-based Internet governance were authoritarian states. This was predictable, because sovereignty provides a blank check for autocratic states to do whatever they want domestically, including regulating and censoring the Internet. The sovereignty advocates reminded everyone involved in ICANN why it had been a good idea to rely on nongovernmental governance in the first place.

While ICANN survived WSIS, it led to a fateful shift in the concepts and rhetoric surrounding Internet community self-governance. Before WSIS, the ICANN model was described as "privatization," "self-governance," or "private sector led." After WSIS, the Internet community fought under the banner of "the multistakeholder model." Embedded within that concept was the inclusion of governments as stakeholders, rather than as a competing governance model.

The story of WSIS and its outcomes has been told in depth elsewhere.[45] This book, however, focuses on its relevance to the ICANN/IANA transition. The WSIS process explicitly recognized and enacted the conflict between Internet community self-governance and state sovereignty. Over the course of three years, thousands of people—including official representatives of most of the world's states, Internet businesses, civil society advocacy groups, and the Internet technical community—openly debated that issue.

WSIS did *not*, however, *resolve* that conflict. It remained unresolved for the following reasons:

First, WSIS did not end US unilateral control of ICANN. Though committed to the goal of privatizing ICANN, the United States refused to consider giving up its control of ICANN and the DNS root during the process. Instead, it agreed to two placebos: a promise of "enhanced cooperation" and the formation of an Internet Governance Forum (IGF) under the auspices of the United Nations. The IGF would provide a venue for continued discussion of the issues, but the discussions would be nonbinding and open to any stakeholder.

Many other governments, including the Europeans, interpreted "enhanced cooperation" as a commitment to move toward some form of multilateral sharing of political oversight over ICANN. That never happened. When it became clear that neither the IGF nor an enhanced cooperation process would shift Internet policy-making authority to states, the conflict over sovereignty, ICANN, and US control of the root continued to fester in other venues.

Second, the political agreement that came out of WSIS, the Tunis Agenda, was only a partial victory for governance by non-state actors. Its call for the involvement of all stakeholders in "the international management of the Internet" seemed inclusive, but it also relegated different stakeholders to different *roles*.[46] In this schema, the role of policy making was reserved for governments. According to the Tunis Agenda, private-sector entities like ICANN could manage technical and operational things, but "authority for Internet-related public policy issues" is "the sovereign right of States."[47] Despite this language, non-state actors in ICANN continued to play the leading role in DNS policy development. The Tunis Agenda's purely verbal assignment of different roles to different stakeholders, however, only heightened the confusion over the proper role of the GAC in ICANN. It encouraged the GAC to assert that it should have the last word in any DNS policy decision if it was a "public policy issue," but it did not and could not clearly define what was public policy and what was not—and in ICANN's processes policy making was decidedly *not* restricted to governments alone. The GNSO continued to run the policy development process, and ICANN's board continued to make the final decisions.

Third, the WSIS process empowered governments within ICANN, intensifying the contradiction generated by the GAC. Post-WSIS, member states—including the United States—felt empowered to intervene in the policy issues ICANN was handling, particularly the creation of new top-level domains. Fueled by the claim that "public policy issues" were the exclusive preserve of states, they demanded special consideration for the views of the GAC in anything that could be deemed a public policy issue—which included, of course, virtually any important issue ICANN considered.

STUART LYNN PROPOSES SURRENDER

The depth of the internal and external problems ICANN faced in its early years was articulated by Stuart Lynn, ICANN's second president and CEO, in a February 2002 report.[48] In a plea that had the flavor of a message from the captain of the *Titanic*, Lynn argued that "the original concept of a purely private sector body, based on consensus and consent, has been shown to be impractical." Lynn's report emphasized especially the need for a greater role for national governments. Lynn also complained of "too much process," and "too little funding."

As a remedy, he proposed an overhaul of ICANN's structure that abandoned the original vision. Arguing that policy making was something governments, not "technical managers," should do, he proposed that governments should appoint one-third of the board. "Governments play a unique role in representing the broad public interests of their populations," he said. Lynn also rejected individual membership and voting as an accountability mechanism. He proposed a self-selecting board based on candidates offered by a nominating committee appointed by the board itself.

Lynn's proposal clashed too directly with ICANN's motivating vision to gain much support. Civil society and industry stakeholders saw it as a step away from participation and accountability, an attempt by ICANN to detach itself entirely from the Internet community and make peace with the status quo.[49] US congressional representatives and the Commerce Department also criticized it.[50] Over the next four years, some of Lynn's "reforms" were made, notably the abandonment of voting membership, the creation of ALAC, and a bylaw revision that gave the GAC the power to tie up ICANN's policy-making process if they did not agree with a policy produced by the GNSO. These changes meant that for the next twelve years, ICANN remained stranded between its original vision, its ties to the

US government, and a privileged role for GAC. The process of institutional-ization had stumbled again.

In sum, in aiming for the goals of the White Paper, the global Internet community set for itself an arduous task. The execution of that task not only created a chaotic process of self-organization around ICANN; it sent ripples throughout the international system, as it challenged one of the foundational institutions of the international order: sovereignty.

7 ICANN IN LIMBO

By 2003, the builders of ICANN had learned, the hard way, that the vision of a private-sector-led global governance institution was more difficult to realize than they had imagined. As a result, US government oversight became regularized and formalized. For the next ten years, ICANN and the US government settled into a pattern in which the Commerce Department used federal contracting and joint project agreements to steer the new institution. As this relationship evolved, the United States tried to incentivize improvements in ICANN by holding out the prospect of independence: *we will loosen your reins if you behave*. The United States also learned, however, that it did not want the Internet community to be *too* independent; it began to leverage its supervisory relationship to advance its own policy objectives.

THE INSTRUMENTS

The National Telecommunications and Information Administration regulated ICANN using two instruments: (1) a memorandum of understanding (MoU) between ICANN and the NTIA, and (2) the IANA contract. A third Commerce Department instrument, the 1993 Cooperative Agreement with the NSI, was also a critical part of the regime.

The original MoU (1998) described itself simply as "an agreement." It defined its purpose as "collaboration on a DNS Project." In the "DNS Project," the NTIA and ICANN would "jointly design, develop, and test the mechanisms, methods, and procedures that should be in place and the steps necessary to transition management responsibility for DNS functions now performed by, or on behalf of, the USG to a private-sector not-for-profit entity." The MoU was amended six times between 1998 and 2006. With the seventh amendment, signed on September 29, 2006, the title "MoU" mysteriously changes to "Joint Project Agreement" (JPA).[1] The JPA had a three-year term and provided for a midterm review. In all these agreements, the NTIA reaffirmed its policy goal of "privatizing the technical management of the DNS."

The MoU was guidance, not a contract; there was no consideration exchanged, and no specific penalty for not making sufficient progress. In congressional testimony, Assistant Secretary John Kneuer described the MoU as "a partnership. . . . us helping them come up with processes [so] that . . . all views are heard and considered through the bottom-up coordination process, and that decision making is accountable."[2]

The IANA contract, on the other hand, was really a contract.[3] It delineated the coordination functions ICANN was supposed to perform. Although the Commerce Department did not pay ICANN (or vice versa), and did not appear to have any alternative contractor, ICANN's designation as IANA had major economic consequences. It officially sanctioned ICANN as the gateway into the DNS root. This meant that all domain name registration businesses had to be licensed by ICANN and regulated by its contracts and policies. The licensing process allowed ICANN to impose fees upon registrars and registries, which in turn funded its growing staff and operations. If the Commerce Department did not designate ICANN as "the IANA," someone else might collect all that money and ICANN, Inc. might go out of existence.

The IANA contract was renewed five times between February 2000 and October 2012. With each renewal, the term of the contract increased: from one year to two years; from two years to three years; from three years to six years. The last IANA contract, finalized on October 1, 2012, was extensively revised. It involved two rounds of public comment and an open call for competing proposals.[4] That episode marked a significant change in the relationship between ICANN and the US government and will be discussed in more depth in the next chapter.

The third Commerce Department instrument, the 1993 Cooperative Agreement with the NSI, was an equally important but often overlooked part of the regime. NSI had been taken over by a company called Verisign. Like the IANA contract, the Cooperative Agreement with Verisign was a form of contractual regulation. Its primary purpose, however, was to ensure that Verisign fully supported and participated in the ICANN regime. While ICANN's GNSO was supposed to be the policy maker for registry contracts, the economic value of Verisign's registration business was so large—it held 80 percent of the entire world domain name market in 2000, and its revenues were many times the budget of ICANN—that only the US government had the authority to keep Verisign in line. When it came to Verisign, the Commerce Department was the real policy maker.

Indeed, it was not until October 2005 that ICANN and Verisign settled the long-running litigation triggered by the rocky start-up process described in the last chapter.[5] Following this truce, the ICANN board of directors made clear the quid pro quo underlying the settlement. In March 2006 it approved a new registry agreement giving Verisign ownership of the .COM registry until 2012 and acknowledging a principle of presumptive renewal beyond that date. Verisign was also explicitly authorized to raise wholesale registration fees in .COM by 7 percent in four of the next six years. Gaining Verisign's full support and participation in the regime required granting it a near-permanent property right over the .COM top-level domain. Despite howls of protest from nearly everyone else in the domain name industry, the NTIA reviewed and approved the agreement and codified it as Amendment 30 to the Cooperative Agreement in November 2006. This crucial policy decision, of course, was not a product of ICANN's GNSO; it was negotiated privately among ICANN, the NTIA and Verisign. Still, it removed one of the most destabilizing factors of ICANN's first six years.

While the contractual forms taken by the NTIA's regulation were relatively primitive and were never grounded in legislation, the scope of this new international regime was impressive. The NTIA-ICANN-Verisign complex regulated a critical part of the global Internet infrastructure. It centralized management of the DNS root zone and controlled entry into the domain name registration industry. This was all done under the aegis of a moderately sized subunit of the Department of Commerce with about four management staff on task.

CONSEQUENCES OF THE US ROLE

Americans involved in the debate over US control of the DNS root at the time often asserted that US supervision was a benign, neutral force and that the NTIA's approval of changes in the root was merely "ceremonial."

This was nonsense, but it was easy to see why so many American stakeholders held this view. Just as the seawater environment is invisible to the fish who live in it, ICANN's embeddedness in Washington politics was an invisible, taken-for-granted aspect of the system to them. It was hard for US-based businesses, intellectual property interests, and civil society groups to recognize how renewal of the MoUs and JPAs were rooted in US governmental processes, how the NTIA's budget was subject to congressional approval, and how any controversial and consequential policy decision in ICANN inevitably triggered lobbying, congressional hearings, or Commerce Department–run public hearings in the US polity.

As US government supervision of ICANN became routinized, and as long as ICANN's policy development processes lacked finality and legitimacy, US-based political interests had an outsize influence over ICANN's policies. Initially committed to a hands-off approach to ICANN's policy development role, the United States gradually became more accustomed to using its control of ICANN to advance its own Internet policy objectives.

The turning point came during the attempt to create a .XXX top-level domain in 2004. The Bush administration NTIA, responding to political pressure from conservative groups, ordered ICANN to put a hold on the contract with a letter from NTIA's director Michael Gallagher.[6] The .XXX incident came in the middle of the WSIS process and illustrated the changing role of the GAC. Instead of merely ordering ICANN to kill .XXX, the United States used the GAC to launder its decision. A day after Gallagher's letter, GAC chair Mohamed Tarmizi of Malaysia, under pressure from Gallagher, sent a letter to ICANN's board advising them that the top-level domain created a "strong sense of discomfort" from many governments, and that "the Board should allow time for additional governmental and public policy concerns to be expressed before reaching a final decision on this TLD."[7] Once seen as an unwanted intrusion into their private-sector led regime, the Tunis Agenda principle that *governments make public policy* helped the NTIA pressure ICANN to do what it wanted.

If .XXX was the most obvious example of US interference, ICANN's Whois policy was a far more important and persistent one. The Internet's Whois service allowed anyone to type a domain name into a Web interface and receive the name, street address, email address, and other personally identifiable information about the registrant. ICANN's earliest registrar contracts made it mandatory for registrars to publish this data. This policy met the demands of trademark holders concerned about legal remedies to domain name trademark conflicts.[8] Later, US government law enforcement agencies—especially the Federal Bureau of Investigation, Drug Enforcement Agency, and Federal Trade Commission—found unrestricted access to this data to be useful. Laws requiring warrants or some other form of due process limited governmental surveillance powers in most communications services. Whois allowed quick and easy collection of identifying information about Internet domains by anyone, without any legal process. Even foreign governments with privacy laws that made Whois illegal, such as Australia and the European Commission, viewed ICANN's Whois as a convenient loophole. They tacitly (and sometimes explicitly) supported US efforts to keep it in place.

As early as 2002, ICANN's Noncommercial Users Constituency (NCUC) led an effort to change Whois policy, calling attention to its conflict with the privacy rights of registrants who were natural persons. In June 2003, the Article 29 Working Group, a committee of European Data Protection authorities, issued an opinion supporting those efforts.[9] The Noncommercials gradually gained the support of domain name registrars, who saw that indiscriminate access to their customers' contact data burdened their information systems, fostered spam, and allowed fake renewal notices to be sent to their customers.

In 2003, ICANN formed a Whois Privacy Steering Group to look into the issue. The group concluded that before ICANN could decide what data to make public or nonpublic, it had to define the purpose of Whois. So, on June 2, 2005 it created a GNSO Task Force on the Purpose of Whois and the Whois Contacts.[10] By January 2006, the task force had produced a preliminary report.[11] Reflecting policy divisions in the community, the report asked for public comment on two competing definitions of the Whois purpose. Formulation 1 said the purpose was to provide contact information needed to resolve technical problems in DNS.[12] Formulation 2 said that the purpose was to provide contact information needed to resolve *any issue* related to the registration and use of a domain.[13] Supporters of Formulation 1 claimed that it was the only definition consistent with the narrow technical mission of ICANN and with national data protection laws worldwide. Formulation 2, by contrast, opened the door to literally any use of Whois data except spamming, which justified unrestricted access to registrants' personally identifiable information. After months of discussion, debate, and public comment, the GNSO Council's March 2006 meeting approved Formulation 1. An alliance of registries, registrars, noncommercial users, and Internet service providers provided the two-thirds majority needed to deem it a "consensus policy" under GNSO operating rules.[14]

ICANN's ability to institutionalize DNS policy making by the global Internet community, however, failed this test. They had not produced the outcome the US government and the law enforcement, trademark, and business interests wanted. The United States simply refused to accept the decision. Suzanne Sene, the NTIA staffer representing the United States in the GAC at that time, worked with the business and trademark constituencies to veto the decision and bury it.[15] They pressured the chair of the GNSO Council, Bruce Tonkin, to reverse the vote. Sene used the GAC to marshal support from other governments. The Australian GAC representative—whose own national privacy laws conflicted with ICANN's Whois policy—sent the GNSO a message announcing that "Australia supported Formulation 2." Eventually, Tonkin (an Australian national) caved. He deliberately failed to forward the decision to the board. The "consensus" definition of Whois purpose died, and in ICANN's accountability-deprived environment, nothing could be done about it.

The US government did not play a "purely ceremonial" role in this drama. Congress, the NTIA, and other agencies got involved. In his July 2006 testimony before the Senate, NTIA head John Kneuer expressed his "strong support" for "continued timely access to accurate and publicly available WHOIS data."[16] In the same hearing, Federal Trade Commissioner Jon Liebowitz said:

> I want to focus my remarks on the importance of continued, unrestricted access to WHOIS information. Simply put, our ability to protect consumers is being placed at risk by a movement within ICANN to limit WHOIS to technical purposes only and, thus, prevent law enforcement and the public from using this critical resource to identify scammers who operate websites.[17]

The Bush administration NTIA and FTC were responding to domestic interest groups, and this did not change in the Obama administration.

ICANN's capture by interest groups favoring its Whois requirements remained in place for more than a decade. Not until May 2018, when the European Union's General Data Protection Regulation (GDPR) came into force, did it make a serious effort to reconcile its policy with privacy norms. That, however, was seventeen months after the transition. Would that have happened if ICANN was still under US control? We will take up that question in chapter 14.

THE JOINT PROJECT AGREEMENT AND TWOMEY'S PRESIDENT'S STRATEGY COMMISSION

The 2006 Joint Project Agreement marks a minor inflection point in the evolution of ICANN's independence. It was negotiated just as ICANN's third CEO and president, Paul Twomey, was beginning to explore options for independence.

Twomey came into ICANN early on as the representative of the Australian government. An ambitious political appointee who in 1997 led the creation of the country's National Office for the Information Economy, Twomey roared into the early days of ICANN as the champion of the GAC and governments. It was he who insisted that states had sovereignty over country code top-level domains. As the first chair of the GAC, he insisted that GAC should meet as if it were an intergovernmental organization, in closed sessions that excluded business and civil society. Everyone in the GNSO hated him, at first. However, Twomey changed. He adapted to the ICANN environment well enough to become its third president. The NTIA people got along with him well, in part because a non-American CEO helped them present a more internationalized ICANN to the world.

Twomey's term as president (2003–2009) started just as WSIS was beginning and ICANN's geopolitical future was in play. The external problem— ICANN's relation to state sovereignty—was uppermost in mind. Ironically, ICANN's first big interaction with the intergovernmental regime subjected Twomey to a form of shock therapy. A WSIS Preparatory Committee meeting excluded Twomey from some of the official deliberations, because he was not part of a government delegation.[18] As president of ICANN, Twomey had cast his lot with the private sector, so he, along with the civil society rabble, was not allowed to be present for key WSIS negotiations, even when they involved ICANN. The contrast between formal, intergovernmental processes and the more open environment of Internet institutions could not have been starker. Twomey became a convert to the cause of nongovernmental governance. It was one of many ways in which the WSIS assault on ICANN unified the Internet governance community around the original vision.

Twomey thus had every reason to be thinking strategically about ICANN's future and its status as a nongovernmental governance institution in December 2005. That is when he formed the President's Strategy Commission (PSC) to help the organization find its way in the post-WSIS environment. The PSC became the vehicle by which ICANN began to explore what it could do about the constraints of US jurisdiction, how it could internationalize its mode of organization, and how it could stabilize and make fairer its internal operations and policy processes. In the PSC reports, there is much discussion about "the international private organization model." An external consultant was engaged to explore this. These very preliminary investigations reflected a tentative, legalistic approach to what was mostly a political problem, but it did broach the subject.

The PSC existed for nearly four years. In some ways, it represented everything that was wrong with ICANN: instead of using established processes and its own representational structure, the CEO had handpicked a gang of people and delegated policy leadership to them—the opposite of bottom-up. On the other hand, at that time and place, Twomey's PSC brought in some external perspectives and might have worked better at providing strategic direction than any formal processes would have.

INCHING TOWARD INDEPENDENCE: SHOULD THE JOINT PROJECT AGREEMENT EXPIRE?

The US government had responded to the challenge of WSIS with an intransigent policy statement that it would not give up control of DNS and did not intend to do so.[19] Before negotiating the 2006 JPA, however, the NTIA showed that it was still fully aware of the overriding policy objective that had led to the creation of ICANN: a transition to the private sector. Having survived WSIS and the intense criticism to which US oversight had been subjected, the big question remained: When and under what conditions would a transition take place?

In May 2006, as the end of the sixth MoU neared, the NTIA issued a formal Notice of Inquiry (NOI), asking for public comment on "The Continued Transition of the Technical Coordination and Management of the Internet Domain Name and Addressing System."[20] The NOI asked for answers to several questions related to the future of ICANN: Were the principles set out in the June 1998 White Paper still relevant? Did they need to be modified?

Was ICANN succeeding in gaining the participation of the key stakeholders? Most importantly, the NTIA sought comment on whether ICANN had achieved sufficient progress for a transition to take place by September 30, 2006.

The community's answer to that last question was, in a word, no. There were 700 comments. Public responses to the NOI expressed widespread support for the original vision underlying ICANN and for a DNS governance regime not tied to one government. Nevertheless, a wide range of interest groups, citing a variety of reasons, demanded a more accountable and representative ICANN before the United States let it go.

The NTIA responded with the September 2006 JPA. Despite the new label, the relationship between the NTIA and ICANN was largely unchanged. The JPA contained the same general policy guidance as the prior MoUs. ICANN still regularly reported to the NTIA. The new agreement lasted for three years, just like the old one. And there was no mention of ending the IANA contract.

There were two changes, however. First, the specific milestones in the MoU were supplemented by a series of broad commitments, memorialized in an ICANN board resolution called an "Affirmation of Responsibilities." The Affirmation of Responsibilities enumerated a general set of responsibilities that ICANN "affirm[ed] and agree[d] to be guided" by. The list included such things as "security and stability," "transparency," "accountability," "root server security and relationships," and "the multistakeholder model."[21] ICANN was promising that as a private sector manager of DNS, it would be a good boy. Second, in announcing the 2006 JPA, the NTIA committed itself to a "midterm review" that would, once again, ask for public comment on the question of whether the agreement should expire at the end of three years.

The midterm review happened in early 2008. The NTIA asked for comments on whether it should let the JPA expire.[22] Many commenters (mis)understood expiration of the JPA to be the equivalent of ICANN independence, but it was not: with the IANA contract and the Verisign Cooperative Agreement still in place, the NTIA would still hold significant unilateral authority over the regime.

In 2008, the domain name industry tended to oppose expiration of the JPA. They were concerned about ICANN's increasingly expansive and arbitrary regulation. The GNSO's attempt to set policies and procedures for the licensing of new top-level domains had metastasized into a bewildering welter of rules, restrictions, and guidelines, many of which were applied or modified arbitrarily. They were also concerned about the growing power of the GAC, which was actively overriding, diluting, or interfering with the GNSO's attempt to set policy for new generic top-level domains. Trademark interest groups also were skeptical of ICANN independence. Their clout in Washington created a major bias for their policy preferences. When they expressed concerns about accountability, it usually meant that the Internet community, left to its own devices, might stop privileging their interests. Civil society groups were divided, with some seeing the US government as the main threat to the public interest in DNS, and others seeing a liberated ICANN as the main threat.

The Internet Governance Project organized a workshop on JPA expiration at the 2008 United Nations Internet Governance Forum in Hyderabad, India. Participants voted 3 to 1 in favor of expiration of the JPA as a "good first step toward internationalization of ICANN."[23] But Jeanette Hofmann, a German academic and IGP member at the time, dissented.

> ICANN's accountability procedures are not sufficient," she said. "There is no independent appeals or review process in place that would meet the standards of due process. . . . I think it would be harder if not impossible to establish a credible external accountability framework around ICANN after the JPA has expired.

A notable feature of the 2008 debate over JPA expiration was that a new argument for US control surfaced—the same argument later made by Republican Senator Ted Cruz during his attempt to stop the transition in 2016. The United States should retain control over ICANN, the argument went, because it shields Internet governance from authoritarian states. In 2008, this argument came not from right-wing nationalists but from the Center for Democracy and Technology, a Washington-based civil society group devoted to online civil liberties. Like many others involved in these debates, the Center for Democracy and Technology seemed to be assuming that JPA expiration meant the end of the IANA contract and Verisign Cooperative Agreement as well. In its public comments, Center for Democracy and Technology wrote,

> The current role of the USG . . . protects the DNS against interference by other governments, some of which are much more likely to try to use any power over the DNS to interfere with innovation, competition and freedom of expression than the U.S. government has done under the present system.[24]

In their view, US oversight was not a form of government control but a shield against the depredations of other governments.

Factually, this claim was wrong. Far from acting as a buffer against state-driven policy influence, US control of ICANN was beginning to encourage interventions by other governments, via the GAC, in the policy process (see chapter 8). Further, the United States' special supervisory status continued to inflame, not defuse, geopolitical tensions. Describing the US role as a shield against Internet control by governments resonated with American audiences, but to anyone who knew what US control meant in practice, it seemed self-contradictory.[25] No one ever explained how ending US control would lead to a takeover of ICANN by authoritarian governments. The US government did not supervise the IETF and World Wide Web Consortium (W3C), yet no one seemed worried that Internet or Web standards would be taken over by Russia or China.

The presence of this sentiment, at this time, and its revival by US right-wing political factions in the final moments of the transition, is a testament to the persistence of nationalistic thinking in Internet governance. It speaks to the difficulty of reconciling the vision of global Internet community self-governance with the existence of geopolitical contention among states.

Summarizing the results of the midterm review, the NTIA stated that "ICANN has made significant progress in several key areas, but most participants agree that important work remains to increase institutional confidence."[26] If ICANN's board and staff wanted to be free of US control, they must gain the confidence of the community, and they didn't have it yet. ICANN's board chair, Peter Dengate Thrush, used that notion to revive the PSC in the second half of 2008. Thrush told the group to "facilitate discussions with the community about the issues raised regarding ICANN's planned transition to the private sector." Later in 2009, the PSC published an "Implementation Plan for Improving Institutional Confidence."[27]

To the PSC, *institutional confidence* implied both liberation from US jurisdiction—an international private organization legal model—and improved accountability.[28] What the PSC meant by "international not for profit organization status" is not entirely clear. What is clear is that the PSC showed little awareness of the political dimensions of that goal. They did not appreciate the way a change in the legal jurisdiction of ICANN's incorporation could be framed as a geopolitical power shift and be contested by politicians. They also did not fully understand its connection to accountability. If ICANN was detached from the US government, the United States would not have veto power over it, and neither would any other government. We would have to trust ICANN's own processes—and everyone at that time believed, not unreasonably, that its processes were flawed. To gain institutional confidence, ICANN needed to gain both the trust of its own participating stakeholder groups and acceptance as a global governance authority by states. In other words, both the internal and external problems were still there.

In the end, the NTIA *did* let the JPA expire. And as soon as it did, the relative insignificance of the MoUs and the JPA became blindingly obvious. Though the JPA had expired, no transition to the private sector had taken place. The United States was still in control of the contents of the root zone file through its Cooperative Agreement with Verisign. Through its power to award the IANA contract, the United States still held life and death power over ICANN's status as a governance authority. The United States was still the primary (if not the only) source of external accountability. The only thing that really changed was that ICANN's Affirmation of Responsibility was replaced by an Affirmation of Commitments.

THE AFFIRMATION OF COMMITMENTS

Like all the memorandums of understanding and the Joint Projects Agreement before it, the Affirmation of Commitments (AoC) was just an agreement, not an enforceable contract. This time, however, the agreement had no expiration date.[29] Its commitments, therefore, could in principle be perpetual. And to whom was ICANN making these perpetual commitments? To the US Department of Commerce. This is evident in the very first sentence: "This document constitutes an Affirmation of Commitments (Affirmation) by the United States Department of Commerce ("DOC") and the Internet Corporation for Assigned Names and Numbers ("ICANN"), a not-for-profit corporation."[30] The AoC was a continuation of the NTIA-ICANN MoUs, a form of policy steering that would never expire but which also allowed either party to terminate it at will, after 120 days' notice.

Unlike the Affirmation of Responsibilities, which was just a set of promises to uphold vaguely defined principles, the Affirmation of Commitments tried to enact specific accountability mechanisms. These accountability "reforms," however, consisted of a series of organizational reviews conducted by ICANN itself. The NTIA did not have a strong grasp of the institutional requirements of accountability. It thought of accountability as a review process, wherein the managers of the organization set up a process to ask for advice about itself. There were still no hard forms of accountability, such as binding external reviews, a voting membership, or competitive discipline.

The AoC established three-year review cycles in four areas of concern: (1) accountability and transparency; (2) security, stability, and resiliency; (3) competition, consumer trust, and consumer choice; and (4) Whois (which was grouped under the consumer trust heading but had its own review process). ICANN was now committed to assembling panels to conduct these four reviews, endlessly, every three years. The AoC's specification of how these panels would be populated reveals the power shift toward governments that had taken place since WSIS, and the US government's complicity in it. Review panel members would be appointed jointly by the chair of ICANN's Governmental Advisory Committee and the ICANN board chair or president. Not very bottom-up. The review teams would develop nonbinding recommendations, but the board had to act on them within six months. In effect, it was just another community consultation, another source of nonbinding advice to an organization with no real accountability. To further dilute accountability, each review panel was required to include the chair of the Governmental Advisory Committee, the ICANN board chair or president, and representatives of ICANN's supporting organizations and advisory committees. In other words, the exact same power structure that was making ICANN policy and governance decisions would be in charge of "reviewing" their own decisions and processes.

The AoC contained two other kickers demonstrating the continued importance of American political influence. ICANN promised to "remain a not-for-profit corporation, headquartered in the United States of America." It could "meet the demands of a global community" by maintaining "offices around the world," but the corporation had to stay in US jurisdiction. Second, the Commerce Department made ICANN commit "to enforcing its existing policy relating to WHOIS." The AoC told ICANN to "implement measures to maintain timely, unrestricted and public access to accurate and complete WHOIS information, including registrant, technical, billing, and administrative contact information." This startlingly specific aspect of the AoC had nothing to do with accountability—it was literally dictating policy to ICANN, even indicating which data elements had to be returned in Whois queries.[31] Far from being a harbinger of independence from US control, the AoC signified perpetual subservience.

Nevertheless, it was in ICANN's organizational self-interest to play up the AoC as an important step toward recognition and independence. In unveiling the AoC on September 30, 2009, ICANN's new CEO, Rod Beckstrom, harked back to the creation of the organization and its goal of a private-sector nonprofit organization for bottom-up policy development. ICANN's news release said,

> The signing of the Affirmation determines once and for all that this model works. . . . It commits ICANN to remaining a private not for profit organization. It declares ICANN is independent and is not controlled by any one entity. It commits ICANN to reviews performed BY THE COMMUNITY—a further recognition that the multi-stakeholder model is robust enough to review itself.[32]

In fact, ICANN was still a long way from being independent, accountable, and not controlled by any one entity.

8   PUTTING THE SCREWS ON ICANN

The US presidential election of 2008, held in the midst of a financial crisis, brought new political leadership to the United States. In March 2009, the Obama administration appointed Lawrence Strickling as the assistant secretary of commerce in charge of the NTIA. This did not, however, produce any immediate discontinuities in the US approach.

Strickling had worked in the Federal Communications Commission during the Clinton administration but focused on telecommunications regulatory issues. He was not part of the process that developed the Framework on Global Electronic Commerce or the White Paper. However, he became a much more visible player in the ICANN process than his predecessors had been. During the Bush administration, four different people rotated into and out of the assistant secretary position.[1] Strickling, in contrast, stayed in place for the full eight years of the Obama administration. He became an enthusiastic supporter of the multistakeholder model and took an avid interest in the development of ICANN.

If anything, the new administration at first increased the governmental role in ICANN. In 2011, the impending expiration of the 2006 IANA contract prompted the NTIA—as well as the IETF—to take a closer look at what the IANA functions were and what was actually in that contract.[2] The NTIA decided to embark on a "comprehensive review of the IANA functions contract," the first since the initial award of the contract in 2000.[3] Not too long after, the US government pushed ICANN into a major revision of its Registrar Accreditation Agreement (RAA), the basic contract governing the retail businesses selling domain names to end users. Both processes reflected a growing US tendency to promote its policy objectives by leveraging its authority over ICANN more aggressively.

The NTIA's leaders were sincere supporters of multistakeholder governance, but they were also employees of a national government agency with its own interests. US policy toward ICANN, moreover, was not narrowly siloed in the NTIA; it went all the way up to the National Security Council, the president's interagency forum for deliberation about national security and foreign policy matters.[4] This made US ICANN policy sensitive to the needs and concerns of the US government and its relationship to other governments. In addition to geopolitical concerns, domestic and international interest groups, notably intellectual property holders and law enforcement agencies, constantly pressured the NTIA about ICANN. The US government's temptation to use its control of ICANN to advance policy objectives was always there.

Sometime in 2011, the NTIA's Vernita Harris met with David Edelman of the National Security Council to discuss the changes they planned to make in the IANA contract. Harris told Edelman that the NTIA wanted several new measures to put the screws on ICANN.[5] The last chapter already documented the importance of Whois to governmental surveillance and law enforcement investigations. In addition to keeping registration data public and accurate, US law enforcement agencies, as well as the copyright and trademark interests, wanted registrars to do more to accurately identify and vet registrants, and they wanted ICANN compliance to force registrars to do this. Already concerned about DNS registrations by botnets, frauds, phishers, and spammers, law enforcement agencies feared ICANN's new top-level domain program would amplify those problems.

As hundreds of applicants for new top-level names surfaced, the United States also became aware that many foreign governments were concerned about what names would be allowed in new top-level domains. Some GAC members—and not just authoritarian states—were demanding veto powers over new names. These demands intensified as ICANN's program to create hundreds of new top-level domains neared completion.

While the United States clearly did use its control over ICANN to pursue its own policies or to respond to the concerns of other states, its commitment to a private-sector governance entity constrained its power. It had to work through ICANN, and that didn't always go according to plan. According to another internal source, "Everybody but NTIA was really unhappy with

ICANN." One pungent comment making the rounds in the interagency group was "the multistakeholder model is just another way of saying, no one's responsible." According to this source, "every attempt by Justice, or State, or NSA or CIA or the DoD folks to push forward their interests would go nowhere. And it drove them crazy. Then they'd yell at Commerce, and Commerce would make suggestions to ICANN, and nothing would happen, and the cycle would repeat."[6] The main source of dissatisfaction was their feeling that ICANN contractual compliance was not doing its job. Clear and obvious DNS abuses, they felt, were not being addressed, and the public policy concerns of governments were not being reflected.

The proposed IANA contract revisions of 2011–2012, and the modification of the RAA in 2013, must be understood in this context. Both the contract revision and the RAA revisions were attempts to use the US government contractual instruments governing ICANN to appease these political interests. Their agenda was opposed, however, by the civil society and some of the domain name industry interests within ICANN's multistakeholder regime.

THE IANA CONTRACT REVISION

In June 2011, the NTIA, drawing on a prior round of public comments, floated a revised IANA contract. The contract revisions added new requirements to the IANA functions' statement of work. This included structural separation of policy making from implementation,[7] a conflict-of-interest policy, provisions reflecting heightened respect for local country laws, and a series of consultation and reporting requirements to increase transparency and accountability to the international community. Another new part of the statement of work would have required IANA to ascertain that a new top-level domain had "consensus support" and was "in the global public interest" before it could be put into in the DNS root.[8]

The demand for structural separation of implementation and policy making conformed to the technical community's understanding of the proper function of IANA. It would reinforce its status as a neutral implementer of policy. The other change, requiring IANA to make a public interest determination before adding new top-level domains, however, pushed in exactly the opposite direction. It would empower IANA to overrule decisions already made in ICANN's policy development process and approved by its board. The "public interest" standard ICANN was being asked to use was undefined. The proposed revisions also included a provision that gave NTIA authority over who ICANN hired as a security director, reflecting a new emphasis on cybersecurity as a critical factor in Internet governance among US foreign policy makers.[9]

Some observers interpreted the proposed IANA public interest review of a new top-level domains as meaning "if the GAC objects, you must reject."[10] There was evidence for that conclusion. In speeches and interviews, the NTIA's Strickling had expressed support for greater deference to GAC.[11] In some comments at an industry conference, he had even defended a GAC veto of top-level domain names, on the grounds that he wanted to limit DNS blocking by national governments:

> If the GAC as a consensus view can't support a [top level domain name], then my view is that the ICANN Board should not approve the string, as to do so in effect legitimizes or sanctions [decisions by national governments to block TLDs] at the root zone level. And I think that is bad for the Internet. Where you're dealing with sensitive strings, where you've engaged the sovereignty of nations, I think it is appropriate to tip the hat a little bit more to governments and listen to what they say.[12]

Here, Strickling tried simultaneously to make concessions to sovereignty and to the Internet community's norm that the DNS should be globally compatible. That attempt was deeply confused. Global uniformity in a world of sovereign vetoes over Internet names (or Internet content, which governments could also block) meant that censorship would be globalized. A lowest common denominator rule would apply, allowing only names unobjectionable to any government in the world. By allowing GAC objections to block a name at the IANA level, DNS blocking would still exist—only it would apply to everyone in the world rather than just the objecting government. Here the contradictions between state sovereignty, global governance, and Internet freedom were evident. Strickling was endorsing exactly the sort of intergovernmental control that ICANN was founded to avoid. Far from using its control of ICANN to "defend the First Amendment," as Republican critics of the transition claimed, the NTIA was considering using ICANN to do the exact opposite.

Contract revisions that would enable IANA to exercise a policy veto generated strong objections from civil society and technical community commentators. Even ICANN's CEO, Rod Beckstrom, publicly pushed back against these changes. In his response to the NTIA's call for comments, he stated,

> The IANA functions contract should not be used to rewrite the policy and implementation process adopted through the bottom-up decision-making process. Not only would this undermine the very principle of the multi-stakeholder model, it would be inconsistent with the objective of more clearly distinguishing policy development from operational implementation by the IANA functions operator.[13]

So intense was the pressure around ICANN in this period that the NTIA was willing to play chicken with the IANA contract. After two rounds of public comment and an open call for applications to be the IANA functions operator, ICANN applied for the renewal.[14] On March 10, 2012, however, the NTIA announced that no acceptable bid for the IANA contract had been received and withdrew the request for proposals.[15] One inside source said that the NTIA was serious about moving the IANA contract and considered awarding it to the Internet Society. Without a credible alternative provider, the NTIA was not in a strong position to threaten removal. Ironically, the announcement that ICANN was not qualified to operate the IANA also contained a notice that NTIA had extended ICANN's existing IANA contract for another six months. As one National Security Council source said, "There was some danger of the contract just not being signed by ICANN." By July 2012, ICANN and the NTIA agreed on a new IANA contract. It did not contain the IANA public interest review.

THE 2013 REGISTRAR ACCREDITATION AGREEMENT

US pressure on the ICANN regime from trademark and law enforcement interests also extended to detailed modifications of the RAA. All domain name registration businesses had to sign this contract before they could sell domains in generic top-level domains. US policy now focused on modifying the RAA to make ICANN compliance force registrars to do more of the work needed to police Internet users. A 2013 report by the US Intellectual Property Enforcement Coordinator made it clear that trademark interests and law enforcement agencies were behind this push:

> NTIA will collaborate with all U.S. stakeholders, including intellectual property stakeholders, as well as other Federal agencies, such as USPTO, and FBI and other law enforcement agencies, to develop positions within ICANN's Governmental Advisory Committee (GAC) to advance access to accurate, complete, and publicly

available WHOIS data, improvements to the Registrar Accreditation Agreement (RAA) between Registrars and ICANN, effective contract compliance by ICANN, and appropriate consideration of intellectual property issues in the context of gTLDs.[16]

One of the new asks was a data retention obligation that would require registrars to retain customer financial data related to their correspondence with registrants, such as timestamps, IP addresses, and credit card data. The data would have to be stored for two years after the last transaction with the customer, even if the customer transferred the domain to another registrar.[17] The Intellectual Property Enforcement Coordinator report went on to note: "NTIA will closely monitor adoption and implementation by Registrars of the revised Registrar Accreditation Agreement (RAA), which will include a specific focus on ICANN's contract compliance capabilities and results to ensure that ICANN holds its accredited Registrars to all of the new commitments included in the RAA."[18]

In the 2013 RAA revision, US leadership in the GAC got ICANN's contract negotiators to give them everything they asked for. The new RAA contained:

- Establishment of a registrar point of contact for abuse reporting
- Annual verification and validation of Whois registrant data
- Registrar responsibility for reseller compliance
- Enhanced compliance tools such as broader suspension and termination tools, clarification of audit rights, and access to information for investigations
- Extensive new data retention requirements

Privacy advocates and data protection authorities objected. "The problem of inaccurate contact details in the WHOIS database cannot be solved without addressing the root of the problem: the unlimited public accessibility of private contact details," said a representative of Europe's data protection authorities, noting that open publication gave registrants an incentive to conceal their contact data.

> The Working Party strongly objects to the introduction of data retention by means of a contract issued by a private corporation in order to facilitate (public) law enforcement. . . . Because there is no legitimate purpose, and in connection with that, no legal ground for the data processing, the proposed data retention requirement is unlawful in Europe.[19]

A digital rights group in Chile wrote to ICANN saying, "Data protection principles . . . are, among others, the Collection Limitation Principle, Purpose Specification Principle, Use Limitation Principle, and Security Safeguards Principle. All of these principles are compromised by the current RAA draft."[20]

In his reply to the European data protection authorities, ICANN CEO Fadi Chehadé cited the approval of the GAC as justification: "The GAC has endorsed the Whois accuracy and data retention requests that stem from recommendations made by law enforcement representatives from across the globe, including the European Union." It was a clear example of how GAC could be used to launder the making of global policies that were not grounded in actual national or international law.

THE NEW TOP-LEVEL DOMAIN PROGRAM

The precipitating cause of governments' intensifying interest was ICANN's complicated, controversial, long-drawn-out program to license new top-level domain names. Like a recurring nightmare, the new TLD program, which had started in 2007, regenerated all the political-economy conflicts that had overwhelmed Jon Postel and the IETF back in 1996–1998. Only now, the economic and political stakes were even higher. The politics were more intense, too, because the United States had given the GAC a green light to interfere with GNSO policy development whenever and however it wanted.[21] Despite the GNSO's attempt to establish clear, predictable criteria for qualification of TLD applications, GAC intervention made all applications part of a beauty contest in which objections could come from any source for almost any reason. As Strickling's comments about a GAC veto and the Intellectual Property Enforcement Coordinator report documented, the United States viewed the GAC as an important means of shaping DNS policy, and the other governments felt the same way.

During the GAC's involvement in new TLD policy, the clash between governments and the non-state actors—between territorial sovereignty and global, bottom-up policy development—reached its greatest intensity. The GNSO's difficult attempts to find consensus policies among contentious private sector stakeholder groups were routinely overridden, arbitrarily modified, and interfered with by the GAC or by the board's response to GAC advice. The GAC had by then successfully transformed "advice" into a government-centered policy development vehicle. During this period, there was no well-defined policy development process. Everything was up for grabs; everything depended on political pull and the board's discretion.

By the beginning of 2013, the ICANN regime embodied a contradiction. One the one hand, it was a multistakeholder regime run by an Internet community that was normatively biased toward open, bottom-up policy development, Internet freedom, and global compatibility. On the other hand, it contained within itself an intergovernmental entity that wanted to play an ever-larger role in domain name policy, and it was beholden to a single, powerful government that wanted to use it to pursue domestic and international policy objectives.

9 THE TRIGGERS

By 2012, it would have been reasonable to assume that ICANN's tether to the US government could continue indefinitely. US supervision was routinized and becoming stronger. Most stakeholders saw few reasons to disturb it. The June 2011 Notice of Inquiry regarding renewal of the IANA contract stated, "NTIA reiterates that it is not in discussions with ICANN to transition the IANA functions nor does the agency intend to undertake such discussions."[1]

Two years later, the NTIA most definitely was in discussions to transition the IANA functions. What changed? What made the original goal of an independent ICANN salient again?

The answer can be found in two watershed geopolitical incidents: the ITU's World Conference on International Telecommunications (WCIT) in December 2012, and Edward Snowden's revelations in June 2013. Coming within six months of each other, these two events pushed the relationship between states and the Internet, between sovereignty and cyberspace, to the forefront of public debate, and did so in a way that made the US government and the Internet community agree that the elimination of US. control of ICANN was the best response.

A new actor entered the scene at this time to facilitate the transition. Fadi Chehadé became the president and CEO of ICANN on September 14, 2012. This happened right in the middle of the WCIT preparatory process, and just before the signing of a new—and what would be the last—IANA contract.

Chehadé seems to have come into ICANN with the goal of internationalizing the organization. Born in Lebanon in 1962 to Egyptian parents, he went to the United States for his education and by 1986 was naturalized as a US citizen. While Paul Twomey had entered ICANN from the world of national governments, Fadi entered from the world of multinational business. After some experience in private firms, Chehadé delved into private-sector-led efforts to globalize standards, becoming the first CEO of RosettaNet, an attempt to facilitate the data exchanges needed to integrate companies' supply chains.[2] His management style reflected his business background. He never quite understood bottom-up policy making, and his top-down initiatives helped unify all stakeholder groups around a demand for harder forms of accountability (see chapter 10). By the same token, he was probably the best political operator ICANN could have found at that moment. Coming from a multicultural background, he maneuvered in the international arena more skillfully than his predecessors. He took diplomatic initiatives in the global governance space and was good at articulating the goals and values of the Internet community. With a big assist from Edward Snowden, Chehadé led ICANN into a state of readiness for the end of US oversight.

THE WORLD CONFERENCE ON INTERNATIONAL TELECOMMUNICATIONS

The WCIT was a formal treaty-negotiating process convened by the ITU in Dubai from December 3 to 14, 2012. Its objective was to revise the ITU's International Telecommunication Regulations (ITRs). Somewhat unexpectedly, it turned into one of the last and most dramatic clashes between the old world of international telecommunications institutions and the globalized world of the Internet.

A revision of the ITRs was an unlikely vehicle for a conflict over Internet governance. The ITRs were a vestige of the age of voice telephones and national post, telephone, and telegraph monopolies. They assumed that telecom companies were part of national governments and that the rules of engagement in global communications were set by formal international treaties, not by markets and contracts. The ITRs had not been changed since 1988—before the development of a new infrastructure of packet-switched data, personal computers, competing private mobile networks, and Internet-enabled smartphones, and before trade agreements in the World Trade Organization had supplanted the ITU as the primary governance model for global information and communication technologies.[3]

The ITRs intersected only tangentially with Internet governance. The regulations could not control the assignment of Internet identifiers or the definition of Internet standards, nor could they directly regulate Internet content, services, and applications. A few vocally pro-sovereigntist states, notably Russia, tried to use WCIT to float proposals that would insert the ITU into matters of Internet governance.[4] But these proposals went nowhere. Some of Europe's incumbent telephone companies, still resistant to competition and innovation from "over the top" services, also tried to use the conference to push for old world settlement and payment models for the exchange of traffic. If implemented, they would not be compatible with the Internet/Web ecosystem.[5] But these proposals died on the vine.[6]

Nevertheless, the Internet community saw in the revision of the ITRs an attempt by the ITU to "take over the internet."[7] That claim became a rallying cry that mobilized the Internet community, which was now financially supported and amplified by a wealthy tech industry.[8] A popular magazine article reflected the prevailing zeitgeist:

> The International Telecommunications Regulations . . . may be extended to cover the Internet, raising questions about who should control it, and how. Arrayed on one side will be representatives from the United States and other major Western powers, advocating what many call "Internet freedom" . . . On the other side will be representatives from countries where governments want to place restrictions on how people use the Internet. These include Russia, China, Brazil, India, Iran, and a host of others.[9]

Framing the battle in this way revived the spirit of 1997. The Internet needed to be defended against governmental encroachments. Transnational, private-sector-led institutions—now recast as a more inclusive "multistakeholder model" that encompassed input from liberal-democratic states—were explicitly linked to the Internet freedom agenda, an agenda still supported by civil society, businesses, and the US State Department at that time.[10] The US Congress passed resolutions condemning the ITRs and holding hearings on the threat posed by the ITU.[11] The ITRs became a proxy battle over competing models of governance.

The Internet community's alarm stemmed in part from underestimating its own strength. WCIT was only the latest in a series of encounters between the global Internet community and legacy intergovernmental organizations. In each of these encounters, sovereignty-based international institutions had lost ground.

The World Summit on the Information Society (2002–2005) was the beginning of the series; it had failed to kill ICANN, failed to dislodge US control over it, and adopted politically binding statements formally approving some form of multistakeholder governance.[12] The subsequent effort to promote "enhanced cooperation" to share more power with governments stalled out and gradually died. The 2010 ITU plenipotentiary meeting in Guadalajara saw proposals to enlarge the role of the ITU in Internet governance, but all failed.[13] Instead, the Guadalajara Plenipotent formally recognized ICANN, mentioning it by name for the first time ever in an ITU resolution.[14] A year before WCIT convened, India, Brazil, and South Africa tried to create a United Nations Committee on Internet-Related Policies. Disappointed with the multistakeholder IGF, they proposed a new UN organization that would put states in control of a (nonbinding) policy development process for the Internet, relegating nongovernmental stakeholders to an advisory role. Even that rather tame idea, opposed by the Internet community, went nowhere.

Despite the manifest weakness of the ITU and the UN system in matters of Internet governance, the alleged threat posed by WCIT revitalized and solidified the Internet community's commitment to nongovernmental governance. In the end, they successfully repelled all ITU incursions into Internet territory. The final text of the ITRs did not even contain the word *Internet*.

That, however, did not satisfy the Internet advocates. They also trashed the ITU's treaty process to drive the point home. The final vote on the revised ITRs split the world into two camps: fifty-five nations refused to sign the revised treaty; another eighty-nine did sign it.[15] The nations that voted against the ITRs did not do so because of any harmful provisions in the revised ITRs themselves. They voted no because of the inclusion of a *nonbinding resolution* in the package of conference outcomes encouraging the ITU to serve as a forum for continued discussions of Internet issues.[16] The message their refusal sent was clear: there was no room whatsoever for the ITU in matters of Internet governance.

That vote count, however, showed that the anti-ITU states were a numerical minority. This further fueled the Internet community's alarm. They concluded that those who understood and believed in the multistakeholder model of governance were a minority. "The model we so believe in is actually not understood or embraced by the world," ICANN's CEO Chehadé lamented later.[17]

This perception contributed to the United States' decision to relinquish control of the DNS root and IANA. If the multistakeholder model meant keeping governments out, how could the United States continue to control the DNS root?

THE SNOWDEN REVELATIONS

In truth, neither the ITRs nor a nonbinding resolution in the ITU could have had much of an impact on Internet freedom. The real threats to Internet freedom were coming not from the ITU or the United Nations but from powerful nation-states acting unilaterally. The US government enjoyed exceptional levers of power over the communications infrastructure and the monetary system.[18] Even outside of the United States, individual states were finding new ways to regulate Internet users and providers, new ways to suppress access to information, new ways to manipulate cyberspace to advance their strategic ends. States were behaving this way not because they were autocracies but simply *because they were states*; they were concerned with their own power and security and their ability to control public policy. That message was brought home by the next incident.

Edward J. Snowden was a subcontractor for the US National Security Agency (NSA) with broad access to classified information. In early June 2013, he fled to Hong Kong and leaked digital copies of thousands of top-secret NSA documents to journalists. In a dialogue that hitherto had put non-state actors at the forefront of Internet governance, the Snowden revelations highlighted the state's role in cyberspace. They documented the massive scale and scope of state surveillance that had developed alongside the Internet in the service of military power and national security. Surveillance of the digital infrastructure was exposed as a fully developed method of espionage, one that respected no territorial boundaries.

If sovereign equality is enshrined in international law, what happens when people discover that it doesn't really exist? The Snowden revelations made it blindingly clear that the scale and scope of US power over the digital environment vastly exceeded that of any other state. The United States had the capability to spy on almost anyone, even allies like German Chancellor Angela Merkel or Brazilian President Dilma Rousseff. The revelations also made it appear as if the preeminence of US businesses in Internet services was linked to their government's military and intelligence superiority. Although US control of ICANN did not intersect with the NSA's global surveillance program, both were instances of an exceptional, wholly globalized form of cyber power held exclusively by the US government. It was therefore inevitable, and not entirely unfair, for the two to be linked politically. The Snowden surveillance scandal forced a choice: the United States had to be consistent about its commitment to a private-sector-led multistakeholder model or risk discrediting it by maintaining its association with US political and military hegemony.

After a global dialogue over WCIT that had targeted authoritarian states as the main threat to the Internet, the Snowden revelations implicated the very state that was touting Internet freedom. This further undermined the claim that the United States had a special status as a neutral steward of ICANN. On the one hand, the revelations prompted other states to move toward a more nationally partitioned Internet; there was suddenly talk of technological sovereignty and restrictions on transborder data flows.[19] But for many non-state actors, it also supported an anti-sovereigntist conclusion: if the Internet was to be free, its users had to adopt a critical stance toward *all* states; its governance needed to be rooted in a transnational, fully multistakeholder polity.

THE MONTEVIDEO STATEMENT

For the Internet technical community, the outrage and panic about WCIT magnified the impact of the Snowden revelations. Already worried about their competition with the ITU and the way WCIT had targeted ICANN's ties to the United States, the organically evolved Internet institutions seem to have felt especially threatened by the ways NSA surveillance undermined their legitimacy and norms. A meeting of its institutional leadership was called. On October 7, 2013, the president of ICANN, all the directors of the five Regional Internet Registries, the chairs of the IETF and the Internet Architecture Board, the president of the Internet Society, and the chief executive officer of the World Wide Web Consortium met in Montevideo, Uruguay. Recognizing the political opportunity, Chehadé insisted that there should be a statement coming out of Montevideo and convinced everyone that it should be published. "We wrangled over the text," said one participant.[20] The outcome was an unusually political communiqué, almost a manifesto, called "The Montevideo Statement on the Future of Internet Cooperation."[21] The statement made it clear that the Internet institutions did not approve of the US government's "pervasive monitoring and surveillance." Those actions were "undermining . . . the trust and confidence of Internet users globally." Note that these leaders could claim to speak for *Internet users globally* and in a way that confronted the world's most powerful state. They went on to make a challenging statement: "They called for accelerating the globalization of ICANN and IANA functions, towards an environment in which all stakeholders, including all governments, participate on an equal footing."

"Globalization of ICANN and IANA functions" was an interesting turn of phrase. What did globalization mean, really? Did it mean privatization as originally envisioned, or something else? Most likely, it was their way of expressing a demand to end the US government's privileged position over the IANA. The Montevideo statement indicated that the entire Internet technical community was ready to untether from the US government. Also noteworthy was the phrase that considered "all governments" as stakeholders that should "participate on an equal footing."

THE DECISION TO "TRANSITION"

The combination of WCIT and Snowden led directly to the US government's decision to complete the privatization of ICANN. Strickling said that, back in 2009, privatization of ICANN "was not a goal going in" to his NTIA office.[22] At that time, he saw a "tremendous amount of dissatisfaction" with the way ICANN ran itself and "serious dysfunction" in the organization. This is what made him an eager participant in the first Accountability and Transparency Review Team (ATRT-1) mandated by the Affirmation of Commitments, which ran from May to December 2010. Strickling approached ICANN, in other words, following the logic of the previous ten years: the NTIA was the parent and ICANN the child who had to be deemed mature enough to leave the house.

The WCIT process, however, changed Strickling's attitude. In Dubai he was confronted with governments who wanted more power over the Internet, and they were using US supervision of ICANN to justify their position. WCIT brought home to him the basic contradiction in the US position: If one government had political oversight over key Internet functions, why shouldn't others? The functions were global, after all, so why not globalize them through the United Nations or an intergovernmental organization?

Chehadé expressed a similar view:

> Post-Snowden, we had two options. Either every government was going to insist
> to sit next to the US government in an equal way at the table to [govern ICANN].
> Or . . . none of them would be in a control position but rather in a co-equal posi-
> tion where they're advising and participating along with the private sector and
> the civic sector.[23]

The choice now seemed binary: go totally multilateral or totally private/
multistakeholder.

In the US government, the interagency committee organized around the
National Security Council now began to see getting rid of the IANA contract as a strategic move. As Strickling put it, "Perhaps this was the time to
demonstrate that the US was so solidly behind the multistakeholder model
that it could transition out of the IANA contract right away."[24] Chehadé,
similarly, said: "Every day the USG held on to ICANN it sent a message that
the multistakeholder model was not legitimate, not really ready to fly."[25]
Another interviewee connected to the NSC agreed with this characteriza-
tion of the decision but gave it a more diplomatic rationale:

> The argument that won the day was: This is a good diplomatic move. We don't
> get any value out of this contract, and it's causing all this consternation. Even some
> allies of ours think it should be moved to the ITU. We don't want to be seen as
> controlling this, but we don't control it really, so it is just bad PR. Snowden in this
> respect was definitely a factor, may have pushed it over the threshold.[26]

In this way of thinking, transition was not a reward for ICANN's good
behavior but a move in the geopolitical game. ICANN would be set free
regardless of whether it had already solved its internal problems. Severing
the connection between IANA and the US government would bolster the
regime's legitimacy and express confidence that it could survive on its own.
That willingness to let it sink or swim without US guardianship had hugely
beneficial effects on ICANN's internal organization: it made everyone take
seriously the need for reforms, and commit to making them. And for the
first time in its history, ICANN's diverse and factionalized stakeholders had
something to unify around: the transition.

Internally in ICANN, they were already ramping up for the IANA transition in October 2013. That is when Grace Abuhamad was hired by Jamie
Hedlund and eventually found herself acting as the lead staff manager of
the transition process (see chapters 10–12).

THE COMMERCE DEPARTMENT "GLOBALIZES" IANA

On March 15, 2014, the US Commerce Department publicly announced its

> intent to transition key Internet domain name functions to the global multi-stakeholder community. As the first step, NTIA is asking the Internet Corporation for Assigned Names and Numbers (ICANN) to convene global stakeholders to develop a proposal to transition the current role played by NTIA in the coordination of the Internet's domain name system (DNS).

ICANN was thus given a key role in organizing and managing the terms and conditions of its future as an independent organization. The NTIA excluded Verisign's role as Root Zone Maintainer from the public, multistakeholder transition process. As noted before, a Cooperative Agreement between the NTIA and Verisign governed the maintenance of the DNS Root Zone. The NTIA stated that there would be a parallel but separate transition to disengage the NTIA from the function it now defined as the *Root Zone Maintainer*.

Note that in the NTIA announcement the change is no longer called *privatization* but *transition*. *Transition* became a stand-alone transitive verb with no information about what noun to attach to the desired end state. The NTIA announcement, however, did include four principles to guide the transition proposal, and an important constraint. The four principles were:

- Support and enhance the multistakeholder model.
- Maintain the security, stability, and resiliency of the Internet DNS.
- Meet the needs and expectations of the global customers and partners of the IANA services.
- Maintain the openness of the Internet.

The constraint—in reality, a fifth principle—was:

- NTIA will not accept a proposal that replaces the NTIA role with a government-led or an intergovernmental organization solution.

The NTIA was thus adhering to the original vision of a self-governing global Internet community. The White Paper plan was finally happening.

PEAK MULTISTAKEHOLDERISM: THE NETMUNDIAL

The road to the ICANN transition unexpectedly went through Brazil. The most immediate manifestation of Snowden's impact on the global politics of Internet governance was a meeting held in São Paulo from April 22 to 24, 2014. This event intersected with and influenced the transition process.[27]

Two weeks before the Montevideo statement was released in Uruguay, ICANN's Chehadé watched on TV as Dilma Rousseff, the Social Democratic president of Brazil, denounced the United States and its spying program before the UN General Assembly.[28] She called for the United Nations to establish "a multilateral civil framework" for Internet governance. In keeping with prior Brazilian positions, Rouseff seemed to be proposing a reassertion of sovereignty. Chehadé decided to make an unplanned visit to Brazil's capital to involve Rouseff in what can only be called a diplomatic initiative. Although Brazil's communications minister initially blocked his access to Rousseff, Hartmut Glaser of Brazil's national-multistakeholder Internet Steering Committee, which ran the .BR domain, helped Chehadé set up a meeting. At that meeting Chehadé succeeded in persuading her to join ICANN in a call for a summit. A global community would be convened to come up with a consensus on two things: Internet governance principles and a Roadmap for the future evolution of the Internet governance ecosystem. In this initiative, Chehadé had the full support of Glaser and the Brazilian Internet Steering Committee (CGI), an institution that combined the IP address registry and country code domain administrator with Internet service providers, civil society, and governmental ministries.

The summit would be organized not by an intergovernmental organization but by a spontaneous alliance between the Internet community and a maverick, relatively Internet-friendly government in the Global South. Reflecting the football culture of its Brazilian hosts, it would be called the NETmundial, the governance equivalent of the World Cup. Its organizing committee would be a combination of Brazil's Internet Steering Committee and the Internet institution leaders who had issued the Montevideo statement.

The NETmundial was one of the most fully developed multistakeholder convenings ever done. It provided an opportunity for the global community concerned with Internet governance to come together to address a wider swath of Internet policy issues than an ICANN meeting could—issues such as surveillance, net neutrality, and privacy. The broader scope helped to clarify ICANN's place in the digital governance ecosystem.

Brazil's buy-in gave the summit the necessary credibility to attract state actors, regardless of which political bloc they were part of. The shock of the Snowden revelations, on the other hand, recruited hundreds of civil society activists eager to use this political opportunity to advance the cause of privacy and Internet freedom. By agreeing that the summit would be a multistakeholder affair, the Internet community could claim that Brazil was edging away from the sovereigntists and supporting a multistakeholder approach. By the same token, ICANN and the Internet organizations were signaling their willingness to bargain with governments who had been critical of the American role in Internet governance and displaying their support for the idea that governments should participate in Internet institutions "on an equal footing."

The NETmundial meeting assembled about 2,000 people. It organized discussions on the floor in a unique way, setting up separate lines for the three stakeholder categories—business, civil society, and government—in a way that evenly distributed speaking time and eliminated discretionary speaker selection. After weeks of preparation and three days of intense meetings, it produced an outcome document that commanded international legitimacy among all three sectors.[29] The aspirations of this meeting were best expressed in the statement's preamble:

> This is the non-binding outcome of a bottom-up, open, and participatory process involving thousands of people from governments, private sector, civil society, technical community, and academia from around the world. The NETmundial conference was the first of its kind. It hopefully contributes to the evolution of the Internet governance ecosystem.

One of the more interesting outcomes was the measured repudiation of the Tunis Agenda's definition of segregated roles for participants in Internet governance. The NETmundial statement said, "The respective roles and responsibilities of stakeholders should be interpreted in a flexible manner with reference to the issue under discussion."

It also backed away from sovereignty. In the Tunis Agenda, states are preeminent and exclusive authorities over the making of international Internet-related public policies. In the NETmundial statement:

> The development of international Internet-related public policies and Internet governance arrangements should enable the full and balanced participation of all stakeholders from around the globe, and [be] made by consensus to the extent possible. . . . Anyone affected by an Internet governance process should be able to participate in that process. . . . Internet Governance should be carried out through a distributed, decentralized and multistakeholder ecosystem.

In its modifications of accepted language and in its process, the NET-mundial statement altered the tone of the global conversation on Internet governance, consolidating the gains associated with the more open participation of non-state actors. Only Russia and Cuba explicitly distanced themselves from the outcome. China, surprisingly, did not. India, on the other hand, eventually decided not to sign the statement, expressing its preference for a multilateral, state-driven approach.[30] But a year later, India flipped to support multistakeholderism during the IANA transition process.[31]

Although the NETmundial statement was nonbinding, it is still interesting to read the "principles" that were memorialized and how they were worded, and it is also instructive to see how much the "roadmap" agreements replayed and revised ongoing controversies from the World Summit and its Tunis Agenda. The most interesting thing about it, however, was the process itself. It was a diplomatic accomplishment similar in scope and significance to the WSIS Tunis Agenda, but it was not hosted by an intergovernmental organization and was not a state-led effort. It was truly the product of a multistakeholder alliance, relying on an ad hoc governance structure mostly rooted in the Internet community. Given the speed with which the group was assembled and the need for process innovations to aggregate the comments of hundreds of people from different stakeholder groups and finalize a document, it was an impressive accomplishment.

Even more striking was the implicit belief of its participants that the digital ecosystem could be shaped by consensus on nonbinding principles agreed at an open, multistakeholder meeting—an aspiration and confidence level that would be hard to find ten years later. That spirit, however, carried over and animated the ICANN transition process.

10   IN TRANSITION

Nine days after the NTIA announcement of March 14, 2014, ICANN convened its scheduled quarterly meeting in Singapore. On Monday morning at 10:30, a two-hour session devoted to the IANA transition started. Two thousand people filled the room: attentive, expectant, and, for the first time in many years, truly focused on a common purpose.

Steve Crocker, author of the first RFC and now the chair of ICANN's board, proudly launched the session. "I'm holding in my hand a press release: 'NTIA announces intent to transition key Internet domain name functions,'" he said, and turned to thank NTIA's Strickling, who was in the audience. Modestly referring to the "small role" he played in the development of the Internet, Crocker referred to ICANN's origins: "More than 15 years ago, the United States government charted a course to give to the world possession of the most remarkable invention of modern time, recognizing the Internet was of the people, by the people, and for the people. And it chose ICANN, now, to oversee that transition."

In a well-planned display of unity, ICANN had arrayed on the stage two dozen people it considered the leaders of the Internet community. Crocker introduced each of them by name and asked them to stand.[1]

Then Chehadé himself took the stage. He began explaining, in his characteristically sincere and persuasive way, what the IANA functions were and "how we understand the scope of the transition." He described each function in a simplified but basically accurate way. He again introduced and praised the institutional representatives of those functions. He outlined his understanding of the community's task and presented it as a cooperative venture that would give all of them a voice.

"Today we discuss process, not substance," Chehadé said.

> ICANN is just the facilitator. We are not the decider. We convene. We engage. We facilitate. We are not running this from a leadership top-down standpoint. And that's an agreement we made with our fellow communities, and I share it with all of you as our ICANN community. We are one of many. We should participate with everyone on an equal footing in this discussion.

An unplanned intervention momentarily interrupted Chehadé's spellbinding talk. Sebastian Bachollet, a board member, blurted out, "I really would like to know if the multistakeholder community is without end users." Barely missing a beat, Chehadé said: "Sebastian was saying the panel does not include users. The user community is not represented." There was scattered applause. Somewhat awkwardly, Chehadé replied, "We are all end users."

THE ACCOUNTABILITY PROBLEM

Beneath the surface of these displays of unity and self-congratulation ran a powerful undercurrent of tension and concern.

From WSIS on, the global Internet community had always rallied behind the multistakeholder model. This implied defending ICANN against governments and intergovernmental institutions. WCIT and NETmundial continued this pattern, and so did the discussions of the NTIA announcement in Singapore. The prospect of a "stewardship transition" heralded the ultimate victory of multistakeholder governance and was greeted with a mixture of excitement and enthusiastic support.

Yet just as support for the multistakeholder model was peaking, so were the community's doubts about ICANN itself. Indeed, concerns about the internal problems facing ICANN—a lack of trust, the inability to operate reliable and fair policy-making processes, the accountability problems—had reached a crescendo just as this critical moment arrived.

ICANN the corporation, or "the Org" as it came to be known after 2016, was not the same as the "multistakeholder community." Though ICANN was the organizational home of IANA, and the vehicle for this community to develop and implement DNS policy, the Org had its own interests, and after fourteen years of tangling with its lawyers and staff, everyone in the community was aware of this. The community and ICANN Org were not the same. ICANN's lawyers in particular had repeatedly put protection of the interests of the corporation, and a desire to insulate it against external challenges and risks, above the demands of the global Internet community.

What would make the Org responsive to the community? Some form of accountability. But the Org's evasion of accountability mechanisms went back to its earliest days. Some said this tendency was "part of its DNA."[2] Its arbitrariness took many forms over many years, but two critical incidents in 2013—the very year ICANN's independence became a real possibility— brought the simmering problem to a boil. One was ICANN's attempt to assert a "unilateral right to amend" the basic contracts it had with registries and registrars. Another was the Org's top-down modification of a policy regarding trademark protection in new top-level domains.

ICANN's unique approach to Internet governance was based on private contracts. Contractual governance, as the Framework for Global Electronic Commerce had proposed back in 1997, served a dual purpose: it was supposed to globalize DNS governance, and it was supposed to empower the global Internet community to shape the policies informing the contracts. In February 2013, however, ICANN made moves that struck at the very heart of contractual governance. After publishing its call for new TLD applications and collecting tens of millions of dollars in application fees, ICANN suddenly altered the applicant guidelines to insist that it could modify their contracts unilaterally.[3] It also insisted that no registrar would be able to register names in any of the new TLDs unless they agreed to the new Registrar Accreditation Agreement discussed in chapter 8. The new RAA, however, was still in the works. The amendments being proposed by law enforcement and intellectual property interests were trying to impose onerous verification procedures on registrars. ICANN seemed to be coercing registrars into signing a blank check, on pain of being excluded from all business in all new top-level domains.[4]

The second triggering instance of arbitrariness was the creation of a trademark clearinghouse (TMCH) in 2012. Trademark owners wanted operators of new top-level domains to give their marks some kind of preemptive protection. The domain name industry and consumers, however, opposed their claim. If such protections were to be granted, they wanted them to be defined narrowly, to minimize their impact on the market and to protect fair use and free expression. With its balanced representation of different stakeholders, the GNSO authorized the creation of a TMCH that would send warnings to registrants of domain names when a user's registration *exactly matched* a trademarked text. But then, beset by lobbying and controversy, CEO Chehadé convened a set of closed, invitation-only meetings with big brand owners.[5] Based on those closed consultations the staff came up with a new policy: the TMCH would now give any registered trademark preemptive warnings on as many as fifty textual variations on their marks. In a stroke, Chehadé had nullified a consensus policy, tilted the playing field to one stakeholder group, and bypassed the GNSO.

As previously noted, the US government was using the IANA contract and the new RAA negotiations to "put the screws" on ICANN. This pressure was probably a factor in ICANN's attempt to get the power to unilaterally amend its contracts.[6] Chehadé's management style exacerbated those problems by trying to cut through problems with quick, top-down initiatives. This culminated in what was widely seen as the "accountability meltdown" of 2013.[7]

ACCOUNTABILITY IS TIED TO THE TRANSITION

Thus, by the time the NTIA announced its intent to "transition" its stewardship, there was a startling degree of unity around the idea that ICANN had a serious accountability problem. It was clear to everyone on the receiving end of these problems that the Affirmation of Commitments and its accountability and transparency review teams were not serious reforms. They were just another form of advisory participation with little effect on the arbitrary exercise of power. Under these circumstances, the prospect of a stewardship transition that would eliminate ICANN's one form of external oversight—the US government—made people take the need for major accountability reforms very seriously indeed.

As a result, the IANA transition became inextricably linked to accountability reforms. The link between the two was first discussed at the Singapore meeting but was cemented into place at the ICANN 50 meeting in London in June 2014. There, the burgeoning movement for accountability led the entire GNSO to agree unanimously on a statement supporting the creation of an independent accountability mechanism. The statement was read in dramatic fashion at ICANN's public forum. Verisign's Keith Drazek, the chair of the Registry Stakeholder Group, came to the microphone flanked by the leaders of all the other stakeholder groups and constituencies in the GNSO: Rafik Dammak from the Noncommercial Stakeholders Group, Elisa

Cooper from the Business Constituency, Michele Neylon from the Registrar Stakeholder Group, Tony Holmes from the Internet Service Providers Constituency, and Kristina Rosette from the Intellectual Property Constituency. Never in ICANN's history had all these constituencies agreed unanimously on a major substantive issue. The prepared statement read:

> The entire GNSO joins together today calling for the Board to support community creation of an independent accountability mechanism that provides meaningful review and adequate redress for those harmed by ICANN action or inaction in contravention of an agreed-upon compact with the community. . . . We need an independent accountability structure that holds the ICANN Board, staff, and various stakeholder groups accountable under ICANN's governing documents, serves as an ultimate review of Board staff decisions, and through the creation of precedent, creates prospective guidance for the Board, the staff and the entire community. As part of the IANA stewardship transition, the multistakeholder community has the opportunity and responsibility to propose meaningful accountability structures that go beyond just the IANA-specific accountability issues. We are committed to coming together and developing those recommendations for the creation of these mechanisms.

After the statement, an impressed Steven Crocker replied, "Boy, that's louder than a hum."[8]

ICANN's supervisors at the NTIA were surprised by this turn of events, and ICANN's management even more so. To their credit, both quickly adjusted to accommodate those concerns. The NTIA had made it clear that it would only accept a transition proposal that gained a broad consensus. The accountability revolt demonstrated that to gain that consensus, ICANN would have to do more than come up with a proposal to replace the NTIA's role in making root zone changes; it would also have to rethink the entire structure of ICANN. The community simply would not allow the transition to happen unless there was a suitable resolution of the accountability problems. While ICANN Org succeeded in fending off the most radical proposals demanded by many in its community, it did lead to a sweeping revision of the corporation's bylaws, as subsequent chapters will show.

THE STEWARDSHIP TRANSITION PROCESS

ICANN quickly set a process in motion. However bad the Org may have been at making consensus policies, it did have in place an established global network of participatory and communicative structures that touched all the primary users/customers of the IANA registries, and many if not most of the stakeholders in their decisions. Recognizing that a moment had come, ICANN could unify and mobilize these structures. The consultations at the Singapore meeting produced a draft proposal from ICANN outlining the "Principles, Mechanisms and Process to Develop a Proposal to Transition NTIA's Stewardship of the IANA Functions."[9] It circulated that draft for public comment on April 6, 2014. Community comments produced many modifications. Reflecting strong concerns about ICANN's dual role as convenor and object of reform, most suggestions reduced the role of the Org in managing the process; others broadened representation.[10] The Org's desire to move ahead expeditiously toward a transition made it highly responsive to the community in this phase. A consensus process was in place by the time the London meeting concluded in June 2014.

The process plan was based on two key decisions. The first was the decision to divide the transition proposal development into three parts, corresponding to the registry trinity: names, numbers, and protocols. The governance of these registries was seen as the product of three distinct "operational communities," which were defined as "those with direct operational or service relationships with the IANA functions operator." Each operational community would organize its own bottom-up process, independently of the others, to propose new governance arrangements to replace the NTIA's role in supervising their distinct registries.

The second key decision was to form a multistakeholder committee to coordinate proposal development. It would receive the three completed proposals and integrate them into a whole before transmitting it to the NTIA. This was dubbed the IANA Functions Stewardship Coordination Group (ICG). The ICG's charter deliberately eschewed centralizing authority. Community comment had objected strongly to ICANN's original idea of a steering committee. Instead, ICG was where the independently developed plans for names, numbers, and protocol governance converged to be assembled into a final proposal. The ICG developed a standard template that outlined the questions that needed to be answered by each proposal, and each operational community would submit transition proposals following this template to the ICG.[11] The ICG would not be empowered to approve or disapprove the substance of the plans based on its own ideas about their merits; it would only be able to assess whether they violated any of the NTIA's conditions and whether there had been appropriate levels of openness and transparency in their processes. The ICG would also look for any incompatibilities among the proposals and act as the intermediary through which the communities reconciled them.

In one sense, the division of the process seemed an obvious, uncontroversial move. It conformed to the accepted norm of bottom-up policy development. It recognized the vast differences between the three operational communities: the geeky protocol and standards developers involved in the IETF; the contentious trademark lawyers, civil society activists, and businesspeople involved with domain names; and the network operators and engineers prominent in the Numbers community. Decentralized development of transition proposals would be more efficient and responsive than a single, centralized process that threw all these stakeholders into the same stew.[12] Isolating the governance issues from each other would simplify their resolution, and the three processes could proceed in parallel.

At the same time, dividing the processes was highly consequential in terms of the outcomes it enabled—even a bit subversive. By recognizing that the three registries were distinct, with different technical characteristics, different policy issues, and a different set of stakeholders, it undermined the myth of a unified, integrated IANA, one of the foundational assumptions behind ICANN's formation. It also raised the possibility that different operational communities could choose different "IANAs," hence reviving debates about whether all the IANA functions needed to be in the same organization.[13] Most important of all, it decentralized power. Each operational community had the power to bargain with ICANN on its own. This had an important impact on the outcomes.

The ICG consisted of thirty people drawn from thirteen different organizational entities of the Internet community, (plus two nonvoting liaisons to the ICANN's IANA department and its board). The composition of the ICG and the numerical representation afforded each stakeholder group within it reflected the broader community's notion of a self-governing global Internet community (table 8.1).

With seven entities (ASO, IAB, IETF, ISOC, NRO, RSSAC, SSAC) and thirteen of the seats, the ICG's representational weighting favored the Internet technical community. Both the Org and the wider community tended to see the technical community as the core of the process and as having high levels of knowledge and legitimacy. The domain name industry (ccTLD managers and gTLD registries and registrars) accounted for seven seats.

Table 8.1

ANA Stewardship Coordination Group (ICG)

Community represented	Seats	People
At Large Advisory Committee	2	*Mohamed El Bashir* (vice chair), Jean-Jacques Subrenat
Address Supporting Organization	1	Hartmut Glaser
Country Code Registry Operators	4	Mary Uduma, Keith Davidson, Martin Boyle, Xiaodong Li
Generic Names Supporting Organization	3	James Bladel, Milton Mueller, Wolf-Ulrich Knoben
GTLD Registry Operators	2	Keith Drazek, Jon Nevett
Governmental Advisory Committee	5	Manal Ismail, Kavouss Arasteh, Michael Niebel, Thomas Schneider, Jandyr Ferreira dos Santos
International Chamber of Commerce	1	Joseph Alhadeff
Internet Architecture Board	2	Russ Housley, Lynn St. Amour
Internet Engineering Task Force	2	Jari Arkko, **Alissa Cooper** (chair)
Internet Society	2	Narelle Clark, Demi Getschko
Number Resource Organization	2	Paul Wilson, Alan Barrett
Root Server System AC	2	Lars-Johan Liman, Daniel Karrenberg
Security and Stability AC	2	*Patrik Fältström* (vice chair), Russ Mundy

Governments were another recognized category of representation and ended up with five seats.[14] A category that might roughly correspond to a notion of end users (ALAC and GNSO's NCUC) was given three seats. Business interests (ICC-BASIS, ISPs in the GNSO) held two seats. With consensus decision-making a requirement, however, voice was more important than numbers, and the diversity of voices was evident.

The ICG did not reflect a demographic-geographic system of representation, nor did it offer the unrealistic promise of representing all five billion Internet users. Rather, it enacted a functional-technical understanding of appropriate representation. Levels of representation were aligned with one's knowledge of, responsibility for, and dependence upon the management of the Internet registries. The process also relied heavily on transparency and public comment for legitimacy and required consensus decision-making. There were no major challenges to the legitimacy of the ICG.

The ICG began meeting in July 2014 and circulated its proposal template along with a call for proposals in September 2014. It set a deadline of January 15, 2015, for receipt of the proposals.

THE ACCOUNTABILITY REFORM PROCESS

The ICG and its three operational communities only addressed the so-called stewardship transition. That label, it became clear, embodied a narrower understanding of the transition and a tacit assumption on the part of the NTIA and ICANN that ICANN would *own* the IANA after the contract with the NTIA expired.[15] Recall that the 1998 White Paper plan had assumed that there was a single, unified IANA that needed to be "privatized" and eventually deemed ICANN the corporate receptacle for it. To the NTIA, the stewardship transition process would complete the privatization process by making ICANN Org, not the NTIA, the steward of the IANA functions. In this view, the main issue to be resolved through the ICG was how each operational community would transmit its policies to ICANN for implementation, and what kind of service-level agreements ICANN would have with these communities.

The accountability process was an entirely different animal. It implied that ICANN Org had to *earn* its stewardship of the IANA functions by agreeing to new institutional mechanisms to guard against arbitrary exercises of power. An implied bargain underlay the process: accountability reforms acceptable to the community had to be in place *before* the stewardship transition. Some proposals emerging from the accountability process even contemplated divesting the IANA from ICANN. This linkage worried ICANN's CEO and some ICANN board members. ICANN's leaders had successfully resisted accountability requirements for years, and now their desire for independence was tied to them. Seemingly unaware of the irony, Chehadé expressed fears that it might threaten the success of the whole endeavor.[16]

The charter governing the accountability reform process adopted a definition of accountability taken from the NETmundial multistakeholder statement: "the existence of mechanisms for independent checks and balances as well as for review and redress."[17] The process thus implicated holistic reform in the relationship between the Org and the community. Reforms could address new limits on ICANN's mission; the way board members could be approved or removed; how decisions might be appealed; how bylaws could be amended. Accountability reform was truly a constitutional moment for the ICANN regime—a "second founding"[18] that relitigated many of the internal issues raised during ICANN's formation in 1998–1999.

Led by the GNSO, the community formed a Cross-Community Working Group on Accountability (CCWG-Accountability) in October 2014 at

ICANN 51 in Los Angeles. Its charter was approved by the relevant SOs and ACs by early December. Its charter authorized it to "investigate accountability mechanisms regarding all of the functions provided by ICANN." It held its first online meeting on December 9, 2014.[19] Thomas Rickert, a lawyer for the German ISP trade association who represented ISPs on the GNSO Council; Mathieu Weill, a country code domain manager for .FR (France); and León Sanchez, an ALAC member from Latin America, co-chaired the working group (table 8.2).

As a working group chartered by ICANN SOs and ACs, CCWG-Accountability initially restricted membership to representatives appointed

Table 8.2
Cross-Community Working Group on Enhancing ICANN Accountability

Category	People appointed
At Large Advisory Committee	**León Sanchez (Latin America)** (co-chair) Sebastien Bachollet (Europe) Tijani Ben Jemaa (Africa) Alan Greenberg (North America) Cheryl Langdon-Orr (Australia)
Address Supporting Organization	Fiona Asonga (AFRINIC) Athina Fragkouli (RIPE-NCC) Izumi Okutani (APNIC) Jorge Villa (LACNIC)
Country Code Names Supporting Organization	**Mathieu Weill (.FR, European Region)** (co-chair) Jordan Carter (.NZ, AP Region) Eberhard Lisse (.NA, African Region) Roelof Meijer (.NL, European Region) Giovanni Seppia (.EU, European Region)
Governmental Advisory Committee	Par Brumark (Niue) Olga Cavalli (Argentina) Alice Munyua (African Union Commission) Suzanne Radell (USA) Julia Wolman (Denmark)
Generic Names Supporting Organization	**Thomas Rickert (CSG)** (co-chair) James Bladel (Registrar SG) Becky Burr (Registry SG) Steve DelBianco (Commercial SG) Robin Gross (Noncommercial SG)
Security and Stability Advisory Committee	Lyman Chapin Julie Hammer
Participants	199 individuals listed

by the chartering organizations but allowed "observers" or "participants" to join its calls and email lists. The original charter specified that "each of the chartering organizations shall appoint a minimum of 2 and a maximum of 5 members to the working group in accordance with their own rules and procedures." As the CCWG progressed, the number of participants expanded to 200. Although voting rights in the determination of "consensus" were still restricted to SOs and ACs, the distinction between "members" and "observers/participants" gradually eroded, and CCWG began to function like an open working group. In the end, there were twenty-six AC/SO members and 199 participants in the CCWG-Accountability group. In addition to a very high-traffic email list, it met monthly in synchronous virtual meetings and held face-to-face sessions at ICANN's quarterly meetings for the next eighteen months. It also spun off five working parties and subgroups focused on specialized issues like "community empowerment," "stress tests," "human rights," and legal advice.

ICANN's accountability reforms and the ICG stewardship transition proposals were interdependent. The ICG could not review and finalize the Names community's stewardship transition proposal until it knew what kind of accountability reforms had been agreed. Indeed, none of the proposals could be finalized until the accountability process had settled on its reforms. The NTIA's Strickling had made it unambiguous: "The two work streams on the IANA transition and enhanced accountability are directly linked and NTIA has repeatedly said that both issues must be addressed before any transition takes place."[20] Both processes wanted the final proposal to be sent to the NTIA in time to complete the transition when the IANA functions contract expired on September 30, 2015.

11 THE THREE PATHS

On September 8, 2014, the ICG released its request for proposals template, setting the transition process in motion. Each operational community then started developing charters and forming working groups to develop a proposal for their piece of the IANA functions. In forming and running their groups, each one scrupulously adhered to multistakeholder procedural norms regarding openness, transparency, and various forms of review and public comment, though the more diverse Names community faced issues regarding timely linguistic translations allowing for public comment.

Although the processes were separate, each community eventually confronted a common question: Was their relationship with ICANN, the existing IANA functions operator, voluntary? If so, could they choose to terminate the arrangement? All three of the working groups expressed satisfaction with the way ICANN was currently handling the IANA functions. In the name of accountability, however, they all pushed for a contractual relationship that would give them the power to choose a different operator if the need arose. The purpose was to fill the vacuum left by the NTIA, which in theory at least had possessed the power to offer the IANA functions contract to another organization.

That issue became known as *separability*. The pursuit of separability, which replaced the NTIA with the operational communities as the contracting authority, generated conflict with ICANN Org. ICANN had expected privatization to mean that IANA would become a permanent part of ICANN. A December 2014 statement by its board directly expressed this sense of entitlement: "ICANN was created and purpose-built to be the permanent and robust home of the IANA functions."[1] This chapter tracks the progress of each operational community individually and shows how these conflicts over separability were resolved.

The narrative also covers the renegotiation of the relationship between Verisign and ICANN regarding the management of the DNS root zone—a critical part of the IANA functions.

PROTOCOL PARAMETERS

As noted in chapter 6, the IETF had already negotiated an agreement with ICANN regarding its management of protocol parameter registries. While the formation of ICANN in 1998–1999 was a major disruption in the IETF's lines of authority, by March 2000 IETF had successfully negotiated a memorandum of understanding (RFC 2860) defining a satisfactory relationship between IANA and the IETF. After some rough patches in the early years after moving IANA to ICANN, in 2004 IETF installed someone known and trusted by the technical community, David Conrad, as the general manager of IANA. Starting in 2007, the IETF memorandum of understanding was supplemented by a service level agreement that was renewed annually.[2] In this respect, ICANN's IANA was already in a quasi-contractual agreement with the IETF.

IETF was happy with this arrangement. It was receiving an important service from ICANN at no cost. Key aspects of Postel's work—coordinating the finalization of standards documents and synchronizing them with the formation of protocol parameter registries—had been offloaded to an organization that could handle them at no cost to IETF, thanks to the substantial revenue stream generated by the fees charged to the domain name industry. In terms of time and human resources, the demands placed upon the IANA department by the protocol parameter registries vastly exceeded the requirements of the other registries. After fifteen years, younger IETF participants now thought of IANA as "a service" provided by ICANN.[3]

The IETF was getting a good deal. Their approach to the transition, therefore, was summarized by the slogan "don't rock the boat." As the protocol parameters operational community formed the IANAPLAN working group to develop a plan for the transition, its charter said:

> minimal change in the oversight of the IETF protocol parameters registries is preferred in all cases and no change is preferred when possible. The working group

will address the implications of moving the NTIA out of its current role with respect to IANA on the IETF protocol parameters registry function in a way that focuses on *continuation of the current arrangements*.[4]

This conservatism surfaced immediately when some members of the working group suggested that the IETF might want to reclaim the intellectual property associated with the IANA label. ICANN held the trademark on IANA, but the term, to recall chapter 4, had been invented by the IETF. Practically every RFC produced after 1988 referred to the IANA in some way or contained an "IANA Considerations" section.[5] If the IANA brand was not owned by the IETF, its RFC series could be in serious trouble. There was also the domain name IANA.org. Postel registered it himself in 1995, but it had been transferred to ICANN by the Commerce Department.[6] If the IETF ever wanted to change its IANA operator, the new operator would need the IANA .org domain and the trademark. If the IETF was serious about using this transitional moment to reclaim its autonomy, separating the IANA mark from a particular IANA functions operator should be at the top of its agenda.

The IETF's leadership in the IANAPLAN working group, however, argued vehemently against this. Their arguments made little sense unless one understood that they were afraid of rocking the boat. They feared that any renegotiation of the IETF's relationship to ICANN that involved taking something away might trigger counterproposals that could include an end to free IANA functions.[7] The IANAPLAN working group's final proposal, therefore, did not ask for any transfer of intellectual property. It said: leave everything as it is and just let the NTIA contract expire.

The "leave it alone" approach suffered from an inconsistency, however. The departure of the NTIA left certain gaps in understanding. The IANA-PLAN working group's proposal to the ICG asked for two simple assurances:

- An acknowledgment that the protocol parameters registries are in the public domain.
- An acknowledgment that if IETF wanted to change operators, ICANN would cooperate with the new operator to achieve a smooth transition and minimize disruption in the use of the protocol parameters registries or other resources currently located at IANA.org.

The IETF soon learned that these clarifications constituted a significant departure from "continuation of the current arrangements." The request for "a smooth transition" implied that IETF could terminate its agreement with

ICANN—in other words, that ICANN was not the owner of the IANA functions, merely a service provider. ICANN's lawyers did not like that language. An April 30, 2014, letter from IETF leadership (Andrew Sullivan, Jari Arkko, and Tobias Gondrom) to the IANAPLAN list reluctantly acknowledged that: "ICANN has informed us that they are unable to agree to that text right now. ICANN told us that, in their opinion, agreeing to that text now would possibly put them in breach of their existing agreement with the NTIA."[8]

Legality or contractual compliance was not really at issue here, because the NTIA would never have used the existing IANA contract to stop the transition process from reaching a conclusion agreed to by its community. The real issue was whether the protocol parameter registries would be delegated to ICANN by the IETF or whether ICANN owned them.

The claims about breach of contract with the NTIA must have puzzled the IETF negotiators. In their request for a commitment to a smooth transition, they had expressed their belief that ICANN was already obligated to achieve a smooth transition under the 2012 IANA functions contract. "It is our view that the substance of the statements above is already part of our agreement with ICANN, and that we are merely elaborating details of that existing agreement."[9]

The IETF representatives were correct that the existing contract could be awarded to another operator and committed ICANN to a "smooth transition." However, the NTIA, not IETF, was the principal of the IANA contract. Once the NTIA was no longer in the picture, who was the principal?[10] The IETF proposal, despite bending over backward to be as conservative as possible, was still shaking things up, due to its unstated premise that IETF was replacing the NTIA as the contracting authority. Likewise, if ICANN denied the IETF a choice of a service provider, it would be in a more powerful position relative to the IETF than it had been before.[11] In effect, this was a debate over who would inherit the NTIA's power. Would it all go directly to ICANN, or would it be divided up among the operational communities?

NUMBERS

IANA plays a much smaller role in the maintenance of IP address registries. It delegated large blocks of numbers from the "free pool" to the Regional Internet Registries as needed; the RIRs were the organizations that maintained detailed registries of which networks were using which numbers.

By the end of 2014, practically all the IPv4 number resources had already been delegated to RIRs; only the vast but underutilized IPv6 number space remained in IANA's hands. ICANN-IANA's top-level address registry was not expensive to maintain. The RIRs, unlike the IETF, were well-funded, legally incorporated organizations that already provided most of the institutional platform for governance of the IP address space. This gave them greater autonomy from ICANN and its IANA.

The Numbers Resource Organization (NRO) is the trade association of Regional Internet Registries. On October 16, 2014, the NRO executive council proposed the formation of a team to develop a proposal for the ICG. The five RIRs agreed to form a single, consolidated group, called the Consolidated RIR IANA Stewardship Proposal (CRISP) team. Each RIR appointed three members (two community members and one RIR staff) to the CRISP team. The fifteen-member team developed a charter and set to work developing a single, agreed Internet numbering community proposal to the ICG.[12]

Unlike IETF, the Numbers community made no pretense that they wanted to continue current arrangements. The CRISP team proposal asserted that the RIRs should have direct contracting authority over the provision of the IANA numbers registry and called for separating the intellectual property associated with IANA from ICANN. Like the IETF, the RIRs had no objections to the way ICANN's IANA department was currently performing those functions but demanded the power to fire IANA. Their proposal stated that they wanted:

> A new contract with the five RIRs and the IANA functions operator as signatories [that] would shift the responsibility for renewing, setting terms or terminating the contract to the RIRs, who would coordinate their decisions via the NRO Executive Council (made up of the RIR Directors and Chief Executives). Decisions made regarding the contract would be based on operational circumstances, past performance and input from open, regional communities.[13]

Once again, ICANN's lawyers were displeased. This was not the transition they were expecting. The transition was supposed to privatize ICANN with IANA remaining in its own hands, not carve it up into service contracts subjecting ICANN to three new forms of external accountability.

In a presentation at an April 13, 2015, meeting of ARIN (the RIR for the North American region), CRISP team representatives reported on how their proposal had been received by ICANN. They projected a slide that said, "ICANN has verbally represented that they will reject any proposed agreement in which ICANN is not deemed the sole source prime contractor for IANA functions in perpetuity." The presentation also stated, "ICANN asserts that neither NTIA nor the US Congress will approve any transition plan which leaves open the possibility of a future non-US IANA Functions Operator."[14]

This statement held great significance. First, it clarified ICANN Org's intentions: ICANN wanted to own the IANA functions, full stop. More revealing still, ICANN seemed to be telling an operational community that it could reject certain proposals and that it could speak on behalf of the US government to veto proposals. Moreover, these private indications (probably from ICANN's lawyers) directly contradicted a statement from Steven Crocker, the chair of the board, who had stated that there was "nothing fundamental in [the Numbers proposal] that we have a problem with."[15]

News of this snag in negotiations spread rapidly throughout all three operational community processes, and to the ICG itself.[16] Commentators began to link the friction the IETF had encountered to ICANN's resistance to the CRISP team proposal and see a pattern. CRISP team member Bill Woodcock claimed that the Internet Architecture Board minutes showed that "ICANN is *refusing to renew* the MOU under which they provide Protocol Registry services to the IETF, because it contains a termination clause" and said he found that "very disturbing."[17]

NAMES

The cross-community working group developing the stewardship transition for the Names community was co-chaired by Lise Fuhr, who was associated with the Country Code Names Supporting Organization (ccNSO) and Jonathan Robinson, representing the Generic Names Supporting Organization (GNSO).[18]

The Names community, to no one's surprise, took the longest time to develop their proposal and proposed the most complicated changes. There was a reason for that. Aside from the fact that domain names engaged the most heterogeneous and contentious community, there was a peculiarity unique to the DNS registry that made the stewardship transition more complex.[19]

The Protocols and Numbers communities could propose a contractual relationship with IANA, because they already had their own policy development institutions outside of ICANN—the IETF and the RIRs/NRO, respectively.[20] The policy development organs of the Names community, on the other hand, were *inside* ICANN. They were creatures of ICANN's own bylaws.

How, then, could the Names community establish an arm's-length contractual relationship with the current IANA functions operator? Both policy development and the names registry operator (IANA) were run by ICANN Org. The policy development organs (GNSO, GAC, ALAC) were unincorporated groups defined by ICANN's bylaws. How could they position themselves as an independent contracting party in a position to hire or fire ICANN to serve as the DNS root zone registry operator? This was the conundrum facing the Names community.

Months before the NTIA announcement of its decision to end the IANA contract, researchers at the Internet Governance Project were wrestling with this problem. On March 3, 2014, they published a paper to submit to the NETmundial meeting as part of its roadmap.[21] The IGP proposal called for structurally separating the DNS-related IANA functions and the root zone maintainer functions from ICANN and Verisign, respectively. It proposed to put them into a new, independent DNS Authority (DNSA), which would be a nonprofit consortium of top-level domain registries and root server operators that would operate the names-related IANA functions. Post-divestiture, ICANN would only manage the policy development process for DNS.

The IGP proposal received some support.[22] ICANN and the Internet technical community, however, did not react favorably and tried to marginalize the proposal at NETmundial. The IGP proposal's clash with ICANN's own expectations about the transition was obvious, but many in the community were also justifiably wary of creating a new institution with responsibilities over something as important as the DNS root. ICANN's own start-up process had generated power struggles and instabilities, and no one wanted a replay of that. The IGP proposal, however, did put the idea of divesting IANA from ICANN on the table, where it stayed in various forms throughout the transition process.

As the cross-community working group (CWG-Names) got underway in October 2014, the idea of finding a way to allow the Names community to contract for the IANA functions took root. Becky Burr, the former NTIA official who helped found ICANN, was now working for registry operator Neustar. Burr linked the power to contract for DNS IANA functions to accountability, just as IGP had. "To accomplish requisite accountability, we need some independent committee, council, unincorporated association, or representative group to have a contract with ICANN/IANA for performing IANA functions."[23] Debate then centered on what this "representative group" would be. A key debate was whether the contracting party would be confined to direct customers of the IANA function (that is, registries) or be more broadly representative.

By mid-November, "separability" was accepted as a principle guiding the CWG, though not without some pushback from ALAC representatives.[24] After a face-to-face meeting in Frankfurt, Germany, the Names community in December 2014 proposed creating a shell company called Contract Co.[25] The brainchild of trademark lawyer Greg Shatan, Contract Co would be a not-for-profit company with no staff whose only function was to be signatory to the contract with the IANA functions operator. It would take its direction from a Multistakeholder Review Team (MRT) drawn from naming community stakeholders and a Customer Standing Committee (CSC) composed of registries. The Contract Co model would enable a switch to a new IANA service provider if the community, as represented by the MRT and CSC, felt that ICANN had failed to perform the naming-related IANA functions properly.

In the public comment period, Contract Co got a mixed reception. There was praise for the way it embodied agreed principles such as separability, multistakeholder representation, and a neutral IANA.[26] Many commenters, however, said the proposal lacked sufficient detail. It left unspecified the contracting entity's jurisdiction, choice of law, and its legal relationship to the MRT. Comments from China, Brazil, and India were mildly favorable, particularly because of the possibility that Contract Co could be incorporated outside US jurisdiction. ICANN, however, was still resisting the principle of separability. Its comments claimed that the proposal overreached and questioned the need for a new entity because "ICANN was created and purpose-built to be the permanent and robust home of the IANA functions."[27] Legitimate concerns were raised, again, about the risks of creating new organizations that duplicated features of existing institutional arrangements.[28] Some claimed that the MRT reproduced ICANN and would bleed into policy.

ALAC members were some of the most strenuous opponents of the proposal. It was already becoming evident that ALAC, itself a creature of

ICANN Org, took positions that upheld the interests of ICANN's staff and board in the transition proceedings. This pattern would become even more prominent during the CCWG-Accountability process (see chapter 12). ALAC representatives now began to promote what became known as an "internal" solution, which meant that the Names IANA would remain inside ICANN but would be functionally separated from the policy process (which it already was). The other camp supported what became known as an "external" solution, which involved structural separation of the Names IANA from ICANN.

The Contract Co idea was effectively killed at the Singapore public meeting in February 2015. After Fuhr and Robinson presented the idea, the NTIA raised doubts about whether the US government would accept it.[29]

In late February 2015, three civil society participants, Avri Doria, Brenden Kuerbis, and Matt Shears, proposed what they called a "New IANA Integrated Model," a middle ground in the debates over functional vs structural separation. They conceived of a structurally separated Post-Transition IANA (PTI) as serving all three of the operational communities. The CWG-Names eventually settled on a complicated variant of that model. A new, separate legal entity—PTI—would be formed as a wholly owned subsidiary of ICANN. The existing IANA functions, administrative staff, and related resources, processes, data, and know-how would be legally transferred to PTI. ICANN would contract with PTI to serve as the IANA functions operator for the naming functions, including service level agreements. A highly complex (and highly unlikely) set of procedures could be invoked to separate PTI from ICANN if deemed necessary.

As a separate legal entity, PTI would have its own board of directors and have the minimum statutorily required responsibilities and powers under California Nonprofit Public Benefit Corporation law. ICANN would be the sole member of PTI, appointing a majority of its board. This model locked in US jurisdiction. Any issues concerning the PTI and the PTI board would be addressed through the ICANN accountability mechanisms. The proposal also called for an IANA Function Review (IFR), which would audit PTI's performance against the ICANN-PTI contract and the statement of work. A Customer Standing Committee was empowered to monitor the performance of the IANA functions and escalate nonremediated issues to the ccNSO and GNSO. The ccNSO and GNSO should be empowered to address matters escalated by the Customer Standing Committee.

In what was becoming an increasingly rushed process, the CWG-Names published its second draft proposal on April 22, 2015, and posted public comments June 9. Chinese stakeholders jointly complained that a Chinese-language version, as well as many other translations, were not provided on time.[30] Still, the public comment process confirmed broad support for PTI and related structures, such as the IANA Function Review and customer standing committee.[31] The proposal concluded with a comment that passed the baton to the ICG:

> While this proposal originates from within the names community, it anticipates that, for reasons of coherence of the IANA function and overall operational logistics, all of the IANA functions will be transferred to PTI. However, it is not clear at the time of writing whether the other operational communities will undertake to contract directly with PTI.

As the Names community was concluding its process, another sign of community convergence emerged. Board member Bruce Tonkin, in his capacity as board liaison, sent a statement to the CCWG-Accountability list addressing "concerns that ICANN will reject community developed proposals."[32] The statement carefully backed away from ICANN legal's reported statement to the Numbers community. Tonkin did not directly repudiate the statements attributed to ICANN legal, nor deny that they had been made, but he did say that "the ICANN Board supports the community processes that have been used to develop proposals for the IANA transition and ICANN's accountability," and "accepts that the community will want to have fall back mechanisms in place should the IANA functions operator not perform its function to the standards required by the community."

On June 11, 2015, CWG-Stewardship (Names) produced a finished proposal, and two weeks later its chartering organizations approved them unanimously at ICANN 53 in Buenos Aires. The ICG now had complete proposals from all three operational communities.

THE ICG TAKES OVER

Now it was ICG's turn to review and reconcile the proposals. The only major incompatibility among the proposals pertained to the intellectual property rights and domain ownership associated with IANA. The ICG had already formally notified the IETF, on February 9, 2015, that it needed to reconcile differences with the CRISP team (numbers) proposal.[33] The IETF quickly ended its resistance to transferring the IANA marks out of ICANN. The chairs of the IANAPLAN working group obtained the consent of the IETF Trust to serve as the organizational holder of the IPR on February 19,[34] allowing the IETF to modify its proposal to align with that of the CRISP team.

The Names community proposal also needed reconciliation on the IPR issue. It allowed ICANN to retain the IPR but required it to license them to any new IANA operator. ICG notified CWG-Names on June 19, 2015, that its proposal was also incompatible with the Numbers and Protocol Parameters proposals.[35] The Names community fell in line with the plan to transfer ownership of the domain name and trademarks to the IETF Trust. On August 15, 2015, the ICANN board indicated that it, too, supported the IPR transfer. Crocker wrote to the IANAPLAN list: "The ICANN Board believes that for stability and pragmatic operational reasons, the IANA Functions Operator must have operational control over the IANA.ORG domain. During the transition, ICANN is prepared to transfer full ownership of the IANA-related trademarks to a neutral third party mutually agreed among the operational communities."[36]

The ICG published its consolidated proposal for public comment on July 31, 2015. It received 159 comments from a diverse array of respondents. Among the issues attracting comment were jurisdiction, the workability and structure of PTI, the relationship between PTI and country code top-level domains, the question of the Root Zone Maintainer (currently Verisign), and dependencies upon the accountability reforms. The ICG found a preponderance of support for the overall proposal: 41 percent of the comments were supportive of the proposal, and another 24 percent offered support but qualified it with questions or requests for clarification.[37] Clear supporters included the main users of the IANA functions from the various operational communities. A minority of the comments (11 percent) opposed the proposal, while a smaller number (9 percent) opposed the IANA stewardship transition completely. Many comments congratulated the ICG on its work and praised the process as showing "how a multistakeholder system works and the remarkable level of dedication of many volunteers around the world."[38]

Half a dozen comments inspired by populist-nationalist opposition in Washington made their way into the transition process for the first time. The proposal "assumes the Internet does not belong to America . . . which it does. All your foreigners should be grateful we let you use it," said one comment. "Modify the proposal to move ICANN to Washington D.C. into a secure facility," said another. Another warned, "The Internet must not become a tool of political agendas generated by other countries, especially non-Western countries. I only want the USA to supervise my internet activity!!!!" A Chinese registry operator, on the other hand, commented, "We do not believe that the proposal sufficiently meets the needs and expectations of the global customers and partners of the IANA service" because of its "failure to actively and effectively engage the Chinese speaking constituency."[39] India expressed general support for the proposal but asked for voting rights for the GAC in PTI's Customer Standing Committee.

Though the reception was mixed, ICG deemed public support sufficient to proceed. The ICG completed its stewardship transition work by October 29, 2015 and awaited the accountability reforms.[40] "Once the CWG confirms that their Accountability needs have been met by the CCWG proposal, the ICG will make a final determination as to whether the combined proposal is complete and ready to be sent to the NTIA."

THE NEW ROOT ZONE MAINTAINER ARRANGEMENT

As noted in chapter 5, neither ICANN nor the pre-ICANN IANA was in direct operational control of the DNS root zone. The Root Zone Maintainer (RZM) was Verisign, the company that ran the .COM and .NET top-level domains. Verisign performed these functions under a cooperative agreement with the NTIA, and that agreement was what gave the US government control over the DNS root zone. The transition therefore required revising that arrangement.

The NTIA, however, did not turn that revision process entirely over to the multistakeholder process. Instead, it asked Verisign and ICANN to submit a proposal for how best to remove the NTIA's administrative role in root zone management. This request tacitly assumed that ICANN would remain as the IANA for names and that ICANN would replace the NTIA as the contracting authority for root zone management. ICANN and Verisign submitted a joint proposal with a high-level plan in August 2015.[41] The proposal resulted in the 2016 development of the Root Zone Maintainer Services Agreement (RZMA), establishing a bilateral relationship between ICANN and Verisign while removing the NTIA from its legacy "approver" role for updates to the root zone file.

Verisign seemed interested in remaining in the role as RZM, but did not view it as a profit center. Under the RZMA, Verisign would be paid a nominal fee (about $250,000 per year), to maintain the root zone in accordance with IANA's decisions, as well as manage the root zone's zone signing key and distribute the root zone file and related files to the root zone operators. The RZMA has an eight-year term, with the intention of promoting the security, stability, and resiliency of root zone maintenance operations. As an important additional accountability mechanism, the RZMA also provides the community with the ability to require ICANN to transition the root zone maintenance function to another service provider after three years. It also allows the community to recommend changes to service level agreements and the RZMA, as root zone management evolves. Via the CWG-Stewardship, the community established a standing Root Zone Evolution Review Committee (RZERC) to provide advice on any future architectural changes. Since its creation in 2016, the RZERC has produced a statement in support of the Key Signing Key rollover, recommendations for adding data protections to the root zone, and recommendations to study signed root zone name server data.

The basic outlines of the structures needed to remove the US government from its role as steward of the DNS root zone and contracting party for the IANA functions were now in place. Now it was time to reform ICANN's accountability arrangements.

12 ACCOUNTABILITY REFORM

In an interview recorded by ICANN's public relations department after the transition, former CEO Fadi Chehadé characterized the accountability process as the product of a "power shift."[1] "No matter what we say about the administrative nature of the U.S. role in the IANA functions," he said:

> it was clear who was defining that whole power structure. It was the U.S. government. Now, when people realized that the U.S. government was going to cede its shaping of that system, this is called a power shift. And any time there's a power shift, accountability and the methods by which we check on it become heightened in the minds of a lot of people. So that's why people woke up and said, hey, we need to look at [accountability] now.

Chehadé's observation contained an interesting oversight. While it was true that a power shift was occurring, accountability concerns did *not* begin with the NTIA announcement. The Internet community did *not* "wake up" to that issue in March 2014. How to make the "new IANA" accountable had preoccupied the International Forum on the White Paper in the summer of 1998. Accountability concerns were the reason the NTIA forced ICANN to agree to establish a voting membership in October 1998 before recognizing it as the new entity contemplated by the White Paper. Ever since ICANN's voting membership was abolished in 2002, law and policy intellectuals had been analyzing and criticizing the board's insulation from accountability.[2] Two legal scholars summed up the thrust of this literature in 2012:

> ICANN's corporate organization vest[s] virtually unconstrained power in its Board of Directors. . . . it remains legally free to remove directors and officers; disregard community consensus; reject recommendations by the Board Governance

Committee or the IRP regarding challenges to a Board decision; and reject policy recommendations from any source, including the GAC and its nation-state representatives.[3]

Far from being provoked by the NTIA's withdrawal, the accountability process was seen as an opportunity to fix design flaws dating back to ICANN's founding.[4] This is why the community's success in getting the NTIA to condition the transition on accountability reforms was so important. In 1998, the NTIA had proceeded with the recognition of ICANN despite unresolved questions about what would keep the new corporation accountable. In a hurry, Commerce chose to rely on promises and, when the promises were broken, on memorandums of understanding and the IANA contract.

This time, the independence ICANN Org wanted so badly would be held hostage until suitable accountability reforms were made. This time, the community itself would be rewriting the rules, and the changes would have to be implemented in the bylaws before a transition took place. The NTIA had made it clear that the new ICANN bylaws needed to have broad community support before the transition could occur. For once, the community had real leverage.

The range of potential bylaw changes was so broad that CCWG-Accountability set up a division between what they called "Workstream 1" and "Workstream 2." Workstream 1 consisted of reforms that had to be made before the NTIA removed itself from its oversight role and the community's leverage was lost. Workstream 2 consisted of issues to consider or desirable changes that could be deferred until after the transition.[5]

The remaking of ICANN from within was a highly complex process. In addition to the main cross-community working group (CCWG-Accountability), nine subgroups spun off to work on specialized problems.[6] As the group encountered complex issues in corporate law and contracts, the CCWG engaged its own independent legal team, which ICANN agreed to pay for. Adler Colvin, specializing in the law of nonprofit organizations, and Sidley Austin, specializing in multinational corporate governance, performed these tasks. Statistics compiled by ICANN staff show that as of February 2016, the 227 participants in CCWG-Accountability had held eighty-three meetings of the full group, and 221 meetings when all the subgroups are included.[7] Taking the number of attendees in each meeting and multiplying by the number of hours in the meeting, the cumulative working hours was 17,368, or about two years. There were 14,000 emails exchanged on multiple lists. These statistics do not include the last two months of the process and the time spent by external counsel, ICANN staff, or observers.

The reform proposals went through four iterations. An open, multistakeholder process conducted under mounting time pressure, it involved not only political bargaining between the community and the corporation's board, lawyers, and management but also a renegotiation of power relations among ICANN's supporting organizations and advisory committees. In particular, the process forced the community to reconsider the role of the Governmental Advisory Committee and its powers and limitations as a stakeholder. The participants recognized and empowered as "stakeholders" in the CCWG-Accountability process, in fact, were in many ways defined by ICANN's existing institutional structure, creating a recursive influence relationship that had a major impact on the outcome.

To simplify the complexity, this chapter breaks down the reform process into four key areas of the Workstream 1 deliberations: empowering the community; re-defining the mission and core values; forming an independent "judiciary"; and circumscribing the role of the GAC.

EMPOWERING THE COMMUNITY

One of the first and most popular ideas for reforming ICANN was to reinstitute some form of membership. California law governing nonprofit organizations has provisions for statutory members, and the law is designed to give them specific rights. From the beginning of ICANN, statutory membership was seen as the most direct way to give the global Internet community control over ICANN Org. Members could be empowered to remove board members, overturn board decisions, or approve bylaw changes, for example. Jordan Carter, one of the managers of the .NZ country code top-level domain, tied membership to the original vision of a self-governing Internet community: "By giving the rights of membership to the community, we are giving the community, in a sense, 'ownership' of ICANN. That's what the NTIA asked for when it said that the stewardship of the DNS was going to the multistakeholder community."[8]

By the same token, ICANN Org—especially its lawyers—saw any form of membership as a threat. They did not want ICANN participants to have enumerated statutory rights. Empowering members, they feared, would allow them to sue the organization, dissolve the corporation, or do other bad things. The circle-the-wagons mentality that permeated ICANN's rocky start-up process still existed. Indeed, the 2015 debates over membership raised bitter memories of ICANN's early days. Avri Doria, an IETF participant who had become involved in the GNSO's Noncommercial Stakeholders Group, wrote to the CCWG list,

> Membership has always been part of the kit that was available to ICANN in the multistakeholder model. An initial experiment met with some issues and instead of fixing that then, they threw the notion away [in 2002] without exploring possible tweaks to the system. As a result, we are living in ICANN 2.0, a system that was imposed in a top-down manner and one that was never fully accepted by those at the bottom.[9]

While the radically democratic idea of individual membership was off the table for most participants, the idea of a new, more aggregated form of membership enjoyed support by mainstream business interests as well as civil society activists and some technical community participants. As ICANN entered the transition process, for example, the Information Technology and Innovation Foundation (ITIF), a pro-business, pro-technology think tank in Washington, DC, favorably promoted a proposal to vest membership rights in the chairs of ICANN's SOs and ACs.[10] A similar notion was proposed by Becky Burr, the former NTIA official who was now working for registry operator Neustar. Burr believed that while the SOs and ACs were part of ICANN, they could become statutory members if they became Unincorporated Associations (UAs).[11]

The first iteration of the CCWG-Accountability's reform proposal developed the idea of making SOs and ACs into members as UAs. This proved legally problematic, because, it was feared, giving SOs and ACs legal personhood might recreate ICANN and generate power struggles over the control of those entities. The idea was dropped.

After several months of intensive debates and deliberations, CCWG turned instead to what it called the Sole Member model. This was an attempt to give ICANN's SOs and ACs statutory membership rights without the problems associated with making them into legal persons. In the words of the CCWG's lawyers,

> The Sole Member would be created as an entity with legal personhood (as an unincorporated association) for the express purpose of holding and exercising

member rights in ICANN through new provisions in the ICANN Bylaws. These Bylaw provisions would be designated as "fundamental" so that any change to them would require approval of the community.[12]

There would be a "community mechanism" for arriving at a consensus involving direct participation by SOs and ACs, but it would not require any of them to have legal personhood. The Sole Member would have no officers or directors and no assets.[13] As the lawyers put it, "The Sole Member would only be able to act as directed by community consensus as defined in the Bylaws."

As ideas of membership gained momentum in the CCWG, ICANN's board, urged on by its legal team, began to propose its own set of "reforms." Anything to avoid membership. ICANN proposed binding arbitration instead of membership, for example. All of the board's counterproposals left considerable discretionary power in the hands of the board. At one point, board chair Steve Crocker even suggested that accountability reforms could be deferred until after the transition, based on a promise to "commit to a future governance structure review."[14] As ICANN Org's push against membership ramped up, it became evident that ALAC participants would echo board/staff arguments.[15] This was not at all surprising, given that the at large was entirely a creature of ICANN Org and its money.

As the CCWG-Accountability's second reform proposal went out for public comment, the spirit of cooperation began to break down. ICANN Org backed away from Chehadé's promises, made in the first blush of the transition, that "we are just the facilitator, we are not the decider." In a leaked memo sent to the CCWG's lawyers, ICANN's lawyers argued aggressively against the sole member model. They assailed the model as "untested," raised fears of "capture," and claimed that it could not be implemented in time for a September 2016 transition.[16] The memo claimed that "a membership model . . . was rejected [in 2002] because it would not best serve the bottom-up, multistakeholder model"—overlooking the vast difference between the individual membership of the 2000 elections and the Sole Member model proposal in 2015.

ICANN's most egregious, yet revealing, argument against membership was that the Sole Member did not owe a fiduciary duty to ICANN.

The shift to the SMM [Sole Member Model] would place a significant amount of power in the hands of individuals and stakeholders that hold no fiduciary obligations to ICANN or the global stakeholder community. These individuals and stakeholders are free to act in their personal interest and are not required to make decisions based on what is best for ICANN, the ICANN community, and the global public interest. The result would be that a limited number of SOs and ACs (which could change over time) would have ultimate power over ICANN for significant matters with literally no accountability.[17]

In effect, ICANN sought to avoid accountability to its community by arguing that its own community was unaccountable. It was also equating fiduciary duty to *ICANN the corporation* with a duty to the *community* and to the *global public interest*. CCWG member Phil Corwin exposed the flaw in this argument on the email list as the debate raged:

> While the Board may credibly state that it has a fiduciary duty to ICANN and makes decisions based upon what is best for ICANN . . . , it cannot claim to make decisions based on what is best for the ICANN community (since its first duty is to the Corporation, and it is quite evident from the current accountability discussion that its views are at significant variance from those of the community members comprising the CCWG). And it has no greater claim to representing the global public interest than the community from which it is drawn.[18]

In its rejoinder to ICANN's legal team that the Sole Member would have unconstrained powers, the CCWG's lawyers argued that "it is possible to constrain the community's internal decision-making . . . by providing very high decision thresholds—even unanimity requirements—for community decisions directing the Sole Member to act."[19]

Disappointment with ICANN's rejection of the Sole Member model ran deep and crossed stakeholder groups and ideologies. It called into question the whole compact underlying the transition. Paul Rosenzweig was a conservative Republican affiliated with the Heritage Foundation who had entered the generally liberal Noncommercial Stakeholders Group to participate in the process but nevertheless shared their concerns about accountability. He said, "The board's rejection [was] an indication that ICANN as an institution really didn't want accountability. This was all about power, and the board was not going to give it up." Rosenzweig saw the rejection as a transformative moment in the process. "You could almost see the people running the CCWG-Accountability deflate, *physically deflate*," he said. "Before that, the meetings were filled with energy, optimism, enthusiasm, intellectual ferment and curiosity. Atmospherically, they were good meetings to go to; they were fun. After that it had the feel of a dead man walking."[20]

Rosenzweig may have overstated the impact of the conflict, but the CCWG mailing list records strong reactions. New Zealand's Jordan Carter fumed, "The Board has abused its role as a decision-maker in this process. In effect, it has sought to replace the open, public, deliberative proposal development process with its own definition of what the community requires, and its own solution that can deliver its evaluation of those requirements."[21]

Guru Acharya, a civil society advocate from India, observed sarcastically, "According to them, ICANN is multistakeholder enough to become the steward of IANA, but the community is not multistakeholder enough to become a member of ICANN. Effectively, we are making ICANN the corporation the steward of IANA and not ICANN the community."[22]

While this was going on, ICANN's CEO was heavily lobbying the three chairs of the CCWG in the background. Chehadé told them that the NTIA or Congress would not accept their proposal and implored them to endorse the board's position. Those who refused were told, "You will have to explain to your children that you made the IANA transition fail." The NTIA's Strickling, in fact, did not back up Chehadé's claims that the US government would not accept their proposal. On the contrary, two congressional leaders who had learned of the controversy, Senators John Thune and Brian Schatz, sent a bipartisan warning letter to ICANN dated October 15, 2015. They wrote, "Significant accountability reforms that empower the community and are developed by the community are necessary for Congressional support of any such transition."[23]

The accountability wars dominated ICANN's annual general meeting in Dublin, Ireland, held October 18–22, 2015. An exhausted and frustrated CCWG tried to reestablish the reform momentum. Eventually, the community salvaged something similar to the Sole Member model by drawing on the "designator" concept in California nonprofit corporate law.

As the community's lawyers explained, ICANN already functioned under a designator model, in that SOs and ACs were already empowered to appoint directors to the ICANN board.[24] Although their statutory powers were a bit weaker than members, most of the powers the CCWG wanted to give the Sole Member could also be held by designators.[25] The lawyers pointed out, however, that under ICANN's existing bylaws these designator powers could be erased by board actions or lead to destabilizing litigation, because "the Bylaws do not specifically expressly acknowledge the legal position of the SOs, ALAC, and the NomCom as designators under California corporate law."

Hence, the CCWG amended its proposal to create an "empowered community," which in essence was a single designator roughly based on the

Sole Member concept. ICANN's revised bylaws defined the empowered community (EC) as a California nonprofit association consisting of the Address Supporting Organization, the Country Code Names Supporting Organization, the Generic Names Supporting Organization, the At Large Advisory Committee, and the Governmental Advisory Committee. Each SO/AC is a "decisional participant" in the empowered community.

The CCWG-Accountability gave the EC new, legally enforceable powers to keep the Org accountable, including the powers to:

- Reject ICANN budgets, IANA budgets, or strategic/operating plans.
- Reject changes to ICANN's standard bylaws.
- Approve changes to new fundamental bylaws, articles of incorporation, and ICANN's sale or other disposition of ICANN's assets.
- Remove an individual ICANN board director.
- Recall the entire ICANN board.
- Initiate a binding independent review process (where a panel decision is enforceable in any court recognizing international arbitration results).
- Reject ICANN board decisions relating to reviews of the IANA functions, including the triggering of post-transition IANA separation.
- Rights of inspection and investigation.

These actions could be taken with the support of any three of the five decisional participants. For the GNSO, which consists of five distinct stakeholder groups with highly divergent interests, support for an action would require all of them to agree on it (or decline to object).

Although the board had expressed opposition to the designator model, too, the warning from the US Senators and pressure from the NTIA and the community eventually led to its compliance with the community's plan for bylaw reform. ICANN accepted the CCWG's empowered community concept. A power shift, to use Chehadé's words, had indeed taken place.

REDEFINING THE MISSION AND CORE VALUES

Revising ICANN's mission was another key area of accountability reform. From the beginning of the DNS wars in the mid-1990s, the Internet community had recognized that the centralization needed to coordinate unique identifiers could be used to undermine the decentralized networking and permissionless innovation enabled by the Internet protocols.[26] Centralized control of DNS, in other words, might be extended into regulation of content, services, and applications by making the award of a domain name contingent on regulations and policies. One way of keeping ICANN away from this temptation was to bind it to a well-defined, narrow mission, and then empowering the community to enforce its boundaries through a quasi-judicial process (the independent review process).

Mission limitation thus became a chief goal of the ICANN reforms. ICANN's mission should be limited to ensuring that the identifiers are unique and that the DNS root zone operates in a secure and stable manner and to providing a contractual legal framework for the operation of the industry that supplies identifier registries. Malcolm Hutty, a manager of one of the earliest Internet service providers in the United Kingdom, expressed the prevailing view of the CCWG-Accountability in December 2015: "CCWG wants to draw a bright line between the area where ICANN is supposed to develop policy (and enforce that policy through contracts) and the area where we believe ICANN should not have a policy. And we want this line to be enforceable by the IRP [independent review process]."[27]

The goal was a kind of First Amendment for ICANN, a fundamental bylaw designed to limit its intervention in Internet activity to narrow forms of DNS-specific governance. ICANN's mission definition was already fairly narrow, but the CCWG proposed to strengthen adherence to its limits by adding a new subsection to the mission statement. In its first four words, this new section paralleled the broad First Amendment prohibition: "(c) ICANN shall not regulate (i.e., impose rules and restrictions on) services that use the Internet's unique identifiers or the content that such services carry or provide, outside the express scope of Section 1.1(a)." Another important limitation added to the mission was that the scope of ICANN's policy making was restricted to policies "that are developed through a bottom-up consensus-based multistakeholder process" (Section 1.1(a)(i)).

There was widespread agreement on this goal in the abstract. As participants began to realize how strong a constraint Section 1.1(c) would be, however, it became contentious. Governments and intellectual property interests began to realize that they had, in fact, been leveraging ICANN's contractual regime to pursue broader regulatory goals, and in some ways they wanted to keep doing that.

Some of the most obvious conflicts with the proposed "content and services" limitation arose from the GAC's interventions in the new top-level domain program. In 2012–2013, ICANN (under pressure from the US government) allowed any GAC member to raise an objection to an application for a new TLD for any reason. From that point on, ICANN's new TLD program departed irrevocably from the GNSO's stated goals of having clear, predictable rules determining which applications would be successful. There were no general policies; it was all political. The GAC then defined a large set of "sensitive strings," which, among other things, recommended that TLDs semantically linked to regulated or professional sectors (e.g., .HEALTH, .BANK, .LAW) should control its content and services in a way that would be consistent with applicable laws. For all intents and purposes, GAC was trying to condition ICANN's grant of a TLD on regulating the services and content offered on the domain. As a result, many new TLD applicants adopted Public Interest Commitments (PICs, manifested as "Specification 11") in their Registry Agreements—promises to operate their services in line with the GAC's stipulations. This was widely considered to be one of the most arbitrary acts of Chehadé's reign. Specification 11 and PICs were introduced into the new gTLD contracts without any pretense that they had been the product of bottom-up, consensus policy making. One cannot blame it entirely on of Chehadé, however. The US government, the GAC, and the applicants' willingness to do anything to win approval for their applications, regardless of its broader policy implications, must share responsibility.

The 2013 modifications of the Registrar Accreditation Agreement also edged up against the mission boundary. The modifications, driven by law enforcement and intellectual property interests as described in chapter 8, were intended to require registrars to prohibit illegal activities in the second-level domains they sold. Some of these included security issues, such as phishing or malware, and thus were arguably within mission, but copyright infringement was also included, which implied that registrars would be committed to content regulation. When lobbyists for intellectual property interests began to question the mission limitation language, David Post, a legal scholar participating in CCWG, acknowledged that the prohibition on content and services regulation might require changing Section 3.18 of the RAA. "I believe we need to insist on a Mission Statement that would negate any use of ICANN's monopoly power to impose an obligation on registrars to revoke domains based on allegations of illegal content."[28]

This problem caused great consternation among the ICANN mission reformers in the CCWG. As time pressure mounted, a compromise was found. The new bylaws would adopt the new first amendment, but it would also add clauses that grandfathered any contracts that contained the transgressing agreements from 2013. Section 1.1 acquired two new subsections. One left the door open to policies that reduce or mitigate trademark–domain name conflicts.[29] The other exempted any contracts written before October 2016 from the new mission limitations.[30] But it also contained a more general statement that "ICANN shall have the ability to negotiate, enter into and enforce agreements, including public interest commitments, with any party in service of its Mission." This was an attempt to legalize PICs indirectly, but its advocates claimed that adding "in service of its Mission" kept the first amendment constraint in place. Anything outside the mission would not be allowed.

Although ICANN's board and staff were not enthusiastic about the new mission limitations, it did not fight them.

INDEPENDENT REVIEW PROCESS

Despite its private sector status, ICANN's function as a governance institution encouraged the application of classical legal-political norms regarding the distinct branches of government and the independence of the judiciary branch. This made the strengthening of ICANN's redress process a key pillar of the accountability push. David Post and Danielle Kehl described an independent review process (IRP) as "the final piece of the constitutional puzzle." It would be "a neutral arbiter in disputes regarding the exercise of [policy making and policy implementation] powers by the other components of the institution."[31] The IRP would decide what was "legal" (i.e., allowed under the bylaws) and what was not.

Why did ICANN need to create another judiciary? Redress to US courts was possible, after all. National courts, however, could not deliver what was needed by an accountable global governance institution. What the reformers were trying to do was make ICANN's bylaws into the real governing structure of the Internet registry communities. The bylaws were supposed to be commitments to the community that the system would operate according to defined, known rules and policies. These rules and policies were supposed to be *generated by the governed community* and capable of being modified *internally* by them as well. An IRP was therefore a critical component of self-governance. ICANN might violate its commitments (break those rules) without necessarily breaking California law, and at any rate California law did not come from and could not be modified by ICANN's community. Binding ICANN to its own rules required it to build its own system of institutional checks and balances. This became one of the main objectives of the accountability reforms.

ICANN already had an independent review process. The bylaws made its rulings advisory, however, not binding. Nevertheless, it had scored one major success. In 2009–2010, the controversy over the .XXX top-level domain led to a successful IRP challenge by ICM Registry, the applicant for .XXX.[32] The panel ruled that ICANN had indeed violated its commitments to registry applicants with its sudden reversal of a positive decision for ICM Registry, based on a last-minute intervention by the US government and the GAC. Though clearly taken aback by the decision, the ICANN board wisely chose to comply with the decision upholding ICM Registry's complaint.

In the 2015 reform push, no one considered purely voluntary compliance with an IRP decision to be acceptable. Moreover, the ICM process was slow and expensive; only a deep-pocketed business could afford it.[33] The biggest flaw in existing institutional arrangements, however, was revealed by what happened after the .XXX case was resolved. ICANN modified its bylaws to narrow the scope of the IRP. After the modification, parties could file IRP disputes only if the board was accused of a small class of procedural misconduct; they could no longer make a substantive claim that the board had violated its bylaws. Under this standard, it was not possible to mount an IRP challenge based on a claim that ICANN had exceeded its authorized powers. The most important kind of accountability checks simply could not happen.

David Post, the law professor who had been one of the original formulators of the idea of a self-governing Internet community in the mid-1990s, allied with Becky Burr to prioritize and define IRP reform during the transition process. Their goals were fourfold: (1) to use the IRP to hold ICANN to "a substantive standard of behavior," rather than just an evaluation of whether or not its actions were taken "in good faith"; (2) to make IRP decisions binding, not merely advisory; (3) to make the process more transparent and accessible, both in terms of cost and standing to bring claims; and (4) to foment precedent-based decisions that would "produce consistent and coherent results that will serve as a guide for future actions."[34]

There were some negotiations and controversies around these reforms, but neither ICANN nor any organized faction fought against them. ICANN's legal team did not closely monitor the IRP reforms, and neither did ALAC. So the reform agenda emerged almost entirely victorious from the transition. The new bylaws created a standing panel of seven arbitrators, selected in consultation with the community. A specific dispute triggers the selection of a three-member panel from the standing panel: one by the claimant, one by ICANN, and the third agreed upon by the previous two. The empowered community and the SOs/ACs automatically have standing to initiate an IRP under the new rules. The new bylaws state, "ICANN intends, agrees, and consents to be bound by all IRP Panel decisions of Disputes of Covered Actions as a final, binding arbitration." The only major deviation from the reformers' proposal was that arbitrations would be conducted by three selected panelists rather than the whole standing panel. Post wanted all standing panel members to hear every case "as an institution," but this did not happen.

THE ROLE OF THE GOVERNMENTAL ADVISORY COMMITTEE

Debates and shifts in the role of ICANN's GAC figured prominently in the accountability reforms. GAC, to recall, is an anomalous entity. ICANN's raison d'être was to provide an alternative to governance by intergovernmental institutions, yet the GAC itself is intergovernmental in structure. There is a single representative from each national government, and each government has an equal vote. Adding to its anomalous character, this intergovernmental entity's existence and powers depend on the bylaws of a private corporation.

Although GAC is nominally advisory, a bylaw modification introduced in 2002 as part of ICANN CEO Stuart Lynn's desire to reinsert governments into the regime required the board to give special deference to GAC advice. If they didn't follow GAC advice, ICANN's bylaws obligated the board to negotiate:

> In the event that the ICANN Board determines to take an action that is not consistent with the Governmental Advisory Committee advice, it shall so inform the

Committee and state the reasons why it decided not to follow that advice. The Governmental Advisory Committee and the ICANN Board will then try, in good faith and in a timely and efficient manner, to find a mutually acceptable solution.

In practice, this meant that anything the GAC put forward as advice could tie up ICANN's policy-making process for months, or even years, as these "good faith" negotiations took place. This back-and-forth had to happen even if GAC advice contradicted the decisions of ICANN's bottom-up multistakeholder policy development processes in the GNSO.

Many reformers wanted to rein in the GAC during the process. Indeed, the NTIA's approach to the transition reflected the classic, Clinton-era policy favoring privatization of governance. The IANA transition proposals would not be acceptable if they "replaced the NTIA role with a government-led or an inter-governmental organization solution."[35] Congress supported this. Senators John Thune and Marco Rubio, in a July 31, 2014, letter to ICANN board chair Crocker stated, "The IANA transition should not provide an opportunity for governments to increase their influence." The letter provided a set of more specific recommendations to achieve that goal: "not permitting representatives of governments to sit on ICANN's board; limiting government participation to advisory roles, such as through the GAC; and amending ICANN's bylaws only to allow receipt of GAC advice if that advice is proffered by consensus."

On the other hand, as we have seen, GAC's influence on ICANN grew consistently over the years, aided and abetted by the US government. The United States endorsed the WSIS claim that GAC advice had a special status in matters of public policy. In 2013, the Commerce Department and US law enforcement agencies used the GAC (as well as direct pressure) to help it shape policy on Whois and the Registrar Accreditation Agreement, and it used the IANA contract award to require ICANN to become more responsive to government concerns. NTIA's Strickling even provided a rationale for a GAC veto of top-level domain applications. The political whiplash around the GAC was in many ways a product of US government policy.

The future of GAC in a reformed, accountable ICANN was thus a decisive battle over the status of sovereignty in Internet governance. Clashes over the role of GAC (or governments generally) in the reformed ICANN occurred on two fronts. The first was "Stress Test 18," which attempted to require GAC advice to be a product of full consensus; the second was whether the GAC should become a "decisional participant" in the empowered community on par with other SOs and ACs.

Stress tests were thirty-eight hypothetical scenarios generated by community members to assess a set of plausible risks or problems that might arise in a reformed ICANN.[36] The CCWG used these stress tests to identify possible changes to ICANN bylaws to meet those challenges.

Stress Test 18 referred to the possibility that the GAC might modify its operating rules to adopt formal advice with only a majority, instead of a consensus.[37] *Consensus*, in GAC as in other intergovernmental organizations, means that no individual government objects to a statement or decision. In effect, it means unanimous support. The GAC, however, had the power, under its own operating rules, to offer formal advice without a consensus.

The board's obligation to negotiate with GAC whenever it deviated from its advice gave the GAC a degree of leverage over policy that no other AC or SO possessed. If the GAC changed its rules to remove the consensus requirement, it could trigger these negotiations even if a significant minority of GAC members opposed the advice. Most participants in the accountability process, particularly nongovernmental actors, felt that removing the consensus requirement for advice would give governments too much power over the policy development process. A numerical majority of governments could pressure ICANN's board to conform to what they found "acceptable," regardless of the wishes of some governments and the other ACs and SOs. Further, there was widespread agreement that "a negotiation between ICANN board and GAC should be reserved for resolving differences between ICANN and governments–not to resolve differences among governments themselves."[38] The CCWG thus amended the ICANN bylaws (Article XI, Section 2, item 1j) to require trying to find a mutually acceptable solution only where GAC advice was supported by GAC consensus. Several GAC members opposed this change, especially Brazil and Argentina, which were sovereigntist in orientation.

The reform process also elevated the GAC's status, however, by making it a part of the empowered community. The process convened by ICANN to develop an accountability proposal included all parts of the existing ICANN structure, including GAC, ALAC, and the supporting organizations for names, addresses, and country code registries. This meant that GAC was embedded within the deliberative process and tacitly recognized as a stakeholder with the same status as other SOs and ACs. Governments were, in this construction, just another stakeholder. Inevitably, then, when it came time to define which entities would comprise the decisional participants in the empowered community, the GAC was included.

Robin Gross, the representative of the Noncommercial Stakeholders Group to the CCWG, objected strongly to the empowered community proposal because it "would allow for fundamental changes to the nature of ICANN's Governmental Advisory Committee (GAC) by endorsing its inclusion in the Empowered Community as a Decisional Participant." Gross noted that this was a major departure from the advisory role originally envisioned for the GAC. She also invoked the many statements by the NTIA and other US government representatives saying that the IANA transition should not provide an opportunity for governments to increase their influence. All to no avail. GAC was already de facto functioning as, and accepted by many other members of the community as, "just another stakeholder." The final recommendations did, however, try to limit GAC's power over policy making with what it called the "GAC carve-out": while the GAC was allowed to become a decisional participant in the empowered community, it was barred from participating in any challenge by the empowered community to the ICANN board's implementation of GAC consensus advice.

The CCWG completed drafting its recommendations in late January 2016. The twelve broad recommendations for bylaw modifications then went through extensive reviews by the CCWG and its legal team in mid-February. A finalized proposal was sent to the chartering organizations for approval. Translations were made available in Arabic, Spanish, French, Portuguese, Russian, and Chinese. On February 29, the chairs of the ICG (CWG-Stewardship) confirmed that the proposed draft met its accountability requirements, which meant that the final proposal was complete.[39]

By March 9, all six of the chartering organizations had approved the proposal. The draft went to a Bylaws Coordination Group for detailed scrutiny of how the bylaw revisions conformed to the intent of the reform recommendations.

Months earlier, it had become evident that a finalized proposal and the required bylaw modifications would not be complete in time for the scheduled September 30, 2015, expiration of the IANA contract. The NTIA had already extended ICANN's contract for another year, making September 30, 2016, the new deadline for completing the transition. With the NTIA receiving a completed proposal in March, it now seemed possible to finalize the process by that date.

The formation of PTI, however, was not engineered by its own legal department. Given the powerful role ICANN legal had played in its corporate governance negotiations, this limited its separation and separability. Lise Fuhr thought the separate legal representation for the community developed for the transition should have continued for PTI.[40] Further limitations on PTI's independence came during the implementation stage. According to leaders in the process, ICANN's CEO Chehadé had no problem with PTI (he was more concerned about the accountability arrangements), but after Chehadé left ICANN in March 2016, much of the implementation was left to his successor, Goran Marby. Marby wanted ICANN, Inc. to stay in control of PTI and resisted its independence during the implementation process.

On May 27, 2016, the ICANN board adopted the new bylaws. On June 9, 2016, the NTIA formally declared that the IANA Stewardship Transition Proposal developed by the global Internet multistakeholder community met its criteria and approved the plan. That paved the way for the expiration of the IANA contract on September 30. But while the NTIA and the multistakeholder process had converged on a solution, certain members of Congress had other ideas.

13   THE ENDGAME

If the transition really was an attempt to detach the IANA functions from nation-states, it would be unrealistic to expect this to happen without a fight. Political power is never yielded without a struggle, especially when it touches on something as fundamental as the hegemonic power of the world's most powerful state.

The fight for independence from international institutions was pretty much over by 2014. From the beginning of the World Summit on the Information Society in 2002 until the World Conference on International Telecommunications and the new International Telecommunication Regulations in 2013, the ICANN regime had tussled with intergovernmental institutions. Each time, it had escaped their grasp. The Internet community's battle with multilateral institutions, however, was always complicated by its connection to the US government. Aside from NTIA oversight, the US economy, law, and technology were so intimately entangled with the global Internet community that it was difficult to know whether autonomy from intergovernmental organizations was a step toward community self-governance or merely the globalization of American law and politics.

Other states understandably resisted an ICANN regime under US control, even if the blow to their authority was softened by ICANN's status as a private corporation with multistakeholder participation and a Governmental Advisory Committee. The ultimate test of the system's independence from state sovereignty, therefore, started when it had to detach itself from the United States government.

THE CHOICE

ICANN was founded on the premise that the Internet's centralized registries should be kept out of governmental hands. Yet it was implemented in a way that gave control to one government. The United States held unilateral veto power over the contents of the DNS root zone; it got to decide who performed the IANA functions; it retained legal jurisdiction over ICANN. That situation persisted for fifteen years.

Suddenly, a commitment to finish the job, to end most of those special powers, had been made by the US Commerce Department itself. While the NTIA could legitimately claim that this had been the policy all along, the long wait and changing geopolitical situation reopened the question politically. Now it was the privatizers who were proposing a change. Should the United States let go?

With full privatization a real prospect, political factions in the United States had to choose whether they were truly committed to a transnational self-governing Internet community or whether they saw ICANN as an extension of the American system. This choice would split the American polity into globalist and nationalist factions.

The technical community's position was unambiguous. They wanted political and operational autonomy for their standards development and identifier registries, as they had all along. Likewise, (most) transnational civil society actors and (many) Internet businesses, especially those directly involved in the regime, still supported private-sector-based, multistakeholder governance.

The US policy community, however—the dense network of legislators, lobbyists, think tanks, media outlets, policy advisors, and national security pundits centered on Washington DC—was not so sure. Among this crowd, there had been overwhelming support for the multistakeholder model when it was under US supervision. Keeping things out of governmental hands had been a good idea as long as it meant keeping it out of the hands of *other governments*. When the United States was included, some in Washington defected from the principle.

That choice came at a time of resurgent populist nationalism in the United States. The movement got political mileage out of challenging both economic globalization and any signs of weakness or deference to foreign powers. This was a transformative moment for American conservatives as well as for the Internet.

Arguments for retaining US control took a common, identifiable form. First, opponents of the transition expressed comfort with the status quo and did not see any problem that would justify a change. Second, in assessing the risks of a transition they would elevate the political significance of the IANA functions, instead of downplaying them as purely technical, as the NTIA had often done. Control of the Internet registries was *control of the Internet*, and that equation was used to link American supervision of ICANN to the cause of Internet freedom. The special US role in ICANN, in this view, was not a form of governmental control; it was a shield against control by *other governments*. Acting as a guarantor of Internet freedom was also an assertion of US sovereignty. Finally, this US-nationalist view was so embedded in the worldview of state sovereignty that it denied the very possibility of making ICANN independent of all governments. If the United States did not govern the system, other sovereigns or multilateral institutions would.

THE US NATIONALIST REACTION

Four days after the NTIA published its historic notice of the transition, L. Gordon Crovitz, a former publisher of the *Wall Street Journal*, penned an editorial designed to rally US nationalists against the transition. Titled "America's Internet Surrender," the widely read piece articulated all the arguments the new conservative nationalism would make over the course of the transition's endgame.[1]

Crovitz described the status quo as a "happy state of affairs" in which "Washington used its oversight only to ensure that the Internet runs efficiently and openly, without political pressure from any country." The Obama administration's move "has now endangered that hallmark of Internet freedom," he warned.

Anyone familiar with the real world of Internet governance could spot many inaccuracies in Crovitz's narrative. It claimed that the new International Telecommunication Regulations adopted by eighty-five of the ITU's member states "grant[ed] authority to governments to close off their citizens' access to the global Internet" and "legitimize[d] censorship of the Web and the blocking of social media." In fact, the words *Internet* and

Web did not appear in the treaty, and governments had been blocking or censoring international communications for more than a century before, based on treaties formally recognizing their sovereignty—behavior that continued during the period the US supervised ICANN. Ignoring the US role in empowering GAC, the article said, "Until late last week other countries knew that Washington would use its control over ICANN to block any [domain name] censorship." In fact, the NTIA had tried to reject the .XXX top-level domain and later encouraged other governments to limit and regulate top-level domains. The article even claimed that the ITU "is now a lead candidate to replace the U.S. in overseeing ICANN." This was pure fiction: the NTIA's transition criteria had explicitly ruled out any plan that transferred control to intergovernmental institutions, and almost no one in the Internet community wanted the ITU involved, anyway.

Crucially, and true to the nationalist logic, Crovitz denied that Internet governance by non-state actors could even exist. "The alternative to control over the Internet by the U.S. is not the elimination of any government involvement," he wrote. "It is, rather, the involvement of many other governments, some authoritarian, at the expense of the U.S."

While distorted, the themes sounded by Crovitz resonated perfectly with conservative Republican hot buttons and the emerging nationalist trend. Partisan politics also played a role, as Republicans could blame the Obama administration for yet another "surrender" of American supremacy.

Within days of the editorial, a member of the House introduced the DOTCOM Act, an attempt to "prohibit the National Telecommunications and Information Administration from relinquishing responsibility over the Internet domain name system until the Comptroller General of the United States submits to Congress a report on the role of the NTIA with respect to such system."[2] On April 2, 2014, Senators Thune and Rubio published a letter asking the NTIA to "explain why it is in our national interest to transition the IANA functions" and how it will ensure "the IANA functions do not end up being controlled, directly or indirectly, by a government or inter-governmental entity."[3] Thirty-three other Senate Republicans signed the letter.

The pressure was on.

CONGRESS JUMPS IN

Over ten bills related to the transition were introduced in the 113th and 114th Congresses.[4] Congressional resistance to the transition was hampered, however, by the government's lack of statutory authority over ICANN or the DNS. Congress did have legislative and budgetary authority over the NTIA, though. Suspicious members used appropriations bills authorizing funds for the Commerce Department, the NTIA, and the national defense to slow down or attempt to stop the transition. While these efforts failed, Congress did have widespread support to closely monitor the transition. During the two-year period, it convened a total of eight hearings in the House and Senate scrutinizing the transition, and it required the NTIA to file quarterly reports on its progress.

In the hearings, representatives of ICANN, the NTIA, and various private sector stakeholders made the multistakeholder model of Internet governance the basis of their defense of the transition. There was, in fact, a reservoir of strong bipartisan support for said multistakeholder model. During WSIS and the WCIT, private-sector-based multistakeholderism had been the flag under which US-backed reactions to the ITU and other intergovernmental institutions had flown.[5]

Nearly all Democrats and several centrist Republicans were on board with the NTIA's "intent to transition." Republican Senator Thune, powerful chair of the Senate Commerce Committee, was a key ally. In one of the earlier Senate hearings (February 2015), Thune stated that concerns about "capture by authoritarian regimes" were valid but said his chief worry was ICANN accountability in the absence of the contract with the US government.[6] Thune promised that he would "scrutinize [the ICG's transition] plan to make sure it both meets the requirements laid out by NTIA and adopts the meaningful accountability reforms that Senator Rubio and I have called for."[7]

Senator Bill Nelson, the ranking Democrat in Thune's committee, said,

> I strongly support the multistakeholder model that ICANN, as an institution, represents: one in which the Internet's diverse stakeholders can come together and make sure that the Internet remains a free, open, and global network. I also support the [NTIA] announcement last year that it would complete the work of privatizing the technical elements of the Internet begun in 1998. I know that there are legitimate concerns . . . but NTIA has been handling this transition in the right way.[8]

The bipartisan bona fides of the transition received a boost from David Gross, a telecommunications industry lawyer with the influential law firm of Wiley Rein. Under the Bush administration, Gross was the State Department's Coordinator for International Communications and Information Policy and the point man for the US government during WSIS. He now spoke in favor of the transition on behalf of an "Internet Governance Coalition" that included AT&T, Cisco, Comcast NBCUniversal, Facebook, GoDaddy, Google, Juniper Networks, Microsoft, Telefonica, Disney, Time Warner Cable, Twenty-First Century Fox, and Verizon.

Some representatives were visibly impressed by the testimony of Internet community members who had been working on the transition plans. Testimony came from Alissa Cooper, the ICG chair from the IETF; Steve DelBianco, a business constituency leader in the CCWG-Accountability; and Matt Shears, a civil society advocate from the Center for Democracy and Technology. After listening to them, California Representative Anna Eshoo gushed that the bottom-up process was "like holding a mirror up to our country, because what we're all working toward, what you have worked so hard to do, is to make sure that the Internet is a reflection of democracy, in its full bloom."[9]

Conservative Republicans were not so thrilled. Stateless multistakeholderism smelled a lot like the "globalism" their base was turning against. ICANN's Chehadé seemed like a suspicious character, a slick corporate globalist. Hadn't he agreed to co-chair a high-level advisory committee for the Chinese government's World Internet Conference?[10] In the February 15, 2015, Senate hearing, Alaska's Dan Sullivan asked Strickling, "What is the problem with one government having a unique role? Particularly when that government has done a fantastic job?" Sullivan was not impressed with reminders that privatization had been the original intent in 1998. "I think we waited for a long time because we didn't see a problem." Calling attention to what he called "the elephant in the room," Sullivan insisted that China and Russia were "determined to gain control of the internet." He saw the transition as "back-pedaling" in the face of this threat.

Whether supportive or suspicious, everyone in Congress was keenly interested in getting commitments from the NTIA and ICANN regarding US interests. Many exchanges focused on how the transition might affect the influence of authoritarian governments on ICANN. Conservatives pressed ICANN repeatedly on whether it might try to leave the United

States after the transition. Another big concern was the fate of the .MIL and .GOV domains. ICANN's leadership had no intention of disturbing existing domains and knew that some concessions to US privilege were unavoidable. Government-run top-level domains and root servers would not be changed, they promised. In his February 2015 testimony, Chehadé said that ICANN would make sure the affirmation of commitments were "enshrined in our bylaws" and that the affirmation was "very clear that the jurisdiction of ICANN shall remain in the U.S.A, and we stand by this."[11]

THE CRUZ CONFRONTATION

By March 2016, both the ICG proposal for transferring the stewardship of the IANA functions and the ICANN accountability reforms were ready. Senator Thune held another hearing in May, "Examining the Multistakeholder Plan for Transitioning the IANA," where opponents of the transition were overshadowed by business, technical community, and civil society supporters.[12] The NTIA reviewed the community's proposals and approved them in June. The plans met the NTIA's criteria and did not run afoul of any US red lines. ICANN said it was ready to implement the required bylaw changes in August. It was now evident that a transition could happen in time for the scheduled September 30, 2016, expiration of the IANA contract.

Opponents of the transition amped up their rhetoric and grasped for tools to slow or stop the transition. According to a news report at the time, "[Senator] Cruz indicated that the Republicans would not give up without a fight against what he described as a 'giveaway' of internet control by the Obama administration."[13] Cruz introduced the Protecting Internet Freedom Act on June 8, 2016, to prohibit the NTIA from relinquishing its authority over the IANA functions and the root zone file unless Congress granted the NTIA such authority. Instead of directly opposing the transition, some conservatives began calling for a "trial period," in which the United States would retain supervisory authority while the new bylaws were "tested." Everyone involved knew that such a delay would amount to the United States reneging on its commitment to a transition and would simply lead to another fight down the road.[14] Opponents also tried to float the idea that the DNS root was US government property, making the transition a "transfer of government property to a private entity," which would require a vote of approval by Congress.[15] The Government Accountability Office report on that topic requested by four congressional representatives was published September 13, 2016; it did not uphold the claim that the DNS root was US government property.

The movement to stop the transition reached its peak on September 14, 2016, in a hearing of a subcommittee of the Senate Judiciary Committee (the hearing with which chapter 2 opened). Unlike the previous hearings, which had been chaired by sympathizers such as Senator Thune or Representative Walden, Senator Cruz chaired this one, and he was out for blood. The hearing contained many dramatic moments, including an angry exchange in which Cruz threatened Strickling and all NTIA employees with criminal prosecution for violating the Antideficiency Act by spending money preparing for the transition. Cruz staffers held up posters with quotes from Chehadé that made it seem as if the former CEO planned to move ICANN to Switzerland. He grilled the new ICANN CEO, Goran Marby, in an attempt to make him say on the record that China was "an enemy of the Internet." While the pressure was intense, Cruz didn't have the votes needed to hold up the transition.

INTERNET FREEDOM AND THE TRANSITION

The opponents of the transition made "Internet freedom" their battle cry. During WSIS and WCIT, however, so had the *supporters* of ICANN's multistakeholder model. A House resolution in 2012 urged the NTIA to "promote a global Internet free from government control and preserve and advance the successful multistakeholder model that governs the Internet today."[16] Underlying this confrontation, then, was a clash between two different visions of how Internet freedom could best be institutionalized. The difference hinged on the appropriate role of national governments.

Supporters of the transition wanted to advance Internet freedom by privatizing and globalizing the IANA functions, detaching them from nation-states and geopolitics as much as possible. NTIA's Strickling opened his testimony in Senator Cruz's hearing by saying, "The best and most effective way to preserve Internet freedom is to depend on the community of stakeholders who own, operate, transact business, and exchange information over the myriad of networks that comprise the Internet." In this view, privatization of the IANA functions would put governance authority in a community that would protect its own interests and freedoms. States were just one of the participants in that community; they did not have hierarchical authority over it but shared power on an equal footing with all the other stakeholders. Post-transition, the US government would become just another state in the GAC along with all the others.

Conservative nationalists, on the other hand, equated Internet freedom with rule by the American government and American law. As one opponent put it, "No multistakeholder system can be devised that will ever be as effective at protecting the free and open Internet as the current U.S. Government and the protections of the U.S. Constitution."[17] Ironically, this made organizations like the Heritage Foundation, Tech Freedom, and Americans for Limited Government advocates for governmental control of a central piece of Internet infrastructure—a precursor of Republicans' abandonment of market liberalism under President Trump. Their support for governmental control of the IANA functions coincided with their resistance to domestic net neutrality regulation, which they claimed would subject the Internet to federal government regulation. Senator Brian Schatz of Hawaii, a liberal Democrat, remarked on this in one of the hearings, asking why "so-called 'small government types' want a Commerce Department bureau to oversee the technical underpinnings of the Internet."[18] The irony, however, worked both ways. Why were Democratic Party liberals so keen on supporting privatization and removing government from the Internet infrastructure when they wanted a bigger federal role in Internet regulation domestically? During ICANN's initial formation in the 1990s, these two sides had been aligned in their approach to privatization; the transition now divided them.

The battle over the transition was highly consequential not only because of the divergent notions of Internet freedom it resolved. An unsuccessful transition would have destroyed ICANN's legitimacy. By making its March 2014 "statement of intent," the NTIA made a commitment that forced the issue and raised the stakes. It laid down specific conditions for the transition and set in motion a labor-intensive, ICANN-administered multistakeholder process involving thousands of participants all over the world. It promised to implement any community-developed transition proposal that met the conditions it had laid down. Once the NTIA certified that the ICG proposal and the accountability reforms met its criteria, failure to make good on its promise because of a roadblock erected by American nationalists in

Congress would have discredited the entire process. The community would feel utterly disempowered, and two years of intense volunteer effort would be thrown down the drain. It would be clear to all that ICANN really was an instrument of one national government and not a delegation of authority to a global Internet community.

Congressional supporters of the transition showed awareness of this problem. Senator Chris Coons of Delaware worried that reneging on the transition might empower authoritarian governments in their effort to foster an institutional alternative to ICANN. The credibility of the multistakeholder governance regime was at stake. Concluding his testimony before the Cruz-led hearing, Strickling made an impassioned plea:

> Mr. Chairman, and members of the subcommittee, I urge you: do not give a gift to Russia and other authoritarian nations by blocking this transition. Show your trust in the private sector, and the work of American and global businesses, technical experts, and civil society who have delivered a thoughtful transition plan.

CLOSING CHAPTER

When it became clear that opponents lacked both the congressional support and the legal grounds needed to block the transition, four attorneys general from the states of Arizona, Texas, Oklahoma, and Nevada filed a last-ditch request for an emergency injunction to stay the transition. The request was filed in the Southern District of Texas on September 28, 2016, only two days before the expiration of the IANA contract. NTIA lawyers and officials rushed to Texas for a hearing before Judge George C. Hanks. On Friday, September 30, Judge Hanks denied the request. His written opinion dismissed the challengers' arguments as flimsy:

> Counsel's statements of what "might" or "could" happen are insufficient to support the extraordinary relief sought in this case. Even if the Court were to find that some past harm or bad acts by [ICANN] impacted the interests of the States in their respective websites and alleged rights at interest, the Court notes that these past harms happened under the exact regulatory and oversight scheme that the States now seek to preserve. This, along with the lack of evidence regarding any predictable or substantially likely events, greatly undermines the States' request for the relief they seek.[19]

ICANN's 57th meeting—the annual general meeting typically held in autumn—took place in Hyderabad, India, from November 3 to 9. At that meeting, there was a curiously muted celebration of the completion of the transition. ICANN staff handed out small buttons marking the event at an outdoor dinner party and recognized some of the leaders of the working groups to a largely inattentive audience. The deed was done; the threat was over.

On the morning of November 9, Hyderabad meeting attendees arose from their beds to learn that Donald J. Trump had been elected president of the United States.

14 POST-TRANSITION ICANN

Post-transition ICANN is as boring as the drama around its separation from the United States was exciting. Overall, the transition accomplished what it intended: the United States no longer controls the DNS root; management of the Internet registries has become more insulated from geopolitical pressures; the community has greater confidence in the regime. On paper, there are strong new accountability mechanisms, but no conflict has come along to trigger their use.

IANA has been officially renamed Public Technical Identifiers (PTI). It got this name because during the transition there was need to discuss the fate of Post-Transition IANA, which inevitably got shortened to PTI. Once the transition was over, we had to find words to match the acronym. Everyone knows PTI is just ICANN's old IANA department, however. PTI has its own board and staff and multiple forms of oversight put in place by the transition, but it is managed by ICANN. Yanking it out of ICANN is possible but would be very difficult politically. PTI would have to do something astoundingly bad to prompt anyone to try it. So far, PTI executes its functions well; having been separated from the policy-making process adequately, its functions really are just clerical.

Domain name policy making, on the other hand, is as messed up as ever. ICANN's policy development process is overly bureaucratized and slow, as the discussion of the GDPR response will show. Its multiple layers of procedure give contending parties opportunities to drag things out or alter substantive policies during implementation. More fundamentally, ICANN's role as policy authority for the DNS root has never recovered from the fights of the mid-1990s. After twenty years, ICANN still has not standardized and routinized the licensing of new top-level domains. Top level domain applications are still beauty contests, in which applicants try to convince GAC and the community that their proposals will serve an undefined "global public interest." Decisions based upon such a subjective standard necessarily become discretionary, which makes political pull the real governor of the process. Investment in a top level domain requires heavy investments in political influence at ICANN. The transition didn't make this much better, but it didn't make it any worse, either. Things may be slightly less arbitrary than the nadir of the Chehadé regime, but they are also slower and more bureaucratic.

The generic TLD space makes for a sharp contrast with the country code TLDs. The ccNSO is an oasis of calm, another boring part of the ICANN regime. That is because ICANN doesn't try to regulate ccTLDs but concentrates instead on its core mission: running a registry that matches a unique character string in the DNS name space to a registrant and a set of IP addresses designated by that registrant. It verifies who is the authorized owner of a domain in the root zone and updates their entries. The ccTLDs' minimalistic relationship with ICANN has left them free to set their own policies in various ways. The global market for names provides alternatives if people do not like their ccTLD.

Post-transition ICANN has faced three big tests:

- The request to delete Russian top-level domains from the root after Russia's invasion of Ukraine (2022)
- The Internet Society's attempt to sell the .ORG domain to a commercial entity for $1 billion, which triggered an intervention by the California Attorney General (2020)
- Europe's General Data Protection Regulation (GDPR), which finally forced ICANN to bring its Whois policies into compliance with basic privacy standards (2018)

Each of these incidents raised important questions about ICANN's relationship to governments and the sovereign system.

GEOPOLITICS AND THE INTERNET REGISTRIES

The most noteworthy aspect of the transition is that the "foreign government takeover" threat heralded by conservative nationalists evaporated as soon as the transition happened. Russia and China have not "taken over." The ITU was not "next in line" to inherit the US role. The ITU is not even trying to play a role in Internet registry governance anymore. The main channel for governmental influence in ICANN, the GAC, operates about the same as it did before, though its influence has waxed and waned in different contexts. Governments' status as "just another stakeholder" inside the ICANN private governance regime has been institutionalized.

Measures of world Internet freedom have been declining both before and after the transition. This is happening primarily due to unilateral actions by sovereign states, not because of the transition. Both democratic and authoritarian states are becoming more aggressive about regulating content, services, and applications on the Internet. Self-governance by the Internet community or misuse of the Internet registries have not played a role in this trend—if anything, the continuing loss of freedom vindicates the initial vision of an Internet governance regime insulated from nation-states.

ICANN's privatization succeeded in insulating it from nation-state rivalries. On February 28, 2022, Ukraine's Vice Prime Minister Mykhailo Fedorov sent a letter to ICANN's Goran Marby asking ICANN to revoke all three Russian top-level domains and to shut down the root server instances located in Russia.[1] It also asked RIPE-NCC, the European IP address registry, to disable all IPv4 and IPv6 assignments to Russian Internet service providers. Only two days later, Marby rejected the request, saying, "We maintain neutrality and act in support of the global Internet. Our mission does not extend to taking punitive actions, issuing sanctions, or restricting access against segments of the Internet."[2] A week later, RIPE-NCC's managing director, Hans Peter Holen, also declined the request, stating, "We . . . believe that Internet number resource registrations should not be used as a means to enforce political outcomes."[3]

The decision to reject Ukraine's request to purge Russian TLDs and IP addresses was a big test of the political independence of the Internet registries. Indeed, given the fate of SWIFT, the Society for Worldwide Interbank Financial Telecommunications, and other nominally neutral international organizations in the US sanctions regime, it might be considered the ultimate test. Theorists of "weaponized interdependence" have documented a vast "underground empire" of seemingly cooperative global infrastructures, from the financial system to intellectual property laws to undersea cables; they explain how the US government leverages its dominant position in this infrastructure to pursue its law enforcement, foreign policy, and military goals.[4] Nevertheless, their story does not mention the governance of the Internet. That is because Internet registry governance has not been subordinated to the underground empire.

When it sanctioned Russia after the invasion of Ukraine, the United States used almost every form of leverage it could get its hands on. Yet Ukraine's request to make the domain name system part of this effort was rebuffed quickly and completely. It had no support in the Internet community, in ICANN Org, or even in the GAC. Geopoliticizing the root clashed too directly with the ethos and mission of the Internet registries. By devolving control of the DNS root to the global Internet community, the transition stacked the deck in favor of neutral global compatibility. Internet registry governance has not been subordinated to the digital neomercantilism of the 2020s, and we have ICANN's unique institutional arrangement to thank for that.

The problem of US jurisdiction, and its possible connection to sanctions, was raised early in the transition process but was pushed into Workstream 2.[5] *Jurisdiction* was a code word for questioning the entire legal framework for the ICANN regime. This concern went deeper than merely ending the US government's ability to award the IANA contract and approve modifications to the DNS root. It called into question ICANN's incorporation in California and its subjection to the laws of a single nation-state.

Contrary to common stereotypes, this anti-US jurisdiction position was articulated most strongly not by authoritarian, adversarial states like Russia or China but by Brazil and, to a lesser extent, by France and Italy. To these states, ICANN could not be equally responsive to all the world's Internet stakeholders unless it was immunized from the application of US laws or politics. In the Brazilian representative's own words,

> as long as ICANN remains a private law entity incorporated under US laws, with no jurisdictional immunity for its core global governance functions, it will be subject to . . . US exclusive enforcement jurisdiction over activities and people within US territory in ways that can adversely affect the Internet worldwide.[6]

There was merit in this argument. Brazil was not asking for a multilateral takeover of ICANN's governance functions but simply for preventing one government—the United States—from interfering in its global governance decisions.

The Office of Foreign Asset Controls (OFAC) is an office of the US Treasury that administers and enforces economic and trade sanctions against targeted individuals and entities. Its bases its decisions on US foreign policy and national security goals. ICANN's activities are heavily affected by OFAC.[7] It needs to manage the ccTLDs of sanctioned nations, for example. ICANN usually succeeded in getting licenses or exemptions from OFAC to engage in such transactions, but there were no guarantees. Aside from OFAC, there was also a threat that new legislation by Congress, regulations by US agencies, or actions by the powerful US president could assert power over ICANN unless there was some form of immunization. As a counter-hegemonic state, Brazil recognized the inherent bias of one nation's jurisdiction.

After the transition, civil society advocates succeeded in bringing the issue of OFAC and US sanctions into the deliberations of the Workstream 2 jurisdiction subgroup.[8] They succeeded in convincing the subgroup to recognize that "there is a tension between the goal of administering the Internet as a neutral global resource and the imposition of sanctions by the U.S. on other countries."[9]

The difference between Brazil's position and that of civil society was that Brazil wanted to achieve immunity more in line with the sovereign system. Brazil put forward the possibility of US congressional action to immunize ICANN under the US International Organizations Immunities Act. It also pointed toward a solution less like ICANN and more like the International Committee of the Red Cross (ICRC). The ICRC and its supporting organization, the International Federation of Red Cross and Red Crescent Societies (IFRC), are products of a humanitarian social movement, similar in some ways to the Internet community and its organic institutions. The ICRC, however, is not incorporated in the traditional sense; it operates based on the legal framework of the Geneva Conventions (a multilateral treaty) and is recognized (by states) as an international humanitarian organization. The IFRC, on the other hand, is a membership organization based on national-level Red Cross/Red Crescent societies. It is organized as a private association formed under the Swiss Civil Code with a special immunity agreement with Switzerland. Reorganizing ICANN on these lines was what Brazil seemed to be asking for. (Interestingly, in its push for a "digital Switzerland," the multinational software company Microsoft also invoked the example of the ICRC in its attempt to protect global users and customers from nation-state-backed cyberattacks.[10])

Pushing jurisdiction into Workstream 2 was sensible, in that achieving the kind of immunity Brazil desired could not take place within the time frame required by the transition process. It would have triggered political opposition in the United States.[11] Worse, it would have made the transition dependent on governmental actions completely outside the control of the Internet community's multistakeholder process.[12] Moving the jurisdiction discussion into Workstream 2, however, also sacrificed the leverage needed to make ICANN implement any recommended reforms. By early 2018, the jurisdiction subgroup agreed that ICANN's Registry and Registrar contracts should be amended to require ICANN to apply for and use best efforts to secure an OFAC license if the other party is otherwise qualified to be a registrar or registry and is not individually subject to sanctions.[13] The subgroup also recommended that ICANN pursue OFAC "general licenses" that would immunize broad categories of its activities from US sanctions.[14]

As of this writing, ICANN has not implemented any of the recommendations of the jurisdiction subgroup.

THE .ORG SALE

On November 13, 2019, Public Interest Registry (PIR), the operator of the .ORG top-level domain, announced that its parent organization, the Internet Society (ISOC), had reached an agreement to sell PIR to a for-profit private equity company called Ethos Capital for $1.135 billion.[15] The deal would convert PIR from a not-for-profit to a for-profit limited liability company. Ethos Capital turned out to be a vehicle of Fadi Chehadé, who was working with other businessmen who had been delegated new top-level domains during the 2011–2013 round when he was ICANN's CEO.[16]

PIR was set up in 2002 by ISOC as a wholly owned subsidiary for the express purpose of applying for the .ORG domain. The .ORG domain was in play because the Commerce Department, seeking to promote competition in the early days of ICANN, forced Verisign to divest the top-level domain to an entity selected by ICANN.[17] The original award to ISOC reflected both ISOC's insider connections with ICANN's board and the kind of outcome one would expect from a beauty contest governed by a "public interest" standard. PIR emphasized its status as nonprofit, its connection to ISOC, and its long-standing ties to Internet pioneers and the IETF. It made promises to support noncommercial stakeholders in the GNSO. Its application was successful for those reasons. While amply recorded in the application materials, however, none of these public interest commitments ended up in its Registry Agreement.

PIR went on to generate a large, highly stable revenue stream, transforming ISOC's previously shaky financial condition. As the number of .ORG domain name registrations surpassed ten million, PIR handed over more than 95 percent of its net income each year to ISOC in the form of a grant. From 2014 to 2016, that was $30 million per year.[18] In 2017 it sent an additional $43 million to ISOC to start the ISOC Foundation. PIR was one of the most highly profitable nonprofits one could imagine.

Negotiations about its sale seem to have begun shortly after Andrew Sullivan became president and CEO of ISOC in September 2018. Sullivan and other ISOC board members wanted to create an endowment that could fund the organization's activities in perpetuity. ISOC's board liked the idea because it would enhance the organization's independence. "While it's true that running .org provided a relatively steady income stream," one ISOC board member wrote, "it effectively staked most of our revenue on a single business. . . . Establishing a more diverse portfolio of investments will allow us to have more predictable revenue over time, and to take a longer-range perspective when it comes to achieving our mission."[19]

ICANN's board probably would have approved the deal as a matter of course had not vocal, widespread opposition ensued. Opposition fed on the terrible optics. There was the clash between the stated "public interest" norms of the original delegation and the enormous rents being made by the registry. That had been happening all along, but the deal explicitly, and likely accurately, attached a monetary value to the top-level domain award ICANN had given to ISOC. A naïve anti-commercialism also animated much of the opposition; as one opponent wrote, "technical entities as important as .org should be kept as far away from private investment money as possible. They're a service to the people, not a product to capitalize on."[20] In fact, a global registry requires substantial capital investment, and all of that money was coming from the private sector. It also looked bad because of the way ICANN insiders seemed to be leveraging their connections. Some critics were moderate: the Noncommercial Stakeholders Group did not oppose the deal but insisted on trying to strengthen .ORG's commitments to civil society by getting them written into its Registry Agreement. Two prominent civil society organizations, however, mounted a campaign to stop the deal that ran roughshod over such subtleties.[21] Eight hundred nonprofit organizations signed letters to stop the deal.

The purpose here is not to assess the merits of the deal, or the validity of the opposition's arguments, but to examine the way this decision tested the capabilities and independence of post-transition ICANN. ICANN did not do well on this test.

Due to a contractual provision in all Registry Agreements, the ownership change needed approval by ICANN's board. Presented with the request, the board and staff were indecisive. They delayed resolution while the advocates made noise and the stakeholders negotiated. Superficially, this could be considered a good thing: it was listening to its community and gathering information. In reality, it appeared that the board was incapable of making a decision that would anger an important stakeholder no matter what decision was made. While it temporized, ICANN received a letter from the California Attorney General's Office on April 15, 2020. The letter cited all the arguments against the deal raised by the opposition and told ICANN that it "must exercise its authority to withhold approval."[22] In what was unmistakably a threat, the attorney general said he would take "whatever action necessary to protect . . . the nonprofit community." Commentators noted that the attorney general had the power to make life difficult for ICANN.[23]

The attorney general's intervention was clearly a product of lobbying by opponents of the deal. His assertion of authority was far outside the remit of California Nonprofit Public Benefit law. ICANN was not accused of violating its bylaws or any specific part of its laws of incorporation; it was considering a policy decision that its board was entitled to make. In effect, the government of California was responding to political pressure from California citizens telling the corporation what policy decision to make about a global resource and threatening it with repercussions if it did not follow his advice.

ICANN's board was intimidated by the letter. Two weeks after its receipt, on April 30, 2020, it denied approval of the deal.[24] The board resolution repeated many of the California attorney general's arguments. There was no assertion that the decision was its own to make. The civil society organizations agitating against the deal tried to downplay its impact on ICANN's status as a global multistakeholder governance institution, but ultimately they were happy to see the California state government override any ICANN policy decision that they thought was not the right one.[25]

The .ORG incident put the spotlight on ICANN's status as the economic regulator of the domain name industry. Despite ICANN's constant claim that it is "not a regulator," its contracts obviously embody policy decisions about pricing, supply, and ownership in an industry that generates billions in value and attracts a proportionate amount of capital from commercial interests. The anti-commercialism harvested by the SaveDotOrg campaign was as absurd as it was politically potent—PIR was rolling in profits and had raised its wholesale rates repeatedly, and the new owners had promised various forms of rate limitation that did not previously exist. But the symbolism of nonprofit versus for-profit carried the day. The .ORG case was also a good example of how local jurisdiction (absent immunity) could affect ICANN's decisions. That outcome was made possible by the board's and CEO's weakness and lack of understanding of the appropriate boundaries between ICANN's global policy-making functions and its need to conform to the corporate law of its jurisdiction.

GDPR AND WHOIS

The GDPR provides a more complex and perhaps more important case study. From 2000 to 2016, ICANN was warned repeatedly that its contracts requiring registrars to publish the personal contact data of all domain name registrants violated data protection laws in Europe and other states. Not only were these warnings ignored, but efforts to remedy the situation through the GNSO's policy process were literally sabotaged by the US government, as noted in chapter 7. While this succeeded in maintaining the policy bubble around ICANN, in the rest of the world data governance concerns were intensifying.

Europe started strengthening its privacy regulations in 2012. As a draft law took shape, collective revulsion at the 2013 Snowden revelations encouraged the European Parliament to make the new regulation stronger. In October 2013, the draft GDPR increased the size of sanctions, extended its territorial scope, limited third-country data transfers, and imposed limits on profiling. In a plenary vote on March 12, 2014—coincidentally only two days before the NTIA announced the IANA stewardship transition—the European Parliament supported GDPR by a vote of 621 in favor, 10 opposed. The final version of GDPR was adopted on April 14, 2016 and became enforceable on May 25, 2018.

The story of ICANN's adjustment to the GDPR could provide the topic for an entire chapter, or perhaps another book. The purpose of this discussion is limited, however. The coming into force of GDPR provided the first major post-independence interaction between the system of sovereign states and the transnational ICANN regime. Here were two competing modes of governance intersecting. As this happened, an interesting historical reversal took place. American websites, cloud, search, and social media firms had globalized the digital economy, and the Framework for Global Electronic Commerce and the ICANN regime that grew out of it institutionalized its governance. ICANN reflected American data governance policies, an approach to publication of domain name registration data that allowed everyone—law enforcement, intelligence agencies, data brokers, platforms, cybersecurity researchers, random end users—to access it at will. Now Europe was globalizing its privacy regulations by asserting a countervailing governmental power to enforce a different policy. GDPR was incompatible with the contractual requirements of the ICANN regime. Like ICANN's Internet registry governance, the GDPR was designed to be nonterritorial in scope, making it in effect a rival to the ICANN regime in the treatment of personal registration data.

Like the Ukraine root zone exclusion request, ICANN's reaction to the GDPR was another big test of the relationship between state sovereignty and the Internet. One question was how ICANN itself would adjust. Another big question was whether Europe's extrusion of its jurisdiction into the global digital economy would lead to counter-assertions of authority by other governments, especially the United States. If so, would this lead to the jurisdictionally fragmented world ICANN was devised to prevent? Once again, ICANN's leadership was weak and did not seem to understand the stakes or have a strategy for handling this problem. Its multistakeholder community, on the other hand, did.

ICANN had two years to prepare for GDPR. It did nothing for a year and a half. Its staff, board, and many stakeholders remained in a state of denial, speaking repeatedly about how important and beneficial the old Whois regime was and exploring ways to keep its essential features in place. Not until March 2018—only two months before severe forms of legal liability would be triggered by GDPR's May 18 effective date—did ICANN release its first proposed interim model for GDPR compliance.

After a flurry of consultations with its constituencies, ICANN took an emergency board action. It did not have time to begin a formal policy development process, so it bypassed the GNSO. On May 17, 2018, only a week before GDPR went into effect, a board resolution created a Temporary Specification (TempSpec) that put Whois requirements into rough compliance with GDPR by authorizing registrars to redact key identifying information about the registrant (name, address, email, phone number) in published responses to Whois queries.[26] The TempSpec also set out a rationale for Whois purpose that showed that ICANN's management had still not internalized the need for change.

To its credit, however, the board recognized the need for community ratification of any modification of policy. It set into motion a policy development process to review the TempSpec and allow all the stakeholders involved in ICANN to accept or alter its terms in ways that would make it a real consensus policy. True to form, however, the always under-institutionalized ICANN did not use its established policy process to revise its Whois policy. It invented an entirely new one, an Expedited Policy Development Process (EPDP), with new modes of representation. The EPDP embarked on a long reform process that occurred in two phases. Phase 1 decided what the purpose of Whois data collection was and which data elements would be redacted from public display. In Phase 2, the EPDP developed policy for the way third parties could request disclosure of the redacted data elements from domain name registrars. Each phase then went into an implementation process. In both phases, an alliance of registrars, registries, Internet service providers, and civil society privacy advocates kept the EPDP focused on the goal of privacy compliance.

In short, it took four years for ICANN to respond to the GDPR—six years if the counting starts from the date the regulation passed. It did bring its regime into compliance, however.

Predictably, some trademark interests pushed the US Congress to pass a law that would assert US jurisdiction over ICANN and force it to bring back open Whois. A rough draft of a "Transparent, Open and Secure Internet Act," circulated around Washington in August 2018, would have required registries and registrars to publish registrant data in a publicly accessible directory.[27] Such a move would have sounded the death knell for the original vision underlying ICANN. It would have reversed the transition and fragmented jurisdiction over DNS, proving the Brazilians right that ICANN's presence in US jurisdiction made it a tool of the American sovereign. This proposal, however, never gained enough support to become a formally submitted bill. The transition mattered.

Though privacy norms played an important role in the reform of Whois, it was the economic interests of ICANN's registrars and registries that made change inevitable. Contracted parties who were domiciled in Europe, or serving European customers, had to choose between complying with ICANN's contracts or complying with their national law. This incompatibility was resolved by ICANN ceding authority to the GDPR standards governing disclosure. ICANN Org never seriously considered using its leverage as gatekeeper into the domain name registration business to impose an open Whois policy on all registrars at the expense of GDPR compliance. In other words, ICANN never asserted that its authority would be supreme. In fact, its CEO at the time, Goran Marby, did not even seem to understand ICANN's policy-making role.[28] In a competition with the European Union over whose rules would apply globally, ICANN pleaded nolo contendere.

The European Union did not win *entirely* because it was a sovereign power, however. It won because it empowered privacy advocates within ICANN. There had always been substantial support for protecting domain name registrants' personal data among ICANN's multistakeholder community. GDPR became a forcing function that allowed them to align domain name policy with privacy rights. ICANN's open Whois policy was never a true product of its multistakeholder regime; it was always an expression of its capture by IPR interests and the US government. Here, the transition made an important difference. The United States was no longer in a position to unilaterally order ICANN to follow its policy preferences on Whois data, and without US backing, the IPR interests could no longer veto a change. Furthermore, the European representatives in the GAC were not consistent supporters of privacy. As often as not, European GAC representatives in the EPDP sided with surveillance interests over privacy interests.[29] It was really the registration businesses and civil society who successfully translated the data protection constraints of the GDPR into the contractual terms of the domain name registries. In this case, it would be fair to say that the apparent triumph of GDPR and globalized European Union law over ICANN's globalized private contractual regime was also a triumph of the transition.

15 ESCAPE FROM SOVEREIGNTY?

This long-term survey of ICANN's relationship to government(s) sheds considerable light on the rhetoric and practice of the so-called multistakeholder model. First, it reveals that the regime's adoption of the label "multistakeholder" and its use as a legitimizing claim came later in its evolutionary road. ICANN originated as an attempt to *privatize* control of the Internet registries. The Framework for Global Electronic Commerce and the NTIA White Paper described the model as "private-sector led." This did not mean placing governance responsibilities in the hands of private industry; rather, it positioned the new institution as an alternative to governance by sovereign states, in which a private nonprofit would provide the organizational framework for policy development. The term *multistakeholder* did not exist in the founding documents.

Beginning in WSIS (2001–2005) and continuing through the transition, the Internet governance community began to use *multistakeholder model* to describe the regime. "Private sector led" did not disappear, but multistakeholder model was the more commonly used term in Internet governance debates. ICANN, the IETF, and the regional number registries started to differentiate themselves from the ITU or other sovereign institutions by describing themselves as multistakeholder models. In line with this trend, the NTIA's 2014 announcement required any transition plan to "support and enhance the multistakeholder model of Internet policymaking and governance."[1]

What is the multistakeholder model" then? A mountain of academic literature on the topic exists.[2] The label is problematic in certain respects. It deemphasizes the departure from sovereign state actors and focuses attention on the multiplicity of stakeholders. One of the better definitions refers to the multistakeholder model as "the idea of assembling actors from diverse societal spheres into one policymaking or rule-setting process, to make use of their resources, competences, and experiences."[3] This definition captures the reasons for including multiple actors in governance but says nothing about what institutional structures, systems of representation, and methods of developing policy are used. It also says nothing about the role of the state. How can one have a "model" of governance that is detached from any specific representational structure, procedure, or source of authority? Almost none of the multistakeholder model literature attempts to answer that question. There is, in fact, no well-defined "multistakeholder model."[4]

Much of the recent literature about multistakeholder models was inspired by discussions of Internet governance. Yet almost all of it misses the most important point about Internet governance. The most salient feature of the Internet governance regime is its independence from established governments, not the participation of multiple stakeholders. New forms of representing stakeholders have emerged, but that is only because they evolved independently of national governments and sovereignty-based international institutions. The three broadly defined communities that converged to institutionalize the Internet registries (technical community, business, and civil society) all agreed on forming a new institution not under the control of a government or an intergovernmental institution. That commitment to keep ICANN away from governments, though eventually taking second place rhetorically to the multistakeholder model, held firm all the way through the transition. The NTIA made it clear that it would "not accept a proposal that replaces the NTIA role with a government-led or an inter-governmental organization solution."[5] Because it explicitly excluded certain outcomes, the transition's mandate of an escape from state sovereignty was a clearer and more binding commitment than the vague command to "support and enhance the multistakeholder model."

Still, ICANN *was* a multistakeholder institution. From its inception, it was conceived as open to anyone in the world. Its representational structures mandated geographic diversity; it offered many channels for stakeholders from different societal sectors and interest groups to have input and, sometimes, real influence. Additionally, accountability reform did enhance ICANN's multistakeholder model by giving the global community more power over ICANN's staff and board.

What needs to be kept in mind is that multistakeholder participation would never have been possible if control of the Internet registries had been forced into the sovereign system. A regime formed in the image of sovereignty would be under the shared control of all governments, through the United Nations or some other intergovernmental institution. That kind of power structure bases representation primarily on national governmental entities. Sovereignty-based governance forces stakeholder communities into segregated units called "nations," and each nation is assumed to have a single, unitary position. That precludes the formation of a multistakeholder governance community because it subordinates the voices and decision-making power of individuals and organizations to the official position taken by their states. Thus, a sovereignty-based institution aggregates and reflects the interests of national governments, not those of autonomous Internet users and developers. If governance of the Internet registries had not been situated in the private sector, *we would never be discussing multistakeholder Internet governance.*

The topic of multistakeholder models appeals to many academics because of the way it reflects aspirations to democratize global governance. As Nicola Palladino and Mauro Santaniello wrote, "Multistakeholderism provides a governance model capable of establishing some form of authority in the transnational sphere and claims to do so through practices embedding the core values and principles of democratic discourse (participation, representativeness, equality, and accountability)."[6]

These scholars are correct that global governance requires new institutional forms if it is to translate the aspirations of liberal democracy to a global scale. Lest we forget, however, the need to "establish some form of authority in the transnational sphere" arises in the first place because there is no global sovereign to which we can turn to govern globalized functions such as the Internet registries or Internet standards. A global public or "stakeholder community" is more than a collection of national publics ruled by territorial sovereigns. It is a polity where stakeholders interact regularly among themselves to form their own norms, rules, decision-making procedures, and policy bargains. Scholars hypnotized by the allure of the multistakeholder model miss the linkage between private-sector leadership and the opportunity for multistakeholder governance.

New problems in deliberative democracy, representation, equality, and accountability arose precisely because the Internet governance institutions were not part of the sovereign system. The engaged community believed—wisely, as it turns out—that established methods of representation, voting, rulemaking, and accountability organized around national governments were not fit for purpose. Early on, this even led it to experiment with a radical form of democratic accountability: offering the world's individuals a right to elect members of the board. To describe ICANN as "multistakeholder" while downplaying or ignoring its shift of power to non-state actors is to put the cart before the horse.

For this reason, the concept of multistakeholder model needs to be carefully distinguished from the concept of *governance by non-state actors*. Both are present in ICANN, but governance by non-state actors is the more important feature. The multistakeholder model emphasizes the *participation* of actors from diverse societal spheres in policy-making or rule-setting processes. Governance by non-state actors, in contrast, supports self-governance by placing real policy-making authority *outside the state*. The collective decision-making unit is not the state or treaty-based international organizations, nor is its membership limited to representatives of sovereign states. Collective action among non-state actors—a category that includes civil society organizations and individuals as well as businesses—displaces or substitutes for decisions that would otherwise be made by states. That is why the transition, which made the ICANN regime fully governed by non-state actors, was so important.

For established liberal democracies, multistakeholder participation by itself is not that revolutionary or disruptive. Practically any governmental legislative body or regulatory agency can (and does) gather input from a diverse set of stakeholders. The same is true of many United Nations–based intergovernmental organizations. It is easy for governments to invite consultations from additional stakeholders—as long as decision-making authority remains with the sovereigns. Multistakeholder consultations may open new channels of influence into sovereign institutions, but the degree of influence is entirely at the discretion of the established power(s). All the input can be ignored, if they wish. Governance by non-state actors, on the other hand, involves a real shift of decision-making authority. It vests authority in collectivities that are not organized around sovereigns, altering the locus of power and the methods by which decisions are made.

Precisely because governance by non-state actors redistributes power, the formation of such institutions must focus attention on the specific

institutional arrangements needed to hold the non-state actors accountable. ICANN was an institutional innovation because it shifted governance
authority from sovereign states to a separate, self-organized community.
The process of translating that community's self-governance into specific
representational structures, policy-making procedures, and accountability
mechanisms was a long, bloody, often disappointing struggle, as this book
has documented. That's what happens, however, when power is moved to
a new space.

There is another serious limitation of the academic discussion of multistakeholder models. It tends to overlook the question of *what* needs to be
governed and *why*. It just assumes that more participation by more stakeholders is a good thing, regardless of the nature of the governance problem.
ICANN formed to address a very specific governance problem: filling the
vacuum in the policy role for the Internet registries. By virtue of its control of key aspects of the Internet registries, and its ability to manage the
policy-making role for those registries, the ICANN regime has real authority
over (one piece of) the Internet. Registry governance is not just a matter
of a bunch of people talking about what they would like to happen. Its
decisions have real consequences for how valuable Internet resources are
allocated and used. The work of Elinor and Vincent Ostrom, which speaks
of self-governance rather than multistakeholder governance, has been especially insightful in the way it ties collective governance structures to the
unique characteristics of the resources being governed.[7]

To the extent that ICANN holds real authority, it holds it largely to the
exclusion of states. Although its Governmental Advisory Committee blurs
the line between states and a private corporation, and some of its policy
decisions may intersect or conflict with national laws, the ICANN board
(and the leaders of the IETF and NRO) hold the authority to make binding policy and governance decisions about the Internet registries. It was
ICANN's status as a private, global corporation governing through contracts, not its openness to multiple stakeholders per se, that made it an
important innovation in global governance.

Governance by non-state actors tends to emerge organically when sovereigns are structurally unable to meet the need for governance. This is most
likely when policy issues transcend jurisdictions. It makes sense, then, that
governance by non-state actors was selected as the initial response to the problem of governing the Internet registries. For the sake of global compatibility,

governance authority needed to be global rather than territorial. Aside from that, the specialized technical expertise required to make good policy decisions was already concentrated in non-state actors. Lack of expertise and the severe policy and political differences among states would have prevented the establishment of an international treaty or other forms of timely collective action among states.[8] Similar conditions have prompted private-sector actors to take the lead in other areas of digital governance, such as content moderation on social media,[9] or governance of the public key infrastructure that supports encryption and authentication on the Web.[10]

The term *multistakeholder* officially entered the language of Internet governance during the World Summit on the Information Society. It was codified in 2005 by the report of the Working Group on Internet Governance (WGIG), which was given the task of coming up with a definition of Internet governance.[11] The resulting definition was a flawed construct. It bolted a state-centric theory of international regimes onto the concept of the multistakeholder model, resulting in the following mélange: "Internet Governance is the development and application by governments, the private sector and civil society, in their respective roles, of shared principles, norms, rules, decision-making procedures, and programmes that shape the evolution and use of the Internet."[12]

This definition is usually interpreted as an endorsement of the multistakeholder model.[13] It would be more accurate to describe it as a verbal construct forged by people trying to find an acceptable diplomatic compromise between traditional sovereigntist theory and a recognition of governance by non-state actors. The phrase "in their respective roles" was slipped into the middle of Stephen D. Krasner's canonical definition of international regimes at the insistence of certain governmental representatives on the Working Group. The definition tried to sort each stakeholder class into different *roles*, reserving "public policy" to governments and consigning the private sector to "technical and operational matters." That bargaining process never quite clarified the "role" of civil society, which was said to "play an important role." What that "important" role was, the WGIG report and Tunis Agenda never specified. Thus, governments formally acknowledged the presence of different stakeholders in Internet governance, but by linking them to distinct, segregated roles, they tried to preserve the sovereign order by excluding business and civil society from making public policy. The definition refused to recognize any sharing or redistribution of political power.

Segregated roles did not work, and could not work, as a means of governing the Internet registries. In the management of the Internet registries, there was no practical way to isolate "public policy" decisions from "technical and operational" concerns. The registries *are* technical facilities, but their operation poses questions that require collectively binding policies to answer. Many of these policy questions are quite "public" in that they define the rights of parties in ways that affect free expression, privacy, and property rights. If one wanted to restrict the policy role to governments, one would have to create a new multilateral organization with hierarchical power over policy decisions in the Internet registries. There was also no practical way to isolate "the private sector" from "civil society" in making policy, as the line between them is inherently blurry. The WGIG definition of Internet governance, while influential and incessantly cited, was a dead end.

Even if one drops the notion of segregated roles, multistakeholderism's tacit promise of perfect inclusiveness avoids or obscures questions of authority, accountability, and practicality. Who, exactly, is a "stakeholder"? The term can mean anything, from someone who owns and operates a piece of critical networking infrastructure, to a holder of IP addresses, to a website operator, to any Internet end user. If anyone "affected" by policy decisions is a stakeholder, even non-Internet users might be considered such, given the broad social impact the Internet governance decisions could have on them. Some of these stakeholders may not even know what an IP address is or how it works. Multistakeholder theory implies—unrealistically—that every individual and group can be represented equally in a governance process, but it never bothers to specify the institutional structures needed to achieve that ideal state.[14] Worse, it encourages an assessment of institutions and policies based entirely on measures of representation, and not on their effects or functionality.[15] It doesn't ask what policies do; it asks only who participated in their making. More participation by more people is presented almost as an end in itself, rather than a means to the end of better governance decisions.

At its most "democratic" extreme, the idea of multistakeholder governance implies that almost any decision affecting the Internet should be made collectively by everyone on the Internet. Yet the Internet and Web protocols were successful precisely because they *decollectivized* so many aspects of networking and content publication. One no longer needed permission from governments or telecom companies to offer a new online service, distribute a new application, or put up a website. Thanks to the end-to-end architecture of the Internet, innovators did not need permission from higher-ups, so private actors would make exchanges with other private actors to make most of the decisions shaping content, services, and applications. Open protocol standards, in other words, delegate a large chunk of Internet governance to voluntary choice, markets, and the price system. Only a few functions need to be centrally coordinated and collectively governed. The Internet registries are among those few. The beauty of the original conception of ICANN was that it recognized that these common functions should be governed not by states but by a private, nonprofit corporation, with a constitution that narrows its remit to basic coordinative functions and structures its bylaws to make it accountable to direct stakeholders in the registries.

The shift in labeling that occurred after WSIS—from "private-sector-led" to "multistakeholder model"—was more than just misguided rhetoric. It was not just a public relations ploy that put a prettier label onto institutions governed by non-state actors. The adoption of multistakeholder rhetoric was, in fact, correlated with an important shift in the nature of the regime. After WSIS—the ICANN regime's first major interaction with the sovereign system—ICANN progressively incorporated governments into the regime as a "stakeholder" on a par with private actors. In other words, the adoption of multistakeholder model rhetoric reflected a new way of integrating state authority and private authority in global governance.

ICANN and the US government began to give more power to governments from 2003 on. GAC "advice" got a higher status than other SOs and ACs. The US government began to use the GAC as a vehicle for shaping ICANN policy and pushed ICANN to accommodate governments' demands for a greater role in policy making. Significantly, states were incorporated into the regime not as sovereigns but as a *stakeholder class* on an equal footing with other private sector stakeholders. None of this happened through formal intergovernmental treaties or United Nations–mediated processes, moreover. It all occurred within ICANN. Governance by non-state actors was still the core of the regime.

To political scientists, defining sovereigns as "stakeholders" on a par with Internet service providers, domain name registries, trademark holders, and civil society advocacy groups is practically incomprehensible.[16] States, in political science, are the supreme and exclusive political power in their jurisdiction. Yet in the governance of the Internet registries, they do not act as sovereigns or negotiate binding intergovernmental treaties; instead, they act as representatives of a certain stakeholder class, based on a private corporation's bylaws. Insofar as the collective, consensus advice of governments in GAC affects policy, it must be approved by the board of a private corporation and implemented through private contracts. The transition, in other words, made the GAC just another stakeholder. This elevated and diminished governments' status at the same time. In the reformed ICANN, national governments are now voting members of an empowered community, which puts them on an equal status with participants in the GNSO, country code registry operators, the ALAC, and the regional IP address registries. But they are not sovereigns. This may clash with political theory, but theoretical inconsistencies must yield to demonstrated fact. Post-WSIS ICANN is an institutional mutation that blurs the lines between private and public authority, in the limited domain of the Internet registries.

In the US political process, the IANA stewardship transition was commonly referred to as an act of privatization all the way to the end. In precise legal terms, it was not a privatization at all. No US government agency ever owned and operated the DNS root or the IANA functions. All the registries were in the hands of different private actors holding government contracts. Insofar as it really existed, the IANA was an invention of the Internet Architecture Board, an unincorporated private association; there was never an "IANA contract" prior to the creation of ICANN. If one defines *privatization* differently, however—as a transference of *policy authority* from the state to a private-sector-led governance regime—the term is appropriate. Policy authority was successfully privatized. An escape from sovereign authority was a critical feature of the transition. ICANN's departure from the sovereign system and its reliance on governance by non-state actors are the core features of the institution. We cannot allow the rhetoric of multistakeholderism to obscure this fact.

Despite the many twists and turns in its evolution, and many compromises and failings, the Internet registries regime has succeeded in creating a global governance institution for the Internet that is outside of the sovereign system. Residents of "cyberspace" cannot say, with John Perry Barlow, that states "have no sovereignty where we gather," but if they are talking only about the governance of the Internet registries, they can. During the transition process, the Internet community held together as an autonomous public capable of self-governance, and states acceded to the status of one stakeholder among many, subordinating their sovereignty to private actors.

16 LOOKING FORWARD

I suspect that many readers of this book may think that ICANN and its governance model are old news, a relic of the 1990s not so relevant to what is happening in the mid-2020s. Yet the more I looked back at the formation of ICANN and its progress toward independence, the more I became convinced that the story is highly relevant to current digital governance debates and a useful aid for looking forward. If we try to imagine a global digital ecosystem without ICANN, the options do not look so good. If we try to imagine governance of some of the newer aspects of the digital economy, then the example of Internet governance, which shifted authority to non-state actors and multistakeholder participation, provides some useful pointers about how to approach—and how not to approach—those problems.

It is obvious that the political trends of 2024–2025 are moving in the opposite direction from the ones that gave birth to ICANN. Almost from the moment the transition concluded, on October 1, 2016, public policies in every major political economy bloc—North America, Europe, China, India, and Russia—started to rotate 180 degrees from the system that was set up in the previous four decades. During the progressive liberalization of the world economy after World War II, the markets for computers, network services, software, and information services became the most liberalized of all. That governance model was tremendously successful. It fostered economic growth, rapidly expanded and democratized access to information technology, and eroded barriers on the flow of information. The policies that supported this trend—the departure from state-owned monopolies in telecommunications, the globalization and privatization of Internet functions, the push for a private-sector-based legal framework, and of course the delegation of Internet registry governance to a nonprofit corporation under the supervision of the global Internet community—were products of optimism and confidence. People were not afraid of where open systems, globalization, free trade, and free expression would lead us. The people who made those policies were also surprisingly confident about the ability of a world community to govern the Internet registries in a new institution. While the problem proved to be much harder to solve than it first appeared, the end goal was reached.

Today, however, there are no bold visions of new governance institutions. There is no confidence in the ability of people to govern themselves. There is fear and loathing of the results of the digital economy due to its alleged concentration of market power, impact on privacy, and the spread of disinformation and misinformation. There are angry, defensive reactions against digital media, technology businesses, and technology itself. There is a general feeling that the governance models meant to support freedom and innovation have had bad results. The usual litany is that social media platforms are monopolies who extract our data and destroy our personal privacy, that the entire system is based on surveillance, and that misinformation, disinformation, fraud, and abuse are pervasive.

Interestingly, some of the worst fears about the dangers of information technology are being spread by the technologists who are developing it! Dozens of computer scientists and prominent businesspeople in information and communications technology, for example, signed a declaration claiming that there is a "risk of extinction from AI," comparing the proliferation of artificial intelligence applications to the risks of "pandemics and nuclear war."[1] This time around, no one is seeking independence from the state; instead, there is a unified chorus calling for more regulation.

One thing our experience with ICANN makes clear, however, is that greater reliance on governance by states would have made all of these problems worse, without the enablement and the innovation. The reactions against ICANN in WSIS and afterward aimed at reducing public participation, increasing state control of content, and enabling state surveillance (or disabling encryption by private firms). The departures from neoliberal globalization are often promoting national champions and domestic market concentration. While many welcome "bringing the state back in," we are also beginning to realize that bringing the state back in also brings in geopolitical rivalries, trade barriers, and increased risks of military conflict.[2] The free trade norms of the 1980s and 1990s are being replaced by populist nationalism and economic protectionism. Some nations act to weaponize digital infrastructure, and others pursue national industrial policies in the digital sectors to preserve their "autonomy." Instead of an escape from sovereignty, China, Russia, the European Union, India, Türkiye, and many other states are openly asserting "digital sovereignty" and do not seem at all worried that their efforts will generate the kind of jurisdictional fragmentation the ICANN regime was designed to avoid.[3] In this context, ICANN's story serves as a valuable reminder of an alternative path for digital governance.

Let's use what we know about ICANN and its history to look forward— not just at Internet registry governance but at the governance of the whole interdependent digital ecosystem. If ICANN's liberal globalism and today's dirigiste nationalism are alternate paths that public policy can take, which path will steer world society better?

It is highly unlikely that ICANN will stay exactly as it is and keep on doing what it's been doing for the last ten years. An important factor leading to change will be the domain name industry itself. ICANN's enormous, complex policy-making apparatus was constructed around the belief that top-level domain names are extremely valuable resources and that the domain name industry is vibrant and growing. It also rested on the premise that critical forms of Internet abuse, especially trademark and copyright infringement, can be combated by regulating domain name registries and registrars. Both of those conditions may no longer be true. If so, the current equilibrium is unlikely to be viable for much longer. Some things will have to change. Consider the following three scenarios.

SCENARIO 1: SURVIVAL AND RIGHT-SIZING

ICANN's domain name policy-making apparatus attenuates and is radically downsized. Yet PTI—the so-called Post-Transition IANA—survives, and so do the regional number registries and the IETF. What's left of ICANN focuses on the management and maintenance of existing registries (the DNS root zone, the unassigned IPv6 number space, if it ever gets used, and the RFC editor for protocol parameters).

In this scenario, ICANN's domain name policy apparatus deflates because of the growing economic irrelevance of new top-level domains. There are now thousands of them. The new ones have only achieved 9 percent of the market, and the possibility that a new one will reach the importance and profitability of .COM is minimal to nonexistent. It is also clear that top-level domains in non-ASCII characters, such as Chinese or Arabic, will probably not become popular because of the limitations on their accessibility to a global audience.

As the market for domain name registrations stops growing or shrinks, the need for ICANN's massive policy development apparatus, subsidized participation efforts, and political maneuvering starts to disappear. A tension begins to develop between touting the multistakeholder model as an inclusive and participatory form of governance and the efficiency and effectiveness of ICANN's policy development process. It also becomes clear that certain economic and political interest groups are striving mightily to leverage ICANN's contractual governance to regulate services and content on the Internet (which would violate its limited mission). By imposing burdensome regulations on newer top-level domain registries and trying to force registrars to comply with them, ICANN could effectively choke off growth in the generic name space and push all growth into legacy TLDs and ccTLDs.

ICANN's Policy Development Processes are already seriously bogged down by the overabundance of review processes, implementation stages, and multiple chances for review and relitigation of issues. With little demand for the licensing of additional top-level domain registries, ICANN has a smaller revenue stream and very little to do. It will have to be downsized. This means—and this will be the hardest part—attenuating or even getting rid of the GAC, as well as reducing the GNSO and some of the highly paid executives devoted to engagement and policy. It also means narrowing the scope of GNSO policy making. Once the process of contracting for new registries is removed from ICANN's remit, most of the policies made by ICANN/PTI would be so narrow and technical that governments need not be there. It also means that constant review and relitigation of issues by business and civil society are not necessary. The contracts should be standardized, the award of new ones entirely routine. Any policy changes could be consigned to ad hoc working groups convened under the downsized ICANN.

In this scenario, however, ICANN retains its status as the globally accepted venue for Internet registry governance. ICANN's policy-making scope is smaller and less controversial, but it is still governance by non-state actors. The world's states continue to accept a California nonprofit as the legitimate authority over registry policy, and the global digital ecosystem accepts the data published by IANA-compliant root servers as authoritative values for the global naming hierarchy. Wars may occur, sanctions may be imposed, but PTI's ICANN floats above all that; it is accepted as a neutral intermediary facilitating global communications. No one really loves ICANN, but they find this open, neutral, demilitarized space useful.

SCENARIO 2: UN-ICANN

Imagine ICANN and IANA taken over by states. Stuart Lynn finally gets his wish, but it is more thoroughgoing and formal than he imagined. ICANN becomes the subject of a new multilateral treaty that formally brings it into the United Nations system. The new UN-ICANN moves its headquarters from Marina del Rey, California, to Geneva, Switzerland, taking over an abandoned ITU building. It allows its former business and civil society constituencies to come to quarterly consultations with its decision makers, but those are informal and advisory. All binding decisions are made by a Council of Governments. The council is appointed by a vote of the national delegations. In effect, the GAC replaces the ICANN board; it rules on policy and chooses the CEO of the corporation.

The new regime marries the revenue-generation capability and executive freedom of a private corporation to the official powers of an intergovernmental organization. It is a bit like the World Intellectual Property Organization, only for techies. Yet now its technical staff, for some reason, seems to have many applicants from the police and intelligence agencies of governments. Policies now tend to veto any changes that might raise national security concerns from any government, threaten sovereign control over information and communications technology policy, or disrupt markets controlled by politically well-connected business interests. The council eventually agrees that the generic top-level domains were a mistake. It divides the naming hierarchy at the top level into countries, like telephone number country codes. Any registrations of individual citizens and businesses within those country codes should require passports or national identity cards with proof of their residence and citizenship. Copyright and trademark interests enthusiastically endorse this, as it strengthens their control over infringement. We must, they all say, bring this dangerous technology under stronger control. Registration contact data is made available to all police and intelligence agencies.

Even so, Council of Government decisions begin to be riven by geopolitical voting blocs. The Five Eyes, Europe, an India-Brazil-South Africa alliance, and a Russia-China alliance all tend to support divergent approaches to registry governance. If the politicization of the Council of Governments reaches a certain level, Scenario 2 could very well morph into Scenario 3.

SCENARIO 3: TECH-FRAG

The United States and China begin to divide themselves into separate technical ecosystems. A digital decoupling process begins. Like the old Cold War, the United States and China compete for the digital allegiance (and business) of other countries, though military conflict is off the table (at least at first). China develops its own new standards, networking protocols, and security arrangements. Europe tries to mount its own ecosystem, but of course it fails as it overloads its standards with social and political goals that are not viable in the market or technically. The US alliance hangs on to most of Europe, Japan, and South Korea, but China's less expensive ecosystem attracts Russia, many African and Latin American countries, and a few Middle Eastern and Southeast Asian nations.

In this scenario, the United States leverages its jurisdictional control of ICANN to reassert policy control over it. It forces ICANN to participate in US sanctions, close offices in adversary nations, and rely on servers and equipment from friendly nations. China responds by creating its own name, number, and protocol registries, splitting the DNS and the IP address spaces. The IETF keeps trying to make standards that enable global compatibility, but standards adoption patterns and registry governance begin to vary widely across the geopolitical blocs. As standards and markets diverge, global compatibility on networks and applications suffers.

The US and Chinese ecosystems are interoperable technically, but political pressure prevents US companies from buying equipment, software, or services from Chinese companies. The US government imposes export controls on advanced electronic components and any other digital technology it thinks will help it maintain a military advantage over China. The Chinese government, for its part, restricts transnational data flows, does not allow its companies or people to buy much equipment, software, or services from the United States and its allies, and China invests heavily in autarkic information and communications technology capabilities. Barriers over trade in information and communications technology become even higher as the two countries confront each other around Taiwan, and the possibility of war makes the national origin of all tech and electronics, from cranes in harbors to drones to EV batteries, a decisive factor in procurement.

THE BIGGER PICTURE

In setting out these scenarios, I have tried to visualize how ICANN might survive and evolve in the future (Scenario 1), as well as plausible and realistic alternatives to ICANN's private-sector-led regime (Scenarios 2 and 3). In all three scenarios, the path taken depends on factors much broader than Internet registry governance alone. It will hinge on the geopolitics of the broader digital ecosystem.

In the first scenario, ICANN's status as a departure from governance by state sovereignty is reinforced; in the other two, it becomes subordinate to state sovereignty and geopolitical tensions.

Thinking about these possibilities reinforces one's sense of the importance of the ICANN experiment. It is difficult to imagine a world in which the ICANN experiment is fully reversed—and when one does, the outcome does not seem promising. Despite the intense devotion to sovereignty, regulation, and state control in recent years, Scenario 1 still appears to be both the *most likely* and the *most desirable* of the three.

For pro-sovereignty governments, Scenario 2 realizes exactly what they have always wanted. Precisely because world politics is so divisive and fraught, however, that outcome seems unlikely. It is difficult to conceive of governments coming together to devise a binding international treaty that would successfully incorporate ICANN. Pro-Western states would fear that a multilateralized ICANN would be too influenced by Russia, China, or the BRICS; the Global South countries would fear that it would be too heavily influenced by the Western liberal democracies or the Global North. When it comes to Internet registry governance, the world's states simply lack the universally shared values and norms and the mutual trust needed to write, ratify, and implement a treaty capable of bringing the Internet registries into the United Nations system. However much today's digital critics might hate the neoliberal order that produced ICANN and see it as an oppressive system imposed on helpless users by evil capitalists, any attempt to reverse it in the context of Internet governance would quickly reveal how much public support it has. Renationalizing the Internet's name and address spaces, especially if it involved overlaying a territorial-sovereigntist structure on them, would greatly restrict user choices and cause enormous disruptions to existing domain name registrants, Internet businesses, and Internet users. Concerns about online civil liberties, privacy, and free expression would surface as states sought more control. There would be intense pushback from business and civil society. States could claim that these changes were in "the public interest," but the public would likely disagree.

Scenario 3, the fragmentation vision, is more plausible. It could happen and may in fact be happening. It is even more difficult to see such an outcome as desirable, however. At best, technical decoupling is a necessary evil, a defensive response to threats posed by hostile foreign powers and attempts at economic or political coercion. At worst, it is an illegitimate attempt by political and military leaders to subject the entire digital economy to their high-level power struggles, regardless of the collateral damage. It is not hard to make the case that these leaders' pursuit of power has made them lose sight of the tremendous benefits of international trade and cooperation, and that the gains of pursuing fragmentation policies will never outweigh the costs.

AI now occupies the same prominent place in the public imagination as the Internet did back in the mid-1990s. What many do not realize is that the same liberal enabling order that gave rise to ICANN and social media is also what enabled AI. In today's negative atmosphere, that is seen as a bad side effect of the open Internet. But is it?

It is common to see the threats or potential harms of AI mentioned in the same breath as the threat of nuclear destruction. Yet nuclear weaponry was a technology developed entirely by states, during a world war involving all the planet's most powerful militaries. Its first practical application at Hiroshima and Nagasaki destroyed 200,000 people in hours. The destructive powers of nuclear bombs were magnified twentyfold in the next few years by a science-and-technology-fueled arms race among the most powerful governments. No product of the private information and communications technology market, no governance arrangement run by non-state actors, has ever posed these risks or come close to this kind of destructive power. Still, privately developed chatbots are now put forward as risks comparable to nuclear destruction. When enumerated, the alleged safety risks of AI are almost comically out of proportion to the damage done by nuclear weapons. We are told that generative AI models can produce incorrect statements or misleading images, for example, or can be used for phishing attempts, malware development, or to spread disinformation—all things that currently happen at scale with existing tools. There is nothing about AI remotely comparable to the dangers of multiple thermonuclear explosions in a war between great powers.

Even more ironic, the comparison of AI to nuclear weapons is used to justify more power for national governments over the entire value chain of digital technology. Proposals for AI governance extend to regulating the cloud, semiconductors, networks, data, and code.[4] Military competition among national governments generated the original nuclear existential threat. That competition still exists. Wouldn't the risk of destructive applications of AI be increased rather than mitigated by more state control over the digital ecosystem? While governments in their domestic policies can and do effectively advance certain kinds of public safety, the pressures of *international* political economy push in the opposite direction. The social institution with the most interest in autonomous weaponry and enhanced powers of surveillance, deception, and espionage is the nation-state. We already know from two decades of cybersecurity threats that state actors are the most dangerous adversaries in the digital ecosystem. ICANN's model of governance by non-state actors in a global Internet community succeeded in limiting the subordination of the Internet registries to geopolitical ends. Wouldn't giving states more control of digital technology steer information and communications technology development in the opposite direction?

Everything that is now being said about the dangers of social media and AI could have been said, and in many cases *was* being said, about "the Internet" twenty-five years ago. Misinformation, disinformation, copyright violations, Internet addiction, harm to children, national security threats, enhanced espionage, financial crashes—all were part of the dialogue. The 1983 film *War Games* even anticipated an AI-controlled nuclear strike triggered by a bright teenager's intrusion into military networks. Social media platforms are simply highly successful commercial applications of the global connectivity fostered by the Internet and the Web. AI, too, is just a compute-intensive, data-intensive derivative of an Internet-enabled digital ecosystem.

Perhaps this is what accounts for the current panic. There is a feeling that the very success of the Internet and its liberal governance model is creating a world out of our control. Are we really losing control? Or is this really a debate about some people losing control over others, about established institutions losing power to the potential for new ones? If digital technology does pose new problems in regulation and control, is it not more important than ever to consider new institutional forms congruent with the nature of the digital ecosystem, instead of reactive calls for intensified national governmental controls? Why not look for new forms of collective action to empower people to confront these problems? Shouldn't we be having a debate about how to demilitarize and denationalize this technology, and shouldn't we be talking about how to put the right amount of control—and the right amount of freedom—in the right hands?

If one looks closely, reports of new ways of influencing or harming Internet users are always accompanied by reports of new tools for managing those problems. Reports of new tools for suppressing communications come with new tools for evading such suppression. New methods of monitoring the outputs of complex information systems seem to surface every day. The same technologies that we fear being out of control are also providing the tools for more accurate information, more efficient cooperation, and enhanced forms of regulation and control. The story told here suggests that we might address the governance problems posed by this evolving system with a more confident vision of human-technical possibilities, as happened in 1998. Certainly, the history shows that new institutions create serious and difficult start-up and accountability issues, but as one well-known political economist said about the relationship between technical change and institutional evolution, "Mankind inevitably sets itself only such tasks as it is able to solve; closer examination will always show that the problem itself arises only when the material conditions for its solution are already present or at least in the course of formation."[5]

APPENDIX A: INTERVIEW SUBJECTS

Completed interviews:

Abuhamad, Grace (ICANN staff): November 10, 2021

Anonymous (former NSC staff): January 20, 2022, and February 2022

Burr, J. Beckwith (ICANN board, Neustar, Commerce Department): July 11, 2023; August 8, 2023

Cerf, Vinton (IAB, Google): July 7, 2023

Conrad, David (APNIC, ICANN): May 2, 2022

Cooper, Alissa (IETF, ICG): February 18, 2022

Drazek, Keith (Verisign): July 28, 2023

Fuhr, Lise (.DK, ETNO): March 3, 2024

Kolkman, Olaf (IETF, ISOC): January 7, 2022

Rickert, Thomas (Rickert Law, GNSO): May 5, 2023

Rosenzweig, Paul, (former DHS, Heritage Foundation, consultant): November 10, 2021

Strickling, Lawrence (NTIA): February 10, 2022

Subjects who declined to be interviewed:

Alexander, Fiona (NTIA)

Beckstrom, Rod (former ICANN CEO)

Subjects who did not respond to requests for an interview:

dos Santos, Jandyr Ferreira (Brazil Ministry of Foreign Affairs, GAC representative on ICG)

Li, Xiaodong (ICG member, former head of CNNIC)

Post, David (US law professor)

APPENDIX B: LIST OF ABBREVIATIONS

AC	Advisory Committee
ALAC	At Large Advisory Committee
AFRINIC	African Network Information Center
APNIC	Asia-Pacific Network Information Center
AoC	Affirmation of Commitments
ARIN	American Registry for Internet Numbers
ARPA	Advanced Research Projects Administration
ASO	Address Supporting Organization
ccTLD	country code top-level domain
CCWG-Accountability	Cross-Community Working Group on Accountability.
ccNSO	Country Code Names Supporting Organization
CRISP	Consolidated RIR IANA Stewardship Proposal
CSC	Customer Standing Committee (of PTI)
CWG-Stewardship	Community Working Group on the IANA Stewardship Transition
DARPA	Defense Advanced Research Projects Administration
DDN-NIC	Defense Data Network—Network Information Center
DNS	domain name system
EC	empowered community
EFF	Electronic Frontier Foundation
EPDP	Expedited Policy Development Process

FGEC	Framework for Global Electronic Commerce
GAC	Governmental Advisory Committee
GDPR	General Data Protection Regulation
GNSO	Generic Names Supporting Organization
gTLD	generic top-level domain
IAB	Internet Architecture Board
IANA	Internet Assigned Numbers Authority
ICANN	Internet Corporation for Assigned Names and Numbers
ICG	IANA Stewardship Transition Coordination Group
IGF	Internet Governance Forum
IETF	Internet Engineering Task Force
IGP	Internet Governance Project
ITU	International Telecommunication Union
IP, IPv4, IPv6	Internet Protocol (version 4, version 6)
IRP	independent review process
ISOC	Internet Society
JPA	Joint Project Administration
LACNIC	Latin America and Caribbean Network Information Center
NomCom	Nominating committee (ICANN)
NRO	Number Resource Organization
NSC	National Security Council
NSA	National Security Agency
NSI	Network Solutions Inc.
NTIA	National Telecommunications and Information Administration
OFAC	Office of Foreign Asset Control
PIR	Public Interest Registry
PSC	President's Strategy Commission (ICANN)
PTI	Public Technical Identifiers; Post-Transition IANA
RAA	Registrar Accreditation Agreement
RFC	Request for Comments
RIPE-NCC	Réseaux IP Européens Network Coordination Centre
RIRs	Regional Internet address registries

RSSAC	Root Server System Advisory Committee
RZM	Root Zone Manager
RZMA	Root Zone Management Agreement
RZERC	Root Zone Evolution and Reform Committee
SOs	Supporting Organizations
SSAC	Security and Stability Advisory Committee
SWIFT	Society for Worldwide Interbank Financial Transfers
TCP/IP	Transport Control Protocol/Internet Protocol
TempSpec	Temporary Specification on Whois and Registration Data
TLD	top-level domain
USC ISI	University of Southern California Information Sciences Institute
WCIT	World Conference on International Telecommunications
WSIS	World Summit on the Information Society

NOTES

CHAPTER 1

1. NTIA Office of Public Affairs, "NTIA Announces Intent to Transition Key Internet Domain Name Functions," March 14, 2014, https://www.ntia.gov/press-release /2014/ntia-announces-intent-transition-key-internet-domain-name-functions.

2. Only a few pieces of scholarly literature examine the transition. Hortense Jongen and Jan Aart Scholte (2021), Nicola Palladino and Mauro Santaniello (2020), M. Becker (2019), and Tobias Mahler (2019) offer more narrowly focused accounts written for exclusively academic audiences. Aside from those, there are only scattered journalistic accounts, records of congressional hearings, and ICANN's own PR. There are many valuable records on ICANN's website about its own history, but ICANN has an organizational interest in framing the narrative in a certain way. ICANN has funded a historical study of the IANA functions, which is mostly correct in factual terms, but the data is often interpreted in a way that reflects ICANN's organizational interest. See Bradley Fidler and Russ Mundy, *The Creation and Administration of Unique Identifiers, 1967–2017* (Los Angeles: ICANN, 2020), https://www.icann.org/en/system /files/files/creation-administration-unique-identifiers-1967-2017-18nov20-en.pdf.

3. Department of Commerce, "Request for Comments on the Registration and Administration of Internet Domain Names," 62 *Fed. Reg.* 35,896 (1997).

4. WSIS and its impact on ICANN and Internet governance are covered in my previous book, *Networks and States: The Global Politics of Internet Governance* (Cambridge, MA: MIT Press, 2010).

CHAPTER 2

1. Subcommittee on Oversight, Agency Action, Federal Rights, and Federal Courts, Subcommittee Hearing: "Protecting Internet Freedom: Implications of Ending U.S. Oversight of the Internet," Wednesday, September 14, 2016.

2. In *McNeil v. Verisign, Inc.*, 127 F. App'x 913, 913 (9th Cir. 2005), a federal court ruled that "The district court correctly held that McNeil cannot assert a First Amendment claim against ICANN because ICANN, a non-profit public benefit corporation established by agencies of the United States government to administer the Internet domain name system, is not a government actor."

3. Dieter Grimm, *Sovereignty: The Origin and Future of a Political and Legal Concept* (New York: Columbia University Press, 2015), 231–233. Janice Thomson argues that "with the institution of sovereignty states are empowered or authorized to decide what is political in the first place." Janice Thomson, "State Sovereignty in International Relations: Bridging the Gap Between Theory and Empirical Research," *International Studies Quarterly* 39, no. 2 (1995): 21.

4. Robert Jackson, "Sovereignty in World Politics: A Glance at the Conceptual and Historical Landscape," *Political Studies* 47, no. 3 (1999): 432.

5. Stephen D. Krasner, *Sovereignty: Organized Hypocrisy* (Princeton, NJ: Princeton University Press, 1999).

6. Trotter Hardy, "The Proper Legal Regime for Cyberspace," *University of Pittsburgh Law Review* 55 (1993); David R. Johnson and David Post, "Law and Borders: The Rise of Law in Cyberspace," *Stanford Law Review* 48, no. 5 (1996): 1367–1402.

7. Johnson and Post, "Law and Borders," 1367.

8. Forrest Hare, "Borders in Cyberspace: Can Sovereignty Adapt to the Challenges of Cyber Security?," in *The Virtual Battlefield: Perspectives on Cyber Warfare*, edited by Christian Czosseck and Kenneth Geers (Clifton, VA: IOS Press, 2009), 88–105; Wolff H. von Heinegg, "Legal Implications of Territorial Sovereignty in Cyberspace," in *2012 4th International Conference on Cyber Conflict (CYCON 2012)*, edited by C. Czosseck, R. Ottis, and K. Ziolkowski (Talinn: NATO CCD COE Publications, 2012), 7–19; Michael N. Schmidt, ed., *Tallinn Manual on the International Law Applicable to Cyber Warfare* (Cambridge: Cambridge University Press, 2013).

9. Milton L. Mueller, "Against Sovereignty in Cyberspace," *International Studies Review* 22, no. 4 (2020): 779–801.

10. Milton L. Mueller, *Will the Internet Fragment? Sovereignty, Globalization and Cyberspace* (New York: John Wiley & Sons, 2017); Wolf J. Schünemann and Marianne Kneuer, "Do Not Disturb! Studying Discourses of Democratic Sovereignty As Potential Drivers of Internet Fragmentation through Online Control," presented at ISA Annual Convention, April 6–9, 2021; Roxana Radu and Giovanni De Gregorio, "The New Era of Internet Governance: Technical Fragmentation and Digital Sovereignty Entanglements," in *Hybridity, Conflict, and the Global Politics of Cybersecurity*, edited by Fabio Cristiano and Bibi van den Berg (Lanham, MD: Rowman & Littlefield Publishers, 2023).

11. Ilona Stadnik, "Sovereign RUnet: What Does It Mean?" *Internet Governance Project*, February 12, 2019, https://www.internetgovernance.org/research/sovereign

-runet-what-does-it-mean; Alexandra Orlova, "'Digital Sovereignty,' Anonymity and Freedom of Expression: Russia's Fight to Re-Shape Internet Governance," *UC Davis Journal of International Law & Policy* 26, no. 2 (2019): 225–247.

12. Roger Creemers, "China's Conception of Cyber Sovereignty," in *Governing Cyberspace: Behavior, Power, and Diplomacy*, edited by Dennis Broeders and Bibi van den Berg (Lanham, MD: Rowman & Littlefield, 2020), 107–145; Anqi Wang, "Cyber Sovereignty at Its Boldest: A Chinese Perspective," *Ohio State Technology Law Journal* 16, no. 2 (2020): 395–466; Yu Hong and G. Thomas Goodnight, "How to Think About Cyber Sovereignty: The Case of China," in *China's Globalizing Internet: History, Power, and Governance*, edited by Yu Hong and Eric Harwit (London: Routledge, 2022), 7–252.

13. In fact, Chinese state-owned telecommunication enterprises had been exploring ways to create a global domain naming system structured on national lines that would give each nation-state its own DNS root and supreme control over all the domain names used in their country. Mueller, *Will the Internet Fragment?*, 37–39.

14. John Perry Barlow, "Declaration of the Independence of Cyberspace," World Economic Forum, February 8, 2018, https://www.weforum.org/agenda/2018/02/a -declaration-of-the-independence-of-cyberspace (originally published online on February 8, 1996).

15. Anthony D. Smith, *Nationalism: Theory, Ideology, History* (Hoboken, NJ: John Wiley & Sons, 2013).

CHAPTER 3

1. O. Kolkman, "Framework for Describing the IANA, draft-iab-iana-framework-02," March 2014, https://datatracker.ietf.org/doc/html/draft-iab-iana-framework-02.

2. "Stable and predictable assignment and registration of protocol identifiers for Internet protocols is of great importance to many stakeholders, including developers, vendors, and customers, as well as users of devices, software, and services on the Internet. These stakeholders use and depend on registries and implicitly trust the registry system to be stable and predictable." Kolkman, "Framework."

3. When the Internet outgrew that number, the IETF created a new standard with a 4-byte ASN space allowing for 4.29 billion unique numbers; when it outgrew the IPv4 address space, it created a new standard, IPv6, which defined an address space with 2^{128} unique values.

4. Kolkman, "Framework," 7. It bears noting that the IAB did not publish a clear definition of "the IANA functions" and the different roles they implied until a few days after the NTIA's announcement that it intended to let go of the IANA functions. This conjunction seems to be coincidental, however, as work on draft-Kolkman began several years earlier as the IETF prepared for the renewal of the IANA contract in 2012.

5. "Liberal" is defined here as the political and social philosophy that promotes individual rights, civil liberties, democracy, and market economy.

CHAPTER 4

1. Jon Postel was a member of the small group of UCLA computer science graduate students who became involved in early work on the ARPANET, a project that later evolved into the development and administration of Internet protocols and registries. Among other accomplishments, he was the editor of the RFC series and a contributor to and editor of RFCs 791, 792, and 793, which define the basic protocols of the Internet protocol suite.

2. Jon Postel, "Proposed Standard Socket Numbers," RFC 349, May 30, 1972. See archive of all RFCs at https://rfc-archive.org.

3. Prior to 1981, these assignments applied to networking configurations that predated Internet protocol and thus cannot be considered "Internet registries." They assigned numbers to protocols such as telnet or to things that no longer exist, such as links, a feature of earlier, pre-IP Internet Messaging Protocol. Later, reflecting the experimental nature of the protocols, numbers were assigned in packets to represent which version of IP it was running, ranging from 0 to 5.

4. Each ARPANET node would tell SRI the name(s) of its computers, and SRI would collect, update, and distribute the host names in a list, making sure there were no duplications. Oral History of Elizabeth (Jake) Feinler, interviewed by Marc Weber, Computer History Museum, September 10, 2009, https://archive.computerhistory .org/resources/access/text/2013/05/102702199-05-01-acc.pdf; Bradley Fidler and Ross Mundy, *The Creation and Administration of Unique Identifiers, 1967–2017* (November 2020), 46, https://www.icann.org/en/system/files/files/creation-administration-unique -identifiers-1967-2017-18nov20-en.pdf.

5. Not until RFC 3232 (January 2002) were the Assigned Numbers documents replaced by "an On-line Database."

6. Documents laying out the design of the DNS were circulated in 1984 (RFC 881, Mockapetris), and in October 1987 the complete specifications for the domain name system were published in RFCs 1034 and 1035.

7. RFC 997, p. 1: "This RFC will be updated periodically, and in any case current information can be obtained from Hostmaster," which was identified as "DDN Network Information Center, SRI International, 333 Ravenswood Avenue, Menlo Park, California 94025, ARPA mail: HOSTMASTER@SRI-NIC.ARPA."

8. Jon Postel and Joyce Reynolds, "Domain Requirements," RFC 920 Internet Society (October 1984). https://datatracker.ietf.org/doc/html/rfc920.

9. In fact, the Internet technical community did not begin to fully articulate that distinction until 2011. Interview with Olaf Kolkman, January 7, 2022. Recording on file with author.

10. The Union of International Associations listing for CCIRN describes its mission as "Stimulate cooperative intercontinental research through enhanced interoperable networking services; achieve *interoperable* networking services between participating entities in support of open research and scholarly pursuit; coordinate development of international network management techniques; optimize use of resources and coordinate intercontinental connections; exchange results of networking research and development." CCIRN included the US Federal Networking Council (see note 15 below) and its counterparts in Canada and Europe.

11. Interview with David Conrad, April 14, 2022. Recording on file with author.

12. The first message on the com-priv listserv, where debates and discussions regarding the commercialization and privatization of various aspects of the Internet raged for nearly a decade, was dated October 5, 1990, only a few months after RFC 1174 was published.

13. The RFC editor function bore certain similarities to registry maintenance, in that there was a need for a single, authoritative version of documents specifying protocols. But while the organizational home for both was USC's ISI, editing and finalizing RFCs was a distinct function from maintaining a registry of unique identifiers, though they needed to be coordinated.

14. Vint Cerf, "IAB Recommended Policy on Distributing Internet Identifier Assignment and IAB Recommended Policy Change to Internet 'Connected' Status," RFC 1174 (August 1990), https://www.rfc-editor.org/rfc/rfc1174.

15. The Federal Networking Council was established as an interagency group of the US government in 1990 and provided policy oversight and guidance to the Internet's developers. It included DARPA, the National Science Foundation, NASA, the Department of Energy, and the Department of Health and Human Services. For a good description of its origins and activities, see Fidler and Mundy, *Creation and Administration*, 81–82.

16. RFC 1174, p. 2.

17. The contract specified that NSI would provide its IP addressing services "in accordance with the provisions of RFC 1174." The relevant provisions of RFC 1174 were these: "The IR would continue to be the principal registry for all network and autonomous system numbers. It would also continue to maintain the list of root Domain Name System servers and a database of registered nets and autonomous systems. In addition, however, the IR would also allocate to organizations approved by the Coordinating Committee for Intercontinental Research Networking (CCIRN) blocks of network and autonomous system numbers, as needed, and delegate to them further assignment authority. It is recommended that, at least initially, the IR serve as the default registry in cases where no delegated registration authority has been identified." Network Information Services Manager(s) for NSFNET and the NREN: INTERNIC Registration Services. COOPERATIVE AGREEMENT NO. NCR-9218742, Effective 1 January 1993. https://archive.icann.org/en/nsi/coopagmt

-01jan93.htm. The NSF contract was taken over by the Commerce Department during the formation of ICANN.

18. Authority over DNS was especially ambiguous. Contractual authority to operate the DNS root registry was shifting from DoD to NSF. Postel had played a role in deciding what top-level domains there would be and in drafting RFCs that set policy for the implementation of DNS—a complex standards migration issue. But other federal contractors were involved.

19. In March 1997, an aspiring operator of new top-level domains pursuing an anti-trust lawsuit against the NSI monopoly asked Postel at USC ISI to instruct NSI to add some top-level domains to the root. The applicant received the following answer from a USC lawyer: "We are aware of no contract or other agreement that gives IANA authority over [NSI's] operations" (*Pgmedia, Inc. v. Network Solutions, Inc.*, Case Text).

20. Conrad, interview.

21. For the complete story, see Milton Mueller, *Ruling the Root: Internet Governance and the Taming of Cyberspace* (Cambridge, MA: MIT Press, 2002).

CHAPTER 5

1. NTIA, "Statement of Policy" (June 5, 1998) (known as the White Paper), https://www.icann.org/resources/unthemed-pages/white-paper-2012-02-25-en.

2. The United States was, at times, a bit of a bully in its trade relationships with other countries, especially when intellectual property was involved, but for the most part, it was opening its own markets as much as it was opening up others'.

3. Prepared statement of Esther Dyson, Domain Name System Privatization: Is ICANN Out of Control? Hearing before the Subcommittee on Oversight and Investigations of the Committee on Commerce, House of Representatives, 106th Congress, First Session, July 22, 1999, https://www.govinfo.gov/content/pkg/CHRG-106hhrg58497/html/CHRG-106hhrg58497.htm.

4. Raymund Werle and Volker Leib, "The Internet Society and Its Struggle for Recognition and Influence," in *Private Organizations in Global Politics*, edited by Karsten Ronit and Volker Schneider (London: Routledge, 2013), 102–123.

5. See International Ad Hoc Committee, https://computer.howstuffworks.com/iahc.htm.

6. The Internet Society tried to collaborate with the grandaddy of all intergovernmental institutions, the ITU, but it boldly did so as a peer. The strange match prompted Pekka Tarjanne, the ITU secretary general, to congratulate Internet Society on the emergence of a new paradigm, which he called "voluntary multilateralism." Tarjanne said, "This process consists of identifying communities of interest who can come together on a voluntary basis to solve problems, and then letting the market

decide whether or not they got it right. Sometimes those communities of interest may use the services of the ITU. Sometimes they will use other bodies such as the WTO or the OECD. Sometimes they will form around a special purpose group, such as the IAHC." Pekka Tarjanne, "Internet Governance: Towards Voluntary Multilateralism," keynote address, Internet Domain Names: Information Session, Meeting of Signatories and Potential Signatories of the Generic Top Level Domain Memorandum of Understanding (gTLD-MoU), ITU, Geneva, Switzerland, April 29–May 1, 1997, https://www.itu.int/newsarchive/projects/dns-meet/KeynoteAddress.html. Unfortunately for the Internet Society, even "voluntary" multilateralism proved to be too much multilateralism for the US government.

7. Information and communications were specific strengths of the US economy. It had hatched the integrated circuit industry, broken up its telecommunications monopoly to create space for hundreds of new businesses, deregulated its mass media industries, and promoted a free market in information services and technologies. It was the home base of the leading software firms. Its universities attracted researchers and professionals from all over the world, especially in engineering and computer science, and its business and investment environment attracted the most innovative entrepreneurs.

8. There were tensions in this alliance, however. Intellectual property interest (IPR) groups, while eager to benefit from the globalizing economy, often viewed the rise of a digital infrastructure as a threat to copyright and trademark protection.

On the other hand, Internet service providers viewed many of the legal and policy demands emanating from the IPR interests, such as strict third-party liability for copyright infringements, as crippling to their industry. In general, the Clinton administration policy makers strongly backed the IPR interests but its commitment to Global Information Infrastructure and Internet development eventually prompted them to find a middle ground in the provisions of the Digital Millennium Copyright Act.

9. Al Gore, "Information Superhighways: The Next Information Revolution," *The Futurist* 25, no. 1 (1991). See also Andrew Targowsky, *Global Information Infrastructure: The Birth, Vision and Architecture* (Idea Group Publishing, 1996).

10. See the General Accounting Office, "Information Superhighway—Issues Affecting Development" (Report to the Congress, September 1994, GAO/RCED-94-285).

11. "Remarks by the President in Announcement of Electronic Commerce Initiative," White House Office of the Press Secretary, July 1, 1997, https://clintonwhitehouse4.archives.gov/WH/New/Commerce/remarks.html.

12. Interview with J. Beckwith (Becky) Burr, July 11, 2023. Recording on file with author.

13. Burr interview, July 11, 2023.

14. A favorable review of the Framework in the *Annual Review of Banking* said, "The fifth principle . . . , to many, is the most important principle in connection with

electronic commerce and the Internet, namely that electronic commerce over the Internet should be facilitated on a global basis." Ernest Patrikis and Stephanie Heller, "The Government's Role in Electronic Commerce," *Annual Review of Banking Law* 18 (1999): 325.

15. Ira C. Magaziner, Ann Grier Cutter, and Len A. Costa, "The Framework for Global Electronic Commerce: A Policy Perspective," *Journal of International Affairs* 51, no. 2 (1998): 527–538. I recall receiving a copy of it from the APPLE email list while living in Hong Kong. (APPLE was the acronym for a listserv called Asia Pacific Policy and LEgal, a list of about 200 people in the region interested in the policy questions of the Internet. In included academics, industry people, and regional and global techies.)

16. "[T]here were a lot of people in the Administration who were extremely skeptical and felt [publishing the draft on the Web] wasn't appropriate for the government. In fact, it turned out to be valuable. We heard from hundreds of people we never would have heard from in Washington. . . . [T]he Vice Minister of MITI, Mr. Nakagawa, who is in charge of this issue for Japan, said that he first heard of our efforts by seeing the original draft on the web. . . . The European Union also saw it on the web. So, in a way, putting the document on the web has accelerated the whole process of international discussion." Magaziner, Cutter, and Costa, "The Framework."

17. Burr interview, July 11, 2023.

18. Commerce Department associate administrator Becky Burr said in testimony before Congress: "The *Framework* sets out a number of principles . . . to guide our approach to a number of important policy issues. In keeping with those principles, President Clinton directed the Secretary of Commerce to work to privatize, increase competition in, and promote international participation in the domain name system." Burr testimony, June 10, 1998, https://www.ntia.gov/speechtestimony/testimony-becky-burr-house-committee-commerce-subcommittee-telecommunications-trade.

19. Barlow, "Declaration."

20. Bobbie Johnson, *Case Study: Private Platforms* (Stanford, CA: Stanford University Ethnics, Technology and Public Policy, 2018), http://ai.stanford.edu/users/sahami/ethicscasestudies/Platforms.pdf.

21. Conrad, interview.

22. Colin J. Bennett, *The Privacy Advocates: Resisting the Spread of Surveillance* (Cambridge, MA: MIT Press, 2010); Michael Froomkin, "Metaphor Is the Key: Cryptography, the Clipper Chip, and the Constitution," *University of Pennsylvania Law Review* 143 (1994); Vanda Pednekar-Magal and Peter Shields, "The State and Telecom Surveillance Policy: The Clipper Chip Initiative," *Communication Law and Policy* 8, no. 4 (2003): 429–464.

23. Alfred C. Yen, "Internet Service Provider Liability for Subscriber Copyright Infringement, Enterprise Liability, and the First Amendment," *Georgetown Law Journal*

88, no. 6 (1999): 1833; Jessica Litman, "The Exclusive Right to Read," *Cardozo Arts & Entertainment Law Journal* 13, no. 1 (1994): 29–54; Pamela Samuelson, "The NII Intellectual Property Report," *Communications of the ACM* 37, no. 12 (1994): 21–28.

24. Coe William Ramsey, "Burning the Global Village to Roast a Pig: The Communications Decency Act of 1996 Is Not 'Narrowly Tailored' in Reno v. ACLU," *Wake Forest Law Review*, 32 (1997): 1283–1325; R. Cannon, "The Legislative History of Senator Exon's Communications Decency Act: Regulating Barbarians on the Information Superhighway," *Federal Communications Law Journal* 49, no. 1 (1996): 51–94.

25. L. Daigle, "Internet Invariants," Internet Society (policy brief), September 26, 2016, https://www.internetsociety.org/policybriefs/internetinvariants.

26. Walter B. Wriston, *The Twilight of Sovereignty: How the Information Revolution Is Transforming Our World* (New York: Scribner, 1992).

27. According to Burr, "Jon Postel came up with a board for ICANN that was *all* technologists—no civil society, no business, it was just his crew. And we said, no, that's not gonna work. We're not picking the board, but you've got to think about diversity in a different way—it is not just geographic diversity, it is structural diversity." By structural diversity, Burr meant what we would now call "multistakeholder representation;" different societal sectors would be represented. She noted that "engineers spoke one language, civil society another, business another" and felt that all three needed to be in direct negotiation with each other. Burr interview, July 11, 2023.

28. The White Paper recorded this principle in this way: "A private coordinating process is likely to be more flexible than government and to move rapidly enough to meet the changing needs of the Internet and of Internet users. The private process should, as far as possible, reflect the bottom-up governance that has characterized development of the Internet to date."

29. John G. Palfrey, "The End of the Experiment: How ICANN's Foray into Global Internet Democracy Failed," *Harvard Journal of Law & Technology* 17, no. 2 (2004): 409–473; Milton L. Mueller, "ICANN Inc.: Accountability and Participation in the Governance of Critical Internet Resources," *Korean Journal of Policy Studies* 24, no. 2 (2009): 91–116.

CHAPTER 6

1. Domain Name System Privatizaton: Is ICANN Out of Control? Hearing before the House of Representatives, Committee on Commerce, Subcommittee on Oversight and Investigations, 106th Congress, First Session, July 22, 1999, https://www.govinfo.gov/content/pkg/CHRG-106hhrg58497/html/CHRG-106hhrg58497.htm.

2. ICANN's written response to questions from Senator Bliley are on the ICANN website as of March 2024. https://www.icann.org/resources/unthemed-pages/bliley-response-1999-07-08-en.

3. Hearing, Domain Name System Privatization, Committee on Commerce, July 22, 1999.

4. Republicans tended to be influenced by NSI and more likely to take its side in what was widely seen as a dispute over competition policy in the DNS registration market. Democrats tended to take ICANN's side, partly for partisan reasons, partly because they bought in to the Internet vision, and partly because they favored undermining the NSI monopoly on DNS.

5. Hearing, House Committee on Commerce, July 22, 1999.

6. Douglass North, "Institutions," *Journal of Economic Perspectives* 5, no. 1 (1991): 97–112; Jack Knight, *Institutions and Social Conflict* (Cambridge: Cambridge University Press, 1992).

7. Stephen D. Krasner, "Structural Causes and Regime Consequences: Regimes as Intervening Variables," *International Organization* 36, no. 2: 185–205.

8. Daron Acemoglu, Simon Johnson, and James A. Robinson, "Institutions as a Fundamental Cause of Long-Run Growth," in *Handbook of Economic Growth*, vol. 1A, edited by Philippe Aghion and Steven N. Durlauf, 385–472 (Elsevier, 2005).

9. In its January 30, 1998, Green Paper, the Commerce Department had proposed a straightforward privatization process based on US law and institutions. It would transfer the IANA functions to a nonprofit organization whose fourteen-member board would consist of three RIR representatives, two selected by the IAB, two representatives of registries and registrars, and seven representatives of "Internet users" drawn from an Internet users' association. Mueller, *Ruling the Root*, 160n42. The Green Paper, however, was widely criticized by the Internet Society and non-US commentators because of its grounding in US government decision-making and law.

10. "Uniform Domain Name Dispute Resolution Policy," ICANN, accessed June 28, 2024, https://www.icann.org/resources/pages/help/dndr/udrp-en.

11. US Senate Committee on Commerce, Science, and Transportation, "Hearing on Internet Corporation Assigned Names and Numbers (ICANN)," July 31, 2003, https://www.commerce.senate.gov/2003/7/internet-corporation-assigned-names-and-numbers-(icann. Confirmed by the Senate in August 2001, Victory had a strong background in international radio spectrum policy and traditional telecommunication issues.

12. The five areas were (1) clarifying ICANN's mission and responsibilities; (2) ensuring transparency and accountability in its processes and decision making; (3) increasing its responsiveness to Internet stakeholders; (4) developing an effective advisory role for governments; (5) ensuring adequate and stable financial and personnel resources to carry out its mission and responsibilities. Testimony of Nancy Victory, Mueller, *Ruling the Root*, 160n42.

13. Control of the DNS root—which had been established for antitrust reasons, not for security reasons—did not provide the US government with any leverage over

terrorism or related global security threats, nor did it give the US any exclusive intelligence.

14. The term has its origin in the expression "pull yourself up by your bootstraps," suggesting the difficulty of starting something from scratch.

15. A commitment to consensus and running code meant that one did not accept a policy or a standard simply because someone higher up in authority told you to; one accepted it if it worked, and no one could make a strong argument against it.

16. Mueller, *Ruling the Root.*

17. The initial board chair, Esther Dyson, was particularly egregious in her tendency to claim "community consensus" for decisions made by the small group around her. She repeatedly dismissed dissenting views by simply asserting that they were "outside the consensus," when there was no formal process for determining consensus.

18. Conrad, interview. ICANN's general counsel was Louis Touton, a Jones Day lawyer who became vice president, secretary, and general counsel of ICANN. Mike Roberts, former head of Educause, was the first CEO of ICANN. Esther Dyson, an organizer of industry conferences, became ICANN's first board chair.

19. A key point of disagreement, according to a report issued by ICANN CEO Stuart Lynn in February 2002, was that the address registries wanted the right to terminate the agreement for ICANN to act as the top-level addressing authority. This issue would return during the transition negotiations in 2014–2015.

20. "NRO Memorandum of Understanding," October 24, 2003, https://www.nro.net /nro-memorandum-of-understanding. The NRO explained why it had made these moves in a November 6, 2003, "Open Letter to ICANN from the Regional Internet Registries." "ICANN is a private corporate entity, and . . . its future is one that is not absolutely assured. There is a risk, as with any private corporate entity, that the entity may fail. Failure of ICANN includes the risk of a freezing of the unallocated number pool, which in turn places a significant risk in the continued operation of the registries and the application of their policies. See https://www.nro.net/open -letter-to-icann-from-the-regional-internet-registries.

21. Postel's USC ISI operation ran only one of the thirteen root servers; the others were run by US government agencies, NSI, and some of Postel's technical community colleagues in the United Kingdom, Japan, and Sweden.

22. ICANN and Commerce/NTIA duly entered into a Cooperative Research and Development Agreement (CRADA) in June 1999 to "study the management of the root server system." The task was supposed to conclude by September 30, 2000, the finalization date envisioned by the White Paper.

23. Geoff Huston, one of the early Internet pioneers, wrote, "A fracture was apparent in the relationship between ICANN the IETF. Attempts to create an agreement between ICANN and the IETF over the IANA function were not recognised by the US administration, who continued to insist that, formally, the IANA function for the

IETF was undertaken at the behest of the US Department of Commerce rather than the IETF. This was not a view shared by the IETF." Huston, "Opinion: ICANN, the ITU, WSIS, and Internet Governance," *The Internet Protocol Journal* 8, no. 1 (2005): 20.

24. Correspondence between IETF and ICANN on Assignment of Protocol Parameters Developed or Maintained by the IETF, February 25, 1999, https://www.icann .org/resources/unthemed-pages/bradner-dyson-1999-02-25-en.

25. It recognized that "the IANA technical team is now part of ICANN" but required ICANN's IANA to manage protocol parameter assignments according to criteria and procedures specified in IETF RFCs. It also gave ICANN-IANA a right to "review all documents in IETF last call to identify any issues of concern." The memorandum of understanding also recognized that the assignment of domain name and IP number blocks raise "policy issues" and that "these policy issues are outside the scope of this MoU." B. Carpenter, IAB; F. Baker, IETF; M. Roberts, ICANN, "Memorandum of Understanding Concerning the Technical Work of the Internet Assigned Numbers Authority," RFC 2860, June 2000, https://www.rfc-editor.org/rfc/rfc2860.

26. It gave ICANN-IANA a right to "review all documents in IETF last call to identify any issues of concern." The memorandum of understanding also recognized that the assignment of domain name and IP number blocks raise "policy issues" and that "these policy issues are outside the scope of this MoU." All quotations are from RFC 2860.

27. The Markle Foundation put together an international study calling for democratic elections and public participation in domain name policy. See https://www .markle.org/about-markle/news-release/markle-foundation-announces-independent -study-icann-elections.

28. Referring to the "Sisyphean effort of searching for a workable public accountability mechanism for ICANN," CEO Stuart Lynn declared in February 2002 that "three years of effort have proven that a global online election of ICANN Board members by an entirely unknown and self-selected membership is not a workable solution to this problem." Ironically, voting membership was replaced by the entirely self-selected— but ICANN-controlled—set of participants in regional at-large organizations. M. Stuart Lynn, "President's Report: ICANN—The Case for Reform," ICANN, February 24, 2002, https://archive.icann.org/en/general/lynn-reform-proposal-24feb02.htm.

29. ALAC, the board claimed, would empower the world's "individual internet users" in ICANN's processes. Representation, however, would be highly indirect and its powers mainly advisory. Organizations known as at -large Structures (not individuals, ironically) would join a regional at-large organization (RALO), and RALOs would then select three representatives to the ALAC. The fifteen-member ALAC would then offer *nonbinding* advice to the board and place five people on a twenty-person committee that selected new board members. Although ICANN spent millions on it, it took another five years just to get the RALOs up and running. With staggered board terms and the ambling, indirect line between at-large participants

and the board selection process, it was impossible for "individual Internet users" to redirect ICANN's policy agenda or even to have a major impact on the composition of the board. In the end, ALAC's main function was to send people to ICANN meetings. ICANN itself refers to RALOs as an "information conduit and facilitators [who] disseminate information from ICANN, promote the participation of their members, and channel the regional user point of view to ICANN." See https://atlarge.icann.org /ralos.

30. Mueller, "ICANN Inc."

31. NSI Cooperative Agreement, https://www.ntia.gov/page/verisign-cooperative -agreement.

32. "NSI must fulfill its obligation to recognize ICANN. This requires NSI and ICANN to reach agreement on a number of contractual issues. The transition of DNS management to the private sector can succeed only if all participants in the domain name system—including NSI—subject themselves to rules emerging from the consensus based, bottom-up process spelled out in the White Paper." Department of Commerce response to letter from the Chairman, Committee on Commerce United States House of Representatives regarding DNS issues, July 8, 1999.

33. This would include the initial registry and registrar contracts, the vertical split between registries and registrars allowing for competition in the .COM and .NET TLDs, and NSI's divestiture of the .ORG registry.

34. Amendment 11 to Cooperative Agreement Between NSI and U.S. Government, October 7, 1998, https://archive.icann.org/en/nsi/coopagmt-amend11-07oct98.htm. From Amendment 11: "While NSI continues to operate the primary root server, it shall request written direction from an authorized USG official before making or rejecting any modifications, additions or deletions to the root zone file."

35. The wording of Amendment 11 (cited in note 34) was motivated primarily by antitrust concerns arising from the case *Pgmedia, Inc. v. Network Solutions, Inc.* Opinion and Order No. 97 CIV. 1946 RPP, decided March 16, 1999. A prospective competitor, PGMedia, had asked NSI to add its TLDs to the root. The Commerce Department action recognized that NSI, an incumbent monopolist in the domain name registration market, could not have the power to determine how many or which new names would go into the root, because that would give it control over the market entry of its own competitors.

36. Claiming that they had their own, independent policy-making procedures based on their local community, and sometimes their governments, the country code managers opted completely out of ICANN's contractual regime; all they wanted from ICANN was the IANA's maintenance of their entries in the DNS root zone file.

37. Mueller, "ICANN Inc."

38. See the records of the "Policy and Implementation Working Group" in 2013, https://community.icann.org/display/gnsoplcyimplmntdrafteam.

39. ICANN bylaws as of November 22, 1998, https://www.icann.org/resources/unthemed-pages/bylaws-1998-11-23-en/.

40. Jonathan Weinberg, "Governments, Privatization, and Privatization: ICANN and the GAC," *Michigan Telecommunication & Technology Law Review* 18, no. 1 (2011): 189, https://repository.law.umich.edu/mttlr/vol18/iss1/5. See also Milton Mueller, "The IANA Transition and the Role of Governments in Internet Governance," *IP Justice Journal*, September 15, 2015, https://www.ipjustice.org/wp-content/uploads/2015/09/IPJustice_Journal_Mueller_IANA_Transition.pdf.

41. The UN Charter Article 2(1) says, "The [United Nations] Organization is based on the principle of the sovereign equality of all its Members."

42. In his 2002 reform proposal, ICANN's Lynn had warned that "the current role of the US Government is not consistent with long-term global stability. ICANN has attracted considerable international participation to date, but this gratifying response has been founded on a belief that it would shortly result in the transition of the DNS away from US Government control to an international policy process, represented by ICANN. . . . The board (and many in the ICANN community) is increasingly restive with continued dependency on unique US government involvement, and if that is seen as an indefinite fact of life, international participation in ICANN will inevitably diminish."

43. World Summit on the Information Society, Draft Declaration of Principles, at 5, Doc. WSIS/PCIP/DT/1-E (Mar. 21, 2003), https://www.itu.int/net/wsis/outcome/booklet/declaration_A.html.

44. Tunis Agenda for the Information Society, WSIS-05/TUNIS/DOC/6(Rev.1), November 18, 2005, https://www.itu.int/net/wsis/docs2/tunis/off/6rev1.html.

45. Jeremy Malcolm, *Multistakeholder Governance and the Internet Governance Forum* (Perth: Terminus Press, 2008); Mueller, *Networks and States*; Hans Klein, "Understanding WSIS: An Institutional Analysis of the UN World Summit on the Information Society," *Information Technologies & International Development* 1, no. 3 (2004); Charlotte Dany, *Global Governance and NGO Participation: Shaping the Information Society in the United Nations* (London: Routledge, 2012); Roxana Radu, *Negotiating Internet Governance* (Oxford: Oxford University Press, 2019), ch. 5.

46. Tunis Agenda, Paragraph 31.

47. Tunis Agenda, Paragraph 35.

48. M. Stuart Lynn, "President's Report: ICANN—The Case for Reform," ICANN, February 24, 2002, https://archive.icann.org/en/general/lynn-reform-proposal-24feb02.htm.

49. "ICANN's Reform Plans Assailed," *NewsMax*, February 26, 2002.

50. S. Stellin, "Plan to Change Internet Group Is Criticized as Inadequate," *New York Times*, April 1, 2002.

CHAPTER 7

1. Probably because the NTIA wanted to make its legal authority clearer by more explicitly connecting the MoU to 15 U.S.C. § 1525, the DOC's Joint Project Authority. A copy of the 2006 JPA is here: https://www.icann.org/en/system/files/files/jpa -29sep06-en.pdf.

2. "Internet Governance and the Future of ICANN: Hearing before the Subcommittee on Trade, Tourism, and Economic Development of the Senate Committee on Commerce, Science, and Transportation," 109th Congress, 2nd Session, September 20, 2006," https://www.govinfo.gov/content/pkg/CHRG-109shrg71638/html/CHRG -109shrg71638.htm.

3. While its contents and duration were decided by NTIA, it was issued by the National Institute of Standards and Technology.

4. See chapter 8 for an analysis of the 2012 IANA contract renewal process.

5. "ICANN and VeriSign Announce End to Long-Standing Dispute," ICANN news release, October 24, 2005, https://www.icann.org/en/announcements/details/icann -and-verisign-announce-end-to-long-standing-dispute-24-10-2005-en.

6. "The Department of Commerce has received nearly 6,000 letters and e-mails from individuals expressing concern about the impact of pornography on families and children," Gallagher wrote to the ICANN board. Declan McCullaugh, "Bush Administration Objects to .xxx Domains," *ZDNet*, August 15, 2005, https://www.zdnet .com/article/bush-administration-objects-to-xxx-domains.

7. "Correspondence from GAC Chairman to ICANN Board regarding .XXX TLD," August 12, 2005, https://www.icann.org/resources/pages/tarmizi-to-board-2005-08 -12-en.

8. Milton L. Mueller and Mawaki Chango, "Disrupting Global Governance: The Internet Whois Service, ICANN, and Privacy," *Journal of Information Technology & Politics* 5, no. 3 (2008): 303–332; Stephanie Perrin, "The Struggle for WHOIS Privacy: Understanding the Standoff Between ICANN and the World's Data Protection Authorities" (PhD thesis, University of Toronto Faculty of Information, 2018). Commercial services developed that aggregated this data over time and sold subscription services that made it searchable and more usable.

9. Article 29 Data Protection Working Party, "Opinion 2/2003 on the application of data protection principles to the Whois directories," adopted June 13, 2003, https://ec.europa.eu/justice/article-29/documentation/opinion-recommendation /files/2003/wp76_en.pdf.

10. The task force was mandated to: "(1) Define the purpose of the WHOIS service in the context of ICANN's mission and relevant core values, international and national laws protecting privacy of natural persons, international and national laws that relate specifically to the WHOIS service, and the changing nature of Registered

Name Holders. (2) Define the purpose of the Registered Name Holder, technical, and administrative contacts, in the context of the purpose of WHOIS, and the purpose for which the data was collected." "Introduction and Background to Whois," ICANN GNSO, last updated September 1, 2009, https://gnso.icann.org/en/issues/whois-privacy/tf-report-15mar06.htm.

11. "Preliminary Task Force Report on the Purpose of Whois and of the Whois Contacts," ICANN GNSO, January 18, 2006, https://gnso.icann.org/en/issues/whois-privacy/prelim-tf-rpt-18jan06.htm.

12. Formulation 1: "The purpose of the gTLD Whois service is to provide information sufficient to contact a responsible party for a particular gTLD domain name who can resolve, or reliably pass on data to a party who can resolve, issues related to the configuration of the records associated with the domain name within a DNS nameserver."

13. Formulation 2: "The purpose of the gTLD Whois service is to provide information sufficient to contact a responsible party or parties for a particular gTLD domain name who can resolve, or reliably pass on data to a party who can resolve, technical, legal or other issues related to the registration or use of a domain name."

14. ICANN's GNSO has deleted all records of this vote. Evidence still exists in the monthly newsletter of the Business Constituency dated April 2006, which recounts the vote and documents how the BC was appealing to the GAC to intervene. "Marilyn Cade and other TF members have now established a dialogue with the GAC working group chair, and will urge the development of a process to ensure GAC input to the Council between now and Marrakech." See https://cbu.memberclicks.net/assets/docs/newsletters/2006_04april_bc%20newsletter.docx.

15. Sene rationalized her intervention by claiming that "GAC didn't know how close to a vote we were," a notably flimsy excuse given that nine months that had passed since the formation of the Whois purpose task force.

16. "Testimony of Acting Assistant Secretary Kneuer on ICANN and WHOIS Before the Subcommittee on Financial Institutions and Consumer Credit of the Committee on Financial Services United States House of Representatives," July 18, 2006, https://www.ntia.doc.gov/speechtestimony/testimony-acting-assistant-secretary-kneuer-icann-and-whois.

17. "Internet Governance and the Future of ICANN: Hearing before the Subcommittee on Trade, Tourism, and Economic Development of the Senate Committee on Commerce, Science, and Transportation," 109th Congress, 2nd Session, September 20, 2006, https://www.govinfo.gov/content/pkg/CHRG-109shrg71638/html/CHRG-109shrg71638.htm.

18. During WSIS Prepcom 3 (September 2003), civil society observers with laptops started blogging live from inside the group sessions—as was common in ICANN meetings. Some governmental participants pushed them out of the room. During

Prepcom3bis (November 2003), ICANN president Paul Twomey had to leave the room where negotiations about ICANN were taking place. Wolfgang Kleinwächter, *A New Diplomacy for the 21st Century? Multi-Stakeholder Approach and Bottom-Up Policy Development in the Information Society* (Geneva: United Nations ICT Task Force, 2005).

19. "U.S. Principles on the Internet's Domain Name and Addressing System," NTIA, June 30, 2005, https://ntia.gov/other-publication/us-principles-internets-domain -name-and-addressing-system.

20. Notices, 71 *Fed. Reg.* 102, Friday, May 26, 2006, https://ntia.gov/files/ntia/NOI_ DNS_Transition_0506.pdf.

21. ICANN Board Resolution 06.71, September 25, 2006, https://www.ntia.doc.gov /legacy/ntiahome/domainname/agreements/jpa/ICANNBoardResolution_09252006 .htm.

22. "The U.S. Department of Commerce's National Telecommunications and Information Administration (NTIA) seeks comment regarding the upcoming expiration of the Joint Project Agreement (JPA) with the Internet Corporation for Assigned Names and Numbers (ICANN). This agreement has been in existence since November 25, 1998, and is scheduled to expire on September 30, 2009." Notices, 74 *Fed. Reg.* 78, Friday, May 24, 2009, https://ntia.gov/sites/default/files/publications/fr_icannvol .74_no78_apr242009_0.pdf.

23. "The Future of ICANN: After the JPA, What?," *Internet Governance Project*, December 15, 2008, https://www.internetgovernance.org/2008/12/15/igf-workshop-report -the-future-of-icann-after-the-jpa-what.

24. Comments of the Center for Democracy and Technology, January 25, 2008. Submitted to the National Telecommunications and Information Administration US Department of Commerce regarding "The Continued Transition of the Technical Coordination and Management of the Internet's Domain Name and Addressing System: Midterm Review of the Joint Project Agreement," https://cdt.org/wp -content/uploads/pdfs/20080128_CDT-JPA-comments.pdf.

25. As I wrote at the time, "It is hard to conceive of a single plausible scenario for governments to exert more power over ICANN that isn't either already happening and being aided and abetted by the USG, or more likely to happen the longer the US stays in control." Milton Mueller, "The Orwellian Meme about the JPA," *Internet Governance Project*, January 28, 2008, https://www.internetgovernance.org/2008/01 /28/the-orwellian-meme-about-the-jpa.

26. NTIA, "Statement on the Mid-Term Review of the Joint Project Agreement (JPA) Between NTIA and ICANN," April 2, 2008.

27. ICANN, "Draft Implementation Plan for Improving Institutional Confidence," February 26, 2009, https://archive.icann.org/en/jpa/iic/. A March 2009 board resolution accepting the report and directing further action is posted at http://www.icann .org/en/minutes/resolutions-06mar09.htm#13.

28. Recommendation 3.9 authorized "discussions with authorities in selected juris-dictions that recognize international not-for-profit organization status to determine whether such jurisdictions would offer a status that would confer the advantages described below."

29. "The agreement is intended to be long-standing, but may be amended at any time by mutual consent of the parties. Any party may terminate this Affirmation of Commitments by providing 120 days written notice to the other party." Affirmation of Commitments, September 30, 2009, https://www.icann.org/resources/pages /affirmation-of-commitments-2009-09-30-en.

30. Affirmation of Commitments, September 30, 2009.

31. These constraints, according to a public video made by ICANN president Rod Beckstrom, were drawn from a letter from Congress. "ICANN CEO Talks About the New Affirmation of Commitments," September 30, 2009, YouTube video 04:57, https://youtu.be/03RvQEaR2bU.

32. "ICANN CEO Talks About the New Affirmation of Commitments," September 30, 2009, https://www.icann.org/en/announcements/details/icann-ceo-talks-about -the-new-affirmation-of-commitments-30-9-2009-en.

CHAPTER 8

1. Nancy Victory, Michael Gallagher, John Kneuer, and Meredith Baker. Baker was only acting assistant secretary, as she was never confirmed.

2. The contract revision triggered the development of RFC 6220 (April 2011) and a draft "Framework for the Evolution of IANA," November 2013.

3. US Commerce Department NTIA, Request for Comments on the Internet Assigned Numbers Authority (IANA) Functions Docket Number 110207099-1099-01, February 25, 2011.

4. Two interviewees referenced the role of the National Security Council in develop-ing the US approach to ICANN. The NSC is chaired by the president, and its regular attendees are the vice president, the secretaries of state, treasury, defense, homeland security, and energy; the attorney general; the US representative to the United Nations, the administrator of the US Agency for International Development, the president's chief of staff, and the assistant to the president for national security affairs. "National Security Council," accessed June 26, 2024, https://www.whitehouse.gov/nsc.

5. Interview with anonymous NSC member, January 20, 2022.

6. Interview with anonymous NSC member, February 2022.

7. It required ICANN to "ensure that designated IANA functions staff members will not initiate, advance, or advocate any policy development related to the IANA functions."

8. Section C.2.2.1.3.2 of the proposed statement of work said, "For delegation requests for new generic TLDS (gTLDs), the Contractor [ICANN] shall include documentation to demonstrate how the proposed string has received consensus support from relevant stakeholders and is supported by the global public interest."

9. Robert Knake, *Internet Governance in an Age of Cyber Insecurity* (New York: Council on Foreign Relations, 2010).

10. Kevin Murphy, "ICANN Fights Government gTLD Power Grab," *Domain Incite*, July 22, 2011, https://domainincite.com/5532-icann-fights-government-gtld-power -grab.

11. "Remarks of Assistant Secretary Strickling at the Internet Governance Forum," July 11, 2011, https://ntia.gov/speechtestimony/remarks-assistant-secretary-strickling -internet-governance-forum-usa.

12. Quoted in Murphy, "ICANN Fights Government."

13. Quoted in Murphy, "ICANN Fights Government."

14. Request for Proposal—Internet Assigned Numbers Authority (IANA) Solicitation Number: SA1301–12-RP-0043 (April 16, 2012), https://www.ntia.gov/page/iana -functions-contract.

15. "Notice—Cancelled Internet Assigned Numbers Authority (IANA) Functions— Request for Proposal (RFP) SA1301–12-RP-IANA," NTIA, March 10, 2012, https://ntia .gov/other-publication/notice-cancelled-internet-assigned-numbers-authority-iana -functions-request.

16. Intellectual Property Enforcement Coordinator (IPEC), *2013 Joint Strategic Plan on Intellectual Property Enforcement* (Washington, DC: Executive Office of the President, 2013), 31, https://obamawhitehouse.archives.gov/sites/default/files/omb/IPEC /2013-us-ipec-joint-strategic-plan.pdf.

17. Perrin, "The Struggle for WHOIS Privacy," 16.

18. US IPEC, *2013 Joint Strategic Plan*, 32.

19. Jacob Kohnstamm, Chairman of the Article 29 Data Protection Working Party to Dr. Steve Crocker and Mr. Akram Atallah, Chairman and interim CEO of the Board of Directors, ICANN, September 26, 2012, https://www.icann.org/en/system/files /correspondence/kohnstamm-to-crocker-atallah-26sep12-en.pdf.

20. Francisco Vera Hott, vice president of ONG Derechos Digitales, to Dr. Steve Crocker, Chair of the ICANN Board, Akram Atallah, interim ICANN CEO. https:// www.icann.org/resources/correspondence/hott-to-crocker-atallah-2012-07-19-en.

21. "GAC Principles Regarding New gTLDs," March 28, 2007, https://gac.icann.org /contentMigrated/gac-principles-regarding-new-gtlds.

CHAPTER 9

1. "Further Notice of Inquiry, The Internet Assigned Numbers Authority (IANA) Functions," 76 *Fed. Reg.* 114, Tuesday, June 14, 2011 [Docket No. 110207099-1319-02] [RIN 066-XA23].

2. The RosettaNet initiative was eventually absorbed by GS1, which still plays an important role in global commerce by administering barcode numbers and Global Trade Item Numbers (GTIN). Just as IP addresses uniquely identify host computers on the Internet, GTINs uniquely identify any products or services that are priced, ordered, or invoiced at any point in the supply chain. Chehadé thus stepped into the ICANN CEO role with expertise in a registry system for globally unique identifiers already governed by the private sector. While RosettaNet was never as important as the Internet protocols, it, too, leveraged compatibility to overcome barriers to trade.

3. There were even some governments and policy makers who didn't think it was necessary to revise them because they didn't matter anymore. For a book-length analysis of the new ITRs, see Richard Hill, *The New International Telecommunications Regulations and the Internet* (Zurich: Springer, 2013).

4. There were proposals for taxes on content providers, over and above what they already pay to carriers; for global Internet quality of service standards; for governmental control over Internet routing; or for new cost-settlement systems. None of these, however, ever gained significant support.

5. These proposals came from the European Telecommunications Network Operators Association.

6. Many of the threatening ITR proposals were a continuation of long-running battles over the way the Internet disrupted traditional telecom businesses and markets. For developing countries that still had monopolies or state-owned champions running their networks, competition from "over the top" applications was an economic threat. For some, the Internet model of paying for your own connectivity to the Internet (sender pays), rather than the old shared-payment model, was also a source of concern. But liberal, competitive arrangements had been institutionalized for two decades, and there was no possibility that WCIT could turn back the clock.

7. For example, the now-defunct website Defund the ITU asserted that "the ITU . . . attempted to seize control of the Internet. . . . Their goal was a coup: to overthrow the open and transparent system of Internet governance that ensures the Internet's freedom and accessibility." The site claimed that "the ITU is spending more than \$180M/year to oppose the Internet." In fact, the ITU's total budget was \$180 million.

8. Civil society organizations such as Public Knowledge and Center for Democracy and Technology, which had been focused primarily on domestic issues and paid no

attention to the ITU, suddenly became active participants in WCIT. Google money was behind their surge of activity.

9. Michael Joseph Gross, "World War 3.0," *Vanity Fair* (May 2012), https://archive .vanityfair.com/article/2012/5/world-war-30.

10. The industry-mobilized civil society groups said that the ITRs might give the ITU the ability to interfere with the free flow of information. But Articles 34 and 35 of the ITU treaty already gave nation-states the power to suspend or cut off international telecommunication connections.

11. : House Energy and Commerce Subcommittee Hearing on Telecom and Technology and Several of the Foreign Affairs Committees, "Fighting for Internet Freedom: Dubai and Beyond," February 5, 2013 https://www.govinfo.gov/content/pkg/CHRG -113hhrg79530/html/CHRG-113hhrg79530.htm.

12. Although, as noted in chapters 6 and 15, its role-based understanding of the multistakeholder model was an incoherent one.

13. There was an attempt to make the ITU an IP address registry; a proposal to transform ICANN's GAC into an intergovernmental organization with oversight powers; a proposal to create a "progressive cooperation agreement between ITU and ICANN and define a mechanism to increase the participation of governments." All were struck from the text.

14. Albeit grudgingly, in a footnote.

15. Mike Masnick, "Who Signed the ITU WCIT Treaty—and Who Didn't," *TechDirt*, December 14, 2012, https://www.techdirt.com/2012/12/14/who-signed-itu-wcit-treaty -who-didnt.

16. The resolution in question, Resolution #3, "To Foster an Enabling Environment for the Greater Growth of the Internet," was an attempt by ITU director general Hamadoun Touré to find a compromise in which the binding ITRs would make no mention of the Internet, but China, Russia, and certain Arab countries would get a nonbinding resolution stating that the ITU should continue to provide a forum for discussion and policy development. Internet advocates saw this as a Trojan horse that would somehow allow the ITU to play a major role in Internet governance. See Wolfgang Kleinwachter, "WCIT and Internet Governance: Harmless Resolution or Trojan Horse?," *Circle ID*, December 17, 2012, https://circleid.com/posts /20121217_wcit_and_internet_governance_harmless_resolution_or_trojan_horse . See also Tim Maurer and Robert Morgus, *Tipping the Scale: An Analysis of Global Swing States in the Internet Governance Debate* (Centre for International Governance Innovation, Internet Governance Paper No. 7, May 2014), https://www.cigionline .org/static/documents/gcig_paper_no2.pdf.

17. "ICANN History Project, Interview with Fadi Chehadé, ICANN CEO (2012–2016)," ICANN, October 16, 2017, YouTube video, 43:07, https://youtu.be/a8hr9FnKSm0&ab.

18. Henry Farrell and Abraham Newman, *Underground Empire: How America Weaponized the World Economy* (New York: Henry Holt and Company, 2023).

19. Multinational corporations started to gain a nationalistic, weaponized identity. An awareness of the espionage potential of trade in digital technologies now could be used, eventually was used, and is still being used, to justify nationalistic regulation, data localization, export controls, and import restrictions. This backlash contained a serious threat to the global nature of the Internet itself.

20. Interview with Alissa Cooper, February 18, 2022.

21. Montevideo Statement on the Future of Internet Cooperation, October 7, 2013. https://en.wikipedia.org/wiki/Montevideo_Statement_on_the_Future_of_Internet _Cooperation.

22. Interview with Larry Strickling, February 10, 2022. Recording on file with author.

23. "ICANN History Project, Interview with Fadi Chehadé."

24. Strickling, interview.

25. "ICANN History Project, Interview with Fadi Chehadé."

26. Interview with anonymous NSC staff member.

27. In a video recording on the ICANN history website, it is said that the US announcement of transition was originally scheduled for September 2014, but it was moved up to March 14 because of the NETmundial meeting and the threat of a leak by a newspaper. Discussions of how to approach the transition, therefore, began in NETmundial. ICANN, "ICANN History Project | Interview with Lawrence Strickling [108E]," YouTube video, 30:39, https://youtu.be/D-SkPc1j1PA.

28. Dilma Rousseff, "United Nations General Assembly Speech," *C-SPAN*, September 24, 2013, https://www.c-span.org/video/?315200-3/united-nations-general-assembly -speech-brazilian-president-dilma-roussef.

29. A good summary of the NETmundial process and outcomes from the perspective of three Global South countries can be found in Anja Kovacs, Grace Githaiga, and Joana Varon, *NETmundial: Reflections from Brazil, India and Kenya* (London: Global Partners Digital, 2014), https://www.gp-digital.org/wp-content/uploads/2014/12 /Netmundial-Reflections-from-Brazil-India-and-Kenya.pdf.

30. Observer Research Foundation, "Indian Stand at NETmundial Surprises Many," May 3, 2014, https://www.orfonline.org/research/indian-stand-at-netmundial-surp rises-many.

31. ICANN Announcements, "Indian Government Declares Support for Multistake-holder Model of Internet Governance at ICANN 53," June 22, 2015. https://www .icann.org/en/announcements/details/indian-government-declares-support-for -multistakeholder-model-of-internet-governance-at-icann53-22-6-2015-en.

CHAPTER 10

1. He began with the Supporting Organizations: Louie Lee, ASO; Byron Holland, ccNSO; Jonathan Robinson, GNSO. Then he turned to the Advisory Committees: Heather Dryden, GAC; Olivier Crepin-Leblond, ALAC; Lars Liman, the RSSAC. Then the regional associations of country top-level domain managers: Peter Van Roste, Europe's CENTR; Paulos Nyirenda, AFTLD; Carolina Aguerre, LACTLD; Don Hollander, APTLD. Then it was the turn of the five IP number registries: Adiel Akplogan, AfriNIC; John Curran, ARIN; Paul Wilson, APNIC; Raul Echeberria, LACNIC; Axel Pawlik, RIPE-NCC. Next he turned to the technical community: Russ Housley, IAB; Jari Arkko, IETF; Kathy Brown, ISOC. Reflecting its role as the root zone maintainer, Pat Kane of VeriSign was also recognized. And then Fadi Chehadé, CEO of ICANN. Brief statements from several of these leaders followed.

2. A. Michael Froomkin, "Plus Ça Change (ICANN Edition)," *Discourse.net*, April 28, 2015, https://www.discourse.net/2015/04/plus-a-change-icann-edition.

3. ICANN had tried to create a unilateral right to amend back in 2010, in the early stages of the new TLD program. There was strong pushback, however, and it agreed to abandon the idea. After the community memorialized its agreement in the Final Applicant Guidebook, ICANN then accepted $185,000 fees from each of 1,900 applications for new gTLDs. A few months after those fees were in hand, and only four months into Chehadé's reign, ICANN jettisoned that compromise. A new version of the Registry Agreement posted on February 5, 2013, gave ICANN Org a unilateral right to amend the basic Registry Agreement based on "a substantial and compelling reason in the public interest" (Section 7.6). ICANN's proposal did not allow its decision to be reviewed by the courts but instead required a one-day arbitration process.

4. See Comments of Google, ICANN list archives, February 5, 2013; comments of Volker Greimann, German registrar, ICANN list archives, February 26, 2013; Jeff Neumann, "Clearing Up the 'Logjam': ICANN Must Drop Its Request for a Unilateral Right to Amend Agreements," *Circle ID*, March 16, 2013, https://circleid.com/posts/20130316_icann_must_drop_request_for_unilateral_right_to_amend_agreements.

5. In mid-2011, it seemed as if the entire ICANN new gTLD policy was finalized. But from August to December of 2011, a group of American brand owners initiated a major public relations campaign against the whole program. The well-financed trade groups unleashed a flurry of lobbying at Congress, the Commerce Department, the Federal Trade Commission, and the ICANN board. Note that all the institutions targeted were American—another indication of the way the IANA contract distorted accountability relationships in ICANN.

6. Suspiciously, the US government (NTIA) was one of the only commentors to express unqualified endorsement of the proposed changes in the registry agreement. Letter from Lawrence Strickling, Department of Commerce, Stephen Crocker, ICANN, February 5, 2013, https://forum.icann.org/lists/comments-base-agreement-05feb13/pdf0yRVbdJtK0.pdf.

7. Milton Mueller, "ICANN's Accountability Meltdown: A Four-Part Series," Internet Governance Project, August 31, 2013, https://www.internetgovernance.org/2013/08/31/icanns-accountability-meltdown-a-four-part-series.

8. This clever comment was a reference to the IETF's measure of working group consensus. Instead of voting, working group participants would "hum" if they were in accord with a document, and the degree of agreement was commonly assessed by the strength of the vibration.

9. "Call for Public Input: Draft Proposal, Based on Initial Community Feedback, of the Principles and Mechanisms and the Process to Develop a Proposal to Transition NTIA's Stewardship of the IANA Functions," ICANN, April 8, 2014, https://www.icann.org/resources/pages/draft-proposal-2014-04-08-en.

10. In its original draft proposal, ICANN had divided the representatives into "affected parties" and "non-affected parties," with "affected" parties including only ICANN SOs and ACs. In a typical top-down move, ICANN had proposed that its board chair and the GAC chair select steering committee representatives from "non-affected" parties. Community comment rejected this idea. The distinction between affected and non-affected parties was eliminated, and all represented entities were empowered to choose their own representatives.

11. The RFP template included the following elements: (a) description of its use of IANA functions; (b) description of existing (pre-transition) arrangements, including their policy sources and oversight and accountability arrangements; (c) description of the proposed new oversight & accountability arrangements; d) transition implications (implementation and continuity implications); (e) did the proposal meet the NTIA requirements?; (f) describe the community processes used to develop the proposal. See https://www.ianacg.org.

12. The protocols and numbers people were particularly concerned about not getting their transition plans dragged into the highly politicized and rancorous debates around domain names.

13. The NTIA Notices of Inquiry around the 2012 IANA contract renewal had explicitly raised this question, and most technical community respondents favored a unified IANA.

14. ICG was originally constituted with only two GAC seats, but the ICG accepted a request to expand it to five, due to the difficulties the GAC had in collapsing its choice of representatives to only two people. Because of the requirement for consensus decision-making, the increase in seats was deemed to not matter much and ICG granted the GAC's request.

15. This assumption became open and explicit once ICANN started negotiating with the operational communities. The Numbers community, for example, was initially told that "ICANN . . . will reject any proposed agreement in which ICANN is not deemed the sole source prime contractor for IANA functions in perpetuity." See chapter 9.

16. "We paired them [the stewardship transition and accountability reforms] in a way that could have put the whole project in danger." "It added a huge new dimension and interdependencies with the technical work and operational work." "We worried that that tight interdependency would delay the transition beyond the point where the moment allowed us." "ICANN History Project, Interview with Fadi Chehadé," https://youtu.be/7Y25IduKSdg.

17. CCWG-Accountability charter, https://community.icann.org/display/acctcross comm/Charter.

18. This is a reference to Eric Foner's prize-winning book *The Second Founding: How the Civil War and Reconstruction Remade the Constitution* (New York: Norton, 2019). While there is no intention to assert an equivalence in social significance between ICANN's accountability reforms and the US Constitutional amendments and political-military processes that abolished slavery, there are important structural parallels. In both cases, the original constitution fell short of the founding ideals and led to an extended reworking.

19. For transcripts, see https://community.icann.org/pages/viewpage.action?pageId= 50823987.

20. "Remarks by Assistant Secretary Strickling at the PLI/FCBA Telecommunications Policy & Regulation Institute," NTIA, December 4, 2014, https://ntia.gov /speechtestimony/remarks-assistant-secretary-strickling-plifcba-telecommunications -policy-0.

CHAPTER 11

1. "ICANN Board Comments on Cross Community Working Group (CWG) Draft Transition Proposal for Naming Related Functions," December 1, 2014, https:// forum.icann.org/lists/comments-cwg-naming-transition-01dec14/pdfqyCZeLL751 .pdf.

2. The 2014 SLA is available here: https://iaoc.ietf.org/documents/2014-ICANN-IETF -MoU-Supplemental-Agreement-Executed.pdf.

3. Interview with Alissa Cooper, February 18, 2022. Recording on file with author.

4. Emphasis added. Final Charter for Working Group, "Planning for the IANA/NTIA Transition," September 8, 2014, https://datatracker.ietf.org/wg/ianaplan/charter/.

5. For a history of how the IPR was transferred from USC ISI to ICANN, see https://mm.icann.org/pipermail/cwg-stewardship/2015-June/003754.html.

6. But indicating the blurred lines of ownership, the first IANA web page visible on the Wayback Machine shows that the domain has been taken over by ICANN: it contains a bulleted link "Visit ICANN" as its main message, and below it a link to a "Tribute to Jon Postel." See https://web.archive.org/web/19990209161256/http://www.iana.org /index2.html.

7. See email from Jon Peterson to IANAPLAN list, November 7, 2014: "There is nothing we need that we stand to gain by negotiating or compromising—but plenty we could lose. Taking us down this path is reckless and unnecessary." See https://mailarchive.ietf.org/arch/msg/ianaplan/eZnoBgkWYs_Ma2aWficaEhCNUsU/.

8. Jeff Arkko, Tobias Gondrom, and Andrew Sullivan, "Update on IANA Transition & Negotiations with ICANN," email to the IANAPLAN list, April 30, 2015, https://mailarchive.ietf.org/arch/msg/ianaplan/suL056OFf20KjHG0ZhJ5D7s_TFg.

9. Arkko, Gondrom, and Sullivan, email to the IANAPLAN list, April 30, 2015, citing sections C.7.3 and I.61 of the 2012 IANA contract.

10. John Klensin, an IETF veteran, wrote to the IANAPLAN list on May 1, 2015, "ICANN appears to have said 'we cannot formally agree, in the SLA, to provisions you have believed were in effect for years.' That does not make me very happy and, IMO, should not make anyone who has been depending on the MOU very happy." https://mailarchive.ietf.org/arch/msg/ianaplan/fSWjy0WymlttKLWVukxPfxsaajw.

11. The NTIA contract provided the US government with reasons for termination similar to those invoked by RIRS (page 2 of the NTIA contract and sections E.2.g.1.ii and I.67.i and sections I.51 and I.52).

12. For the CRISP team and charter, see https://www.nro.net/internet-governance/iana/iana-stewardship-transition/stewardship-transition-archive/crisp-team/. Archives of email list: https://www.nro.net/pipermail/crisp.

13. "Final Proposal of the Internet Number Community for the IANA Stewardship Coordination Group," NRO, January 15, 2015, https://www.nro.net/final-proposal-crisp.

14. As of May 2023, the CRISP team's presentation was still accessible at the ARIN website: https://www.arin.net/participate/meetings/reports/ARIN_35/PDF/monday/crisp_panel.pdf.

15. CRISP team presentation, ARIN website.

16. See Milton Mueller, "ICANN Wants an IANA Functions Monopoly: Will It Wreck the Transition Process to Get It?," *Internet Governance Project*, April 28, 2015, https://www.internetgovernance.org/2015/04/28/icann-wants-an-iana-functions-monopoly-and-its-willing-to-wreck-the-transition-process-to-get-it.

17. IAB meeting minutes, April 8, 2015, https://www.iab.org/documents/minutes/minutes-2015/iab-minutes-2015-04-08/. Woodcock's comments were made in reply to the IGP blog post of April 28, 2015, cited above.

18. Fuhr was the CEO of DIFO, the Danish Internet Forum, which operates the .DK top-level domain and owns DK Hostmaster. With a background in the Danish telecommunications ministry, she read the White Paper in 1998 and attended the second ICANN meeting in Berlin in May 1999 as a founding member of the GAC.

After working for Telia for ten years, she was recruited to DIFO. She was hired to her current position as CEO of the European Telecommunications Network Operators Association by the same headhunter who had found the same headhunter who had found Chehade. Robinson worked for Afilias, a gTLD registry, was a GNSO council representative of the Registry Constituency, and chaired the GNSO at the time of the transition.

19. DNS policy involved gTLDs under contract to ICANN; ccTLDs whose delegations had predated ICANN; ccTLDs that had been delegated by ICANN, trademark, and copyright owners; other business users of domains; suppliers of DNS registration services; civil society advocates; governments via the GAC; and putative representatives of "individual Internet users."

20. Both the IETF and the RIRs were external to ICANN and predated its creation. The same could be said for country code name registries, whose delegations usually preceded ICANN and who developed policies through their local communities with no subjection to ICANN's formal contracts.

21. Milton Mueller and Brenden Kuerbis, "Roadmap for Globalizing IANA: Four Principles and a Proposal for Reform: A Submission to the Global Multistakeholder Meeting on the Future of Internet Governance," Internet Governance Project, March 3, 2014, https://www.internetgovernance.org/wp-content/uploads /ICANNreformglobalizingIANAfinal.pdf.

22. Internet NZ, a country code operator.

23. Burr, email to CWG-Stewardship (Names) list, October 23, 2014, https://mm .icann.org/pipermail/cwg-stewardship/2014-October/000228.html.

24. Lise Fuhr, "Draft of Principles and Criteria that Should Underpin Decisions on the Transition of NTIA Stewardship," email to CWG-Stewardship (Names) list, November 14, 2014, https://mm.icann.org/pipermail/cwg-stewardship/2014 -November/000553.html.

25. "Cross Community Working Group (CWG) on Naming Related Functions Public Consultation on Draft Transition Proposal," ICANN, December 2014, https://mm .icann.org/pipermail/cwg-stewardship/attachments/20141126/d6cae841/CWG -Dec01PublicConsultV116-0001.pdf.

26. Comments of CDT, citing its independence of IANA function operator oversight; separability of the IANA contract from the IANA functions operator; a clear commitment to multistakeholder principles; and a desire to see a noncapturable, neutral, and robust IANA going forward.

27. ICANN comments on first draft proposal.

28. Comments of Andrew Sullivan: "The MRT is to be 'a multistakeholder body with formally selected representatives from all of the relevant communities.' The

MRT is to develop contract terms, make decisions for another entity, perform budget and performance reviews, manage a bidding process, and receive escalation from the CSC. The CSC is made up of registry operators. These two structures appear set respectively to replicate, only perhaps with different personnel, the ICANN Board on the one hand and CCNSO and GNSO (henceforth, the NSOs) on the other."

29. Interview with Lise Fuhr, March 3, 2024.

30. Joint comment of China Academy of Information and Communication Technology (CAICT), CNNIC, Internet Society of China.

31. Kieren McCarthy, "Let It Go, Let It Go: How global DNS Could Survive in the Frozen Lands outside US Control: Public Comments on Revised IANA Transition Plan," *The Register*, May 26, 2015, https://www.theregister.com/2015/05/26/iana_icann_latest/. Another summary of public comment on the proposal can be found in Milton Mueller, email to CWG-Stewardship (Names) list, May 28, 2015. https://mm.icann.org/pipermail/cwg-stewardship/2015-May/003411.html.

32. Tonkin, email to CCWG-Accountability list, "Further comment on concerns that ICANN will reject community developed proposals," May 6, 2015, https://mm.icann.org/pipermail/accountability-cross-community/2015-May/002889.html.

33. Alissa Cooper, email to IANAPLAN list, February 9, 2015, https://mailarchive.ietf.org/arch/msg/ianaplan/PVotlV4DYqAVFoxjiPt_Sc-FgYM.

34. Tobias Gondrom, email to IANAPLAN WG list, February 20, 2015, https://mailarchive.ietf.org/arch/msg/ianaplan/TyGHyx8Ik0Xy-EkICG3yCP5eenU. "In accordance with Article 5.2 of the Trust Agreement the IETF Trust would be willing to hold intellectual property rights relating to the IANA function, including the IANA trademark and the IANA.ORG domain name. I am pleased to report that the Trustees approved that motion. The IETF Trust Agreement is located here: http://trustee.ietf.org/documents/IETF-Trust-Agreement-Amended-and-Restated-02-20-2014.pdf."

35. Alissa Cooper, email to CWG-Names list, "ICG request concerning IANA trademark and iana.org domain name," June 19, 2015, https://mm.icann.org/pipermail/cwg-stewardship/2015-June/003841.html.

36. Steven Crocker, email to IANAPLAN WG list, August 15, 2015, https://mailarchive.ietf.org/arch/msg/ianaplan/49VgmxMZUA-ZaZ_aTLnyKZ18r6s/. The IETF Trust memorialized the IPR transfer agreement in April 2016. See https://www.ietf.org/proceedings/95/slides/slides-95-ianaplan-0.pdf.

37. "ICG Summary Report on Comments Received during the Public Comment Period on the Combined Transition Proposal" (undated), https://www.ianacg.org/icg-files/documents/Public-Comment-Summary-final.pdf. A complete record of the comments can be found here: https://www.ianacg.org/calls-for-input/combined-proposal-public-comment-period/.

38. Comments of ICANN, https://comments.ianacg.org/pdf/submission/submission 121.pdf.

39. Comments of Huyi Global Information Resources (Huyi Global).

40. Final ICG proposal, http://www.ianacg.org/icg-files/documents/IANA-transition -proposal-v9.pdf.

41. "Verisign/ICANN Proposal in Response to NTIA Request. Root Zone Administrator Proposal Related to the IANA Functions Stewardship Transition" (undated), accessed June 29, 2023, https://www.ntia.doc.gov/files/ntia/publications/root_zone_adminis trator_proposal-relatedtoiana_functionsste-final.pdf.

CHAPTER 12

1. ICANN PR, Interview with Fadi Chehadé, ICANN CEO (2012–2016), https://youtu .be/7Y25IduKSdg.

2. Froomkin, "Wrong Turn in Cyberspace" (2000), and "ICANN 2.0: Meet the New Boss" (2002); S. P. Crawford, "The ICANN Experiment," *Cardozo Journal of Internal & Comparative Law* 12 (2004): 409–448; Mueller, "ICANN Inc."; Rolf H. Weber and R. Shawn Gunnarson, "A Constitutional Solution for Internet Governance," *Columbia Science & Technology Review* 14 (2012).

3. Weber and Gunnarson, "A Constitutional Solution."

4. The CCWG-Accountability process pulled in many of the intellectuals who had helped articulate the original vision, such as David Johnson and David Post. See, e.g., David G. Post and Danielle Kehl, "Controlling Internet Infrastructure Part 1: The 'IANA Transition' and Why It Matters for the Future of the Internet," July 27, 2015, https://ssrn.com/abstract=2636417; "Controlling Internet Infrastructure: The 'IANA Transition' and ICANN Accountability, Part II," September 16, 2015, https://ssrn .com/abstract=2671343.

5. According to the scope section of the charter, Workstream 2 was "focused on addressing accountability topics for which a timeline for developing solutions and full implementation may extend beyond the IANA Stewardship Transition." https:// ccnso.icann.org/sites/default/files/filefield_46603/ccwg-accountability-charter -20nov14-en.pdf.

6. ICANN budgeted $15.7 million for the accountability process, including legal, travel, and staff support: https://community.icann.org/download/attachments /56142788/Letter%20to%20CCWG%20co-chairs%20151012.pdf?version=1 &modificationDate=1444738946000&api=v2.

7. CCWG Statistics & Diversity, created by Berry Cobb, last modified by Brenda Brewer on June 3, 2016, https://community.icann.org/pages/viewpage.action?pageId= 50823970.

8. Jordan Carter, email to CCWG-Accountability list, June 1, 2015, https://mm.icann.org/pipermail/accountability-cross-community/2015-June/003217.html.

9. Avri Doria, email to CCWG-Accountability list, October 1, 2015, https://mm.icann.org/pipermail/accountability-cross-community/2015-October/005943.html. See also Nigel Roberts, email to CCWG-Accountability list, October 15, 2015, "ICANN made a mis-step in 1998 in not having members at the outset and we are paying the price."

10. Daniel Castro, "ICANN Transition Plan Needs New Ideas to Ensure Accountability," *The Hill*, December 17, 2014, https://thehill.com/blogs/pundits-blog/technology/227375-icann-transition-plan-needs-new-ideas-to-ensure-accountability. Castro cited the article by Weber and Gunnarson, "A Constitutional Solution."

11. Becky Burr, email to CCWG-Accountability, May 20, 2015, https://mm.icann.org/pipermail/accountability-cross-community/2015-May/003030.html.

12. Memorandum from Sidley Austin LLP and Adler & Colvin to the CCWG-Accountability, October 2, 2015; link unavailable from ICANN website, but source is on file with author.

13. "Californian law would recognise the Single Member as having legal personality. But it still doesn't need any of the normal accoutrements of artificial persons (such as registration, officers, etc) that might otherwise make this problematic." Malcolm Hutty, email to CCWG list, October 1, 2015, https://mm.icann.org/pipermail/accountability-cross-community/2015-October/006006.html.

14. "This can be enshrined in a new fundamental bylaw that would require the holding of a future governance structure review if SOs and ACs agree to kick off that review." Crocker, email to CCWG list, October 6, 2015, https://mm.icann.org/pipermail/accountability-cross-community/2015-October/006233.html.

15. See Olivier MJ Crepin-Leblond, chair of ALAC, who was arguing as late as October 10, 2015, that "the overall proposal that has gone through the ICG is what's going to be sent to NTIA. The CCWG Accountability is a separate process that has NOTHING to do with NTIA apart from a small part of the CCWG's work that has to feed into the CWG's work. But the CCWG's work has to go through the Board first and the Board has every right to veto it, if it feels the proposal is incompatible with the public interest"; see https://mm.icann.org/pipermail/accountability-cross-community/2015-October/006537.html. See also Alan Greenberg, ALAC chair, explaining the committee's withdrawal of support for a membership model in an October 18, 2015, email to the CCWG list: https://mm.icann.org/pipermail/accountability-cross-community/2015-October/006927.html.

16. The original memo cannot be found, but its content was sent to the CCWG list by James Gannon under the heading, "FW Continued Counsel Dialogue," October 2, 2015, https://mm.icann.org/pipermail/accountability-cross-community/2015-October/006040.html.

17. Gannon, email to CCWG-Accountability list.

18. Corwin, email to CCWG-Accountability list, October 6, 2015, https://mm.icann .org/pipermail/accountability-cross-community/2015-October/006308.html.

19. Sidley Austin/Adler Colvin memorandum to CCWG-Accountability.

20. Interview with Paul Rosenzweig, November 10, 2021. Recording on file with author.

21. Carter, email to CCWG-Accountability, October 6, 2015, https://mm.icann.org /pipermail/accountability-cross-community/2015-October/006234.html.

22. Acharya, email to CCWG-Accountability, October 6, 2015, https://mm.icann.org /pipermail/accountability-cross-community/2015-October/006249.html.

23. Letter from John Thune and Brian Schatz, Chairman and Ranking Member, US Senate Committee on Commerce, Science and Transportation, to Stephen Crocker, October 15, 2015, https://mm.icann.org/pipermail/accountability-cross-community /attachments/20151015/114466f4/Thune-SchatzlettertoSteveCrocker10-15-15.pdf.

24. Sidley Austin/Adler Colvin Memorandum to CCWG-Accountability.

25. Under California Corporation Code, a designator is an entity that is given the right to select one or more directors by the corporation's articles or bylaws. It differs from board selection by members.

26. Post and Kehl, "Controlling Internet Infrastructure, Part II."

27. Hutty, email to CCWG-Accountability list, December 16, 2015, https://mm.icann .org/pipermail/accountability-cross-community/2015-December/008872.html.

28. David Post, email to CCWG-Accountability list, December 1, 2015, https://mm .icann.org/pipermail/accountability-cross-community/2015-December/008592.html.

29. Subsection (d)(i) says, "the foregoing prohibitions are not intended to limit ICANN's authority or ability to adopt or implement policies or procedures that take into account the use of domain names as natural-language identifiers;

30. Subsection (d)(ii) is complex and says, "(ii) Notwithstanding any provision of the Bylaws to the contrary, the terms and conditions of the documents listed in subsections (A) through (C) below, and ICANN's performance of its obligations or duties thereunder, may not be challenged by any party in any proceeding against, or process involving, ICANN (including a request for reconsideration or an independent review process pursuant to Article 4) on the basis that such terms and conditions conflict with, or are in violation of, ICANN's Mission or otherwise exceed the scope of ICANN's authority or powers pursuant to these Bylaws ("Bylaws") or ICANN's Articles of Incorporation ("Articles of Incorporation"): (A) (1) all registry agreements and registrar accreditation agreements between ICANN and registry operators or registrars in force on 1 October 2016, including, in each case, any terms or conditions therein that are not contained in the underlying form of registry agreement and registrar accreditation agreement; (2) any registry agreement or registrar accreditation

agreement not encompassed by (1) above to the extent its terms do not vary materially from the form of registry agreement or registrar accreditation agreement that existed on 1 October 2016; (B)any renewals of agreements described in subsection (A) pursuant to their terms and conditions for renewal; and (C)ICANN's Five-Year Strategic Plan and Five-Year Operating Plan existing on 10 March 2016. (iii) Section 1.1(d)(ii) does not limit the ability of a party to any agreement described therein to challenge any provision of such agreement on any other basis, including the other party's interpretation of the provision, in any proceeding or process involving ICANN. (iv) ICANN shall have the ability to negotiate, enter into and enforce agreements, including public interest commitments, with any party in service of its Mission.

31. David G. Post and Danielle Kehl, Comments on CCWG-Accountability Initial Draft Proposal, June 3, 2015. https://mm.icann.org/pipermail/accountability-cross -community/2015-June/003267.html.

32. See ICM v. ICANN web page, accessed June 23, 2023, https://www.icann.org /resources/pages/icm-v-icann-2012-02-25-en. The author was engaged as an expert witness in this case.

33. The ICM Registry case consumed two years (from 2008–2010) to rectify an error made in 2005. The applicant spent at least a million dollars on the case.

34. ICM v. ICANN web page.

35. NTIA, "Transition of NTIA's Stewardship of the IANA Functions," https://www .icann.org/resources/pages/process-next-steps-2014-06-06-en.

36. CCWG-Accountability: Using Stress Tests to evaluate existing & proposed accountability measures [Draft v8], March 20, 2015, https://community.icann.org /download/attachments/52232556/Applying%20Stress%20Tests%20%5BDraft%20 v8%5D.pdf.

37. CCWG-Accountability, Stress Test 18 and proposed bylaws change regarding GAC advice, Draft v1, March 31, 2015, https://community.icann.org/download /attachments/52232556/Stress%20Test%2018%20and%20bylaws%20proposal.pdf.

38. CCWG-Accountability, Stress Test 18.

39. Lise Fuhr and Jonathan Robinson, email to CWG-Stewardship list, February 29, 2016, https://mm.icann.org/pipermail/cwg-stewardship/2016-February/004756.html.

40. Fuhr, interview.

CHAPTER 13

1. L. Gordon Crovitz, "America's Internet Surrender: By Unilaterally Retreating from Online Oversight, the White House Pleased Regimes That Want to Control the Web," *Wall Street Journal*, March 18, 2014.

2. Representative John Shimkus (R.-IL), "H.R. 4342, Domain Openness Through Continued Oversight Matters." On April 2, 2014, the Subcommittee on Communications

and Technology held a hearing on the DOTCOM Act. This hearing seems to be origin of the "stress test" idea that was taken into the CCWG-Accountability.

3. US Senate Committee on Commerce, Science and Transportation, "Thune, Rubio Demand Answers from Administration on Internet Transition," April 2, 2014, https://www.commerce.senate.gov/2014/4/thune-rubio-demand-answers-from -administration-on-internet-transition.

4. Lennard G. Kruger, *The Future of Internet Governance: Should the United States Relinquish Its Authority Over ICANN?* (Congressional Research Service, September 2016), 11–16, https://sgp.fas.org/crs/misc/R44022.pdf. This March 15, 2016, document from the House Energy and Commerce committee contains a summary of legislative efforts around the transition as well as a list of the witnesses and a summary of ICANN process.

5. See *House Report 112–564—Expressing the Sense of Congress Regarding Actions to Preserve and Advance the Multistakeholder Governance Model Under Which the Internet Has Thrived,* June 29, 2012, https://www.congress.gov/congressional-report/112th -congress/house-report/564/1.

6. "ICANN could become an organization like FIFA—the international soccer organization that is flush with cash, unresponsive to those it supposedly serves, and accountable to no one." Majority Statement, Chairman John Thune, Senate Committee on Commerce, Science, and Transportation, "Preserving the Multistakeholder Model of Internet Governance," February 25, 2015, https://www.commerce .senate.gov/2015/2/preserving-the-multistakeholder-model-of-internet-governance.

7. Thune, "Preserving the Multistakeholder Model."

8. Minority Statement, Senator Bill Nelson, Senate Committee on Commerce, Science, and Transportation, "Preserving the Multistakeholder Model of Internet Governance," February 25, 2015, https://www.commerce.senate.gov/2015/2/preserving -the-multistakeholder-model-of-internet-governance.

9. Spoken comments of Rep. Anna Eshoo (D.-Cal.), March 17, 2016, the House Committee on Energy and Commerce, Subcommittee on Communications and Technology, "Privatizing the Internet Assigned Number Authority," https://youtu .be/icE4ZrrmS2s.

10. Letter from Senators Cruz, Lankford, and Lee to Commerce Secretary Penny Pritzker, May 20, 2016, "We Must Protect Internet Freedom: Cruz, Lankford, and Lee outline concerns for Department of Commerce and NTIA," https://www.cruz.senate .gov/newsroom/press-releases/we-must-protect-internet-freedom.

11. Recording of Senate Committee on Commerce, Science, and Transportation, "Preserving the Multistakeholder Model of Internet Governance," February 15, 2015, https://www.commerce.senate.gov/2015/2/preserving-the-multistakeholder -model-of-internet-governance.

12. Senate Committee on Commerce, Science, and Transportation, Hearing, "Examining the Multistakeholder Plan for Transitioning the Internet Assigned

Number Authority," May 24, 2016, https://www.govinfo.gov/content/pkg/CHRG -114shrg23872/pdf/CHRG-114shrg23872.pdf.

13. J. Ribeiro, "Internet Naming System Not US Property, Says Congressional Watchdog," *Computerworld*, September 13, 2016, https://www.computerworld.com/article /3119890/internet-naming-system-not-us-property-says-congressional-watchdog .html.

14. At the hearing, Steve DelBianco compared the "test period" to making the US Constitution a test drive while maintaining its status as British colonies.

15. A September 22, 2015, letter from Senator Grassley, Senator Cruz, Representative Goodlatte, and Representative Issa to the Comptroller General asked for a GAO report on whether the transition would involve a transfer of government property to a private entity. The Congress members claimed that under Article IV Section 3 of the US Constitution, such a transfer would require congressional approval. Grassley, Cruz, Goodlatte, and Issa, Letter to Comptroller General Gene Dodaro, September 22, 2015, https://www.cruz.senate.gov/imo/media/doc/Letters/20150922%20Grass-ley%20Cruz%20Goodlatte%20Issa%20GAO%20Request%20ICANN.pdf.

16. 112th Congress, 2nd Session, House Concurrent Resolution 127, "Expressing the sense of Congress regarding actions to preserve and advance the multistakeholder governance model under which the Internet has thrived," https://www.govtrack.us /congress/bills/112/hconres127/text.

17. Statement of Richard Manning, President, Americans for Limited Government, before the Senate Committee on Commerce, Science, and Transportation hearing, "Examining the Multistakeholder Plan for Transitioning the Internet Assigned Number Authority," May 24, 2016, https://www.govinfo.gov/content/pkg/CHRG -114shrg23872/pdf/CHRG-114shrg23872.pdf.

18. Senate Committee on Commerce, Science, and Transportation hearing, "Examining the Multistakeholder Plan for Transitioning the Internet Assigned Number Authority," May 24, 2016, https://www.govinfo.gov/content/pkg/CHRG -114shrg23872/pdf/CHRG-114shrg23872.pdf.

19. State of Arizona, et al., Plaintiffs, vs. National Telecommunications and Information Administration (NTIA), et al, Defendants. Civil Action No. 3:16-CV-274. US District Court, Southern District of Texas, entered October 3, 2016, https:// domainnamewire.com/wp-content/hanks-iana.pdf.

CHAPTER 14

1. Vice Prime Minister Fedorov of Ukraine to Goran Marby, February 28, 2022, https://www.icann.org/en/system/files/correspondence/fedorov-to-marby-28feb22 -en.pdf.

2. Goran Marby to Vice Prime Minister Fedorov, March 2, 2022, https://www.icann .org/en/system/files/correspondence/marby-to-fedorov-02mar22-en.pdf.

3. Hans Peter Holen to Vice Prime Minister Fedorov, March 10, 2022, https://www
.ripe.net/publications/news/announcements/ripe-ncc-response-to-request-from
-ukrainian-government.

4. Farrell and Newman, *Underground Empire*.

5. An email list for the CCWG-Accountability subgroup on jurisdiction was started
July 12, 2016, shortly after the transition proposal was finalized.

6. Dissenting statement of Brazil in the CCWG-Accountability WS2 subgroup on
jurisdiction, October 13, 2017, https://mm.icann.org/pipermail/ws2-jurisdiction
/attachments/20171015/436b7873/StatementofBrazil-0001.pdf.

7. See Samantha Eisner, Deputy General Counsel, slide presentation, "WS2 Jurisdiction: Presentation on OFAC," August 1, 2017, https://community.icann.org
/download/attachments/69272128/OFAC%20Presentation.pdf.

8. Farzaneh Badii, an exiled Iranian NCSG member associated with Georgia Tech's
Internet Governance Project, had been tracking the way US sanctions affected
innocent Internet users of domain name services in the Middle East. She succeeded
in getting a statement from Middle East Space, Abu Dhabi, United Arab Emir-
ates, November 1, 2017 in support of immunizing ICANN from OFAC sanctions,
http://mm.icann.org/pipermail/ws2-jurisdiction/attachments/20171120/d5a1c33a
/ME-Statement-Final-20-11-2017-0001.docx.

9. CCWG-Accountability Jurisdiction subgroup, "OFAC Recommendations First
Draft," August 30, 2017, https://community.icann.org/download/attachments/5964
3282/OFAC%20Recommendation%20First%20Draft.pdf.

10. See Brad Smith, "The Need for a Digital Geneva Convention," Microsoft (blog),
February 14, 2017, https://blogs.microsoft.com/on-the-issues/2017/02/14/need-digital
-geneva-convention.

11. While some US stakeholders thought their own state was the only trustwor-
thy jurisdiction, there were less chauvinistic reasons to oppose a change. It risked
generating uncertainty around the contracts governing existing domain name
businesses. Despite support for the transition and improved accountability from
the US Congress, various hearings had made it clear that any transition plan that
involved moving ICANN's headquarters out of the United States would not be
received favorably. This concern went all the way back to the 2009 Affirmation of
Commitments, in which ICANN promised the Commerce Department it would
keep its headquarters in the United States. This was probably one reason why business interests pushed for incorporating the Affirmation into ICANN's fundamental
bylaws as part of the transition.

12. Even if Congress hadn't already signaled its unwillingness to allow ICANN's
headquarters to move out of the United States, the prospect of an act of Congress
immunizing ICANN under the International Organizations Immunity Act was virtually impossible in a Trump administration. Indeed, in 2017 some in the new Trump
administration were talking about legislation to reverse the transition.

13. CCWG-Accountability WS2 Jurisdiction Subgroup Recommendations, March 2018, https://community.icann.org/display/WEIA/Jurisdiction?preview=/59643282 /79440995/CCWG-Accountability-WS2-Jurisdiction-FinalRecommendations-Clean -AfterSecondReading.pdf.

14. The Recommendation instructed ICANN to "first prioritize a study of the costs, benefits, timeline and details of the process. ICANN should then pursue general licenses as soon as possible, unless it discovers significant obstacles." CCWG-Accountability WS2 Jurisdiction Subgroup Recommendations, February 2018, https:// community.icann.org/display/WEIA/Jurisdiction?preview=/59643282/79436137 /WS2-Jurisdiction-Final%20Draft%20v1.2.3.PDF.

15. PIR, "The Internet Society & Public Interest Registry: A New Era of Opportunity," November 13, 2019, https://thenew.org/the-internet-society-public-interest-registry -a-new-era-of-opportunity.

16. In September 2018, Chehadé, then a partner or senior advisor at Abry, helped Abry close their acquisition of a majority stake in Donuts. Donuts had raised $300 million and spent much of it buying some 250 TLDs. Brooks took a board seat at Donuts in October 2018, while Donuts cofounder and chief counsel Jon Nevett became the new CEO of PIR in December 2018.

17. Mueller, *Ruling the Root*.

18. PUBLIC INTEREST REGISTRY, full text of "Form 990" for fiscal year ending Dec. 2017, https://projects.propublica.org/nonprofits/organizations/331025119/2018415 69349300514/IRS990.

19. Richard Barnes, "Why I Voted to Sell .ORG," *CircleID*, November 27, 2019, https://circleid.com/posts/20191127_why_i_voted_to_sell_org.

20. Hacker News, November 2019, https://news.ycombinator.com/item?id=21667355.

21. Access Now and the Electronic Frontier Foundation, two prominent civil society advocacy groups, mounted a SaveDotOrg campaign, despite having played no role in ICANN policy making or in the transition. The narrative promulgated by the anti-.ORG sale agitators was this: .ORG was a safe, protected place for noncommercial domain name registrants; it was now being taken over by soulless capitalists who were going to take advantage of ICANN's decision to eliminate price caps on the wholesale price of registration and start gouging .ORG registrants with thousand dollar renewal fees; there were even claims that the evil capitalists would bow to the demands of China to eliminate dissenting civil society groups from their domains.

22. Xavier Becerra, California AG, to Maarten Botterman and Goran Marby, April 15, 2020, https://www.icann.org/en/system/files/correspondence/becerra-to-botterman -marby-15apr20-en.pdf.

23. Jonathan Zuck, "ICANN and Attorneys General: Ends, Means and Unintended Ends," *CircleID*, April 27, 2020, https://circleid.com/posts/20200427-icann-attorney -generals-ends-means-and-unintended-ends.

24. Maarten Botterman, "ICANN Board Withholds Consent for a Change of Control of the Public Interest Registry (PIR)," ICANN, April 30, 2020, https://www.icann .org/en/blogs/details/icann-board-withholds-consent-for-a-change-of-control-of-the -public-interest-registry-pir-30-4-2020-en; board resolution, April 30, 2020, https:// www.icann.org/en/board-activities-and-meetings/materials/approved-resolutions -special-meeting-of-the-icann-board-30-04-2020-en.

25. "ICANN cannot avoid California law enforcement officials acting to make sure that ICANN is using its valuable registry agreements to further its mission, except by proactively and clearly staying true to that mission." Mitch Stolz, "Preserving ICANN's Independence through Bold Action," *CircleID*, April 29, 2020, https://circleid.com /posts/20200429-preserving-icanns-independence-through-bold-action-not-inaction.

26. "Temporary Specification for gTLD Registration Data," adopted by resolution of the ICANN Board of Directors May 17, 2018, https://www.icann.org/resources/pages /gtld-registration-data-specs-en.

27. The "Transparent, Open and Secure Internet Act of 2018," https://www .internetgovernance.org/wp-content/uploads/Draft-WHOIS-Legislation-as-of-Aug-16 -2018.pdf.

28. In an interview with the European Internet Forum, Goran Marby characterized Whois policy as "a balancing act between the right to privacy and the need for information" but went on to say, "I believe that the answer to that question belongs to the legislature, it belongs to the [European] parliament. ICANN as a technical organization has a problem coming up with that answer." Milton Mueller, "Europe Flip-Flops on Privacy," Internet Governance Project (blog), April 30, 2021, https:// www.internetgovernance.org/2021/04/30/europe-flip-flops-on-privacy-icann-ceo -abdicates.

29. Mueller, "Europe Flip-Flops."

CHAPTER 15

1. News Release, "NTIA Announces Intent to Transition Key Internet Domain Name Functions," US Department of Commerce, National Telecommunications and Information Administration, March 14, 2014.

2. Palladino and Santaniello, *Legitimacy, Power, and Inequalities*; Jeanette Hofmann, "Multi-stakeholderism in Internet Governance: Putting a Fiction into Practice," *Journal of Cyber Policy* 1, no. 1 (2016): 32; Rohan Grover, "The Geopolitics of Digital Rights Activism: Evaluating Civil Society's Role in the Promises of Multistakeholder Internet Governance," *Telecommunications Policy* 46, no. 10 (2022): 102437; Laura DeNardis and Mark Raymond, "Thinking Clearly About Multistakeholder Internet Governance" (paper presented at 8th National GigaNet: Global Internet Governance Academic Network, Annual Symposium, Bali, Indonesia, October 21, 2013); Roxana Radu, Nicolo Zingales, and Enrico Calandro, "Crowdsourcing Ideas as an Emerging

Form of Multistakeholder Participation in Internet Governance," *Policy & Internet* 7, no. 3 (2015): 362–382.

3. Hofmann, "Multi-stakeholderism," 32.

4. Laura DeNardis and Mark Raymond have even defined the concept in a way that suggests that the ITU and other intergovernmental organizations could be classified as multistakeholder. They call it an "institution, consisting of two or more classes of actors engaged in a common governance enterprise concerning issues they regard as public in nature, and characterized by polyarchic authority relations constituted by procedural rules" (DeNardis and Raymond, "Thinking Clearly," 2–3).

5. News Release, "NTIA Announces Intent to Transition Key Internet Domain Name Functions." One could claim that this was a unilaterally imposed constraint on the community by the US government, to be sure, but it was also politically necessary to get the transition get through Congress. In fact, it wasn't much of a constraint, because no organized constituency involved in the transition wanted to turn it all over to governments. A few governments did, of course, but they were outside of the ICANN regime. Even the GAC did not agitate for that.

6. Palladino and Santaniello, *Legitimacy, Power, and Inequalities*, 25.

7. A good overview of this literature can be found in Jayme Lemke and Vlad Tarko (eds.), *Elinor Ostrom and the Bloomington School: Building a New Approach to Policy and the Social Sciences* (Montreal: McGill-Queen's Press, 2021).

8. US fears of bogging down Internet development in intergovernmental politics made it act unilaterally, and quickly, to put the ICANN regime in place.

9. The Global Internet Forum for Counter Terrorism (GIFCT) and the Facebook Oversight Board are examples.

10. K. Grindal, M. Mueller, and V. Srivastava, "Non-governmental Governance of Trust on the Internet: WebPKI as Public Good," WEIS, 2024.

11. Report of the Working Group on Internet Governance, July 2005, http://www.wgig.org/docs/WGIGREPORT.pdf.

12. Report of the Working Group on Internet Governance, 4. Note how this matches Stephen D. Krasner's canonical definition of an international regime as "sets of implicit or explicit principles, norms, rules, and decision-making procedures around which actors' expectations converge in a given area of international relations" (Krasner, "Structural Causes and Regime Consequences").

13. Palladino and Santaniello, for example, wrote that the WGIG definition "represents the full acknowledgment by a broad and variegated Internet community, including governments and intergovernmental organizations, that the complexity of Internet governance does not allow the leadership of a single class of actors, but rather requires decentralized, bottom-up, inclusive policy development, and

decision-making processes with the collaboration of all affected parties." Palladino and Santaniello, *Legitimacy, Power, and Inequalities*, 4.

14. It is neither possible nor desirable for everyone in the world to have exactly equal levels of input and authority over what everyone else on the Internet does. There are also severe practical constraints on the ability of large-scale global publics to converge for deliberation—such as different languages and time zones.

15. Palladino and Santaniello's negative assessment of the transition, for example, is based entirely on showing that the participation of actors from North America and Europe was proportionally somewhat larger than participation from actors in the Global South. Ironically, their conclusion ignores empirical findings about the perceived legitimacy of ICANN based on surveys of people in the so-called Global South (*Legitimacy, Power, and Inequalities*). Jongen and Scholte found the highest legitimacy (confidence) from Asians and Africans relative to North Americans and whites, because those are the people who feel most empowered by the regime; see Hortense Jongen and Jan Aart Scholte, "Legitimacy in Multistakeholder Global Governance at ICANN," *Global Governance: A Review of Multilateralism and International Organizations* 27, no. 2 (2021): 298–324. Surprisingly, the same is true for governments. As noted in my own observations, GAC members often feel empowered by GAC and support the multistakeholder model.

16. Becker, e.g., views ICANN as an act of delegation by states rather than a surrender of power to the global Internet community. M. Becker, "When Public Principals Give Up Control over Private Agents: The New Independence of ICANN in Internet Governance," *Regulation & Governance* 13, no. 4 (2019): 561–576.

CHAPTER 16

1. Center for AI Safety, "Statement on AI Risk: AI Experts and Public Figures Express Their Concern about AI Risk," accessed June 28, 2024, https://www.safe.ai/statement -on-ai-risk#open-letter. See also Jonathan Grieg, "CISA Director: AI Cyber Threats the 'Biggest Issue We're Going to Deal with This Century,'" *The Record*, April 6, 2023, https://therecord.media/cisa-director-ai-cyber-threats-the-biggest-of-the-century.

2. The phrase is a reference is to Skocpol (1985) and was applied to Internet governance in Drezner (2004).

3. Creemers, "China's Conception of Cyber Sovereignty"; Ilona Stadnik, "Russia: An Independent and Sovereign Internet," in *Power and Authority in Internet Governance: Return of the State*, edited by Blayne Haggart, Natasha Tusikov, and Jan Aart Scholte (London: Routledge, 2021), 147–167; Luciano Floridi, "The Fight for Digital Sovereignty: What It Is, and Why It Matters, Especially for the EU," *Philosophy & Technology* 33 (2020): 369–378; Jyoti Panday, *India Stack: The Public-Private Roads to Digital Sovereignty* (Internet Governance Project, 2023), https://www.internetgovernance

.org/wp-content/uploads/India_stack_9_1_2023.pdf; Stockholm Center for Freedom, "Social Media Platforms Pose Threat to Turkey's Sovereignty: Ruling Party Spokesman," February 11, 2021. https://stockholmcf.org/social-media-platforms-pose-threat-to-turkeys-sovereignty-ruling-party-spokesman.

4. Girish Sastry, Lennart Heim, Hadyn Belfield, Markus Anderljung, Miles Brundage, Julian Hazell, et al. "Computing Power and the Governance of Artificial Intelligence." arXiv preprint, February 13, 2024. arXiv:2402.08797.

5. Karl Marx, *A Contribution to the Critique of Political Economy* (Moscow: Progress Publishers, 1977).

BIBLIOGRAPHY

Acemoglu, Daron, Simon Johnson, and James A. Robinson. "Institutions as a Fundamental Cause of Long-Run Growth." In *Handbook of Economic Growth*, vol. 1A, edited by Philippe Aghion and Steven N. Durlauf, 385–472. Amsterdam: Elsevier, 2005.

Appelman, Daniel. "Internet Governance and Human Rights: ICANN's Transition Away from United States Control." *The Clarion, a journal of the American Bar Association's International Human Rights Committee* 1, no. 1 (Spring–Summer 2016).

Becker, M. "When Public Principals Give Up Control over Private Agents: The New Independence of ICANN in Internet Governance." *Regulation & Governance* 13, no. 4 (2019): 561–576.

Bennett, Colin J. *The Privacy Advocates: Resisting the Spread of Surveillance*. Cambridge, MA: MIT Press, 2010.

Broeders, Dennis. *The Public Core of the Internet: An International Agenda for Internet Governance*. Amsterdam: Amsterdam University Press. 2016

Cannon, R. "The Legislative History of Senator Exon's Communications Decency Act: Regulating Barbarians on the Information Superhighway." *Federal Communications Law Journal* 49, no. 1 (1996): 51–94.

Carr, Madeline. "Power Plays in Global Internet Governance." *Millennium* 43, no. 2 (2015): 640–659.

Christou, George, and Seamus Simpson. "Gaining a Stake in Global Internet Governance: The EU, ICANN and Strategic Norm Manipulation." *European Journal of Communication* 22, no. 2 (2007): 147–164.

Coe, William Ramsey. "Burning the Global Village to Roast a Pig: The Communications Decency Act of 1996 Is Not 'Narrowly Tailored' in Reno v. ACLU." *Wake Forest Law Review*, 32 (1997): 1283–1325.

Cogburn, D. L., M. Mueller, L. McKnight, H. Klein, and J. Mathiason. "The US Role in Global Internet Governance." *IEEE Communications Magazine* 43, no. 12 (2005): 12–14.

Crawford, S. P. "The ICANN Experiment." *Cardozo Journal of International & Comparative Law* 12 (2004): 409–448.

Creemers, Roger. "China's Conception of Cyber Sovereignty." In *Governing Cyberspace: Behavior, Power, and Diplomacy*, edited by Dennis Broeders and Bibi van den Berg, 107–145. Lanham, MD: Rowman & Littlefield, 2020.

Daigle, Leslie. "Internet Invariants." Policy Brief. Internet Society, September 26, 2016. https://www.internetsociety.org/policybriefs/internetinvariants.

Dany, Charlotte. *Global Governance and NGO Participation: Shaping the Information Society in the United Nations*. London: Routledge, 2012.

DelBianco, Steven, and Braden Cox. "ICANN Internet Governance: Is It Working?" *Pacific McGeorge Global Business & Development Law Journal* 21, no. 1 (2008). https://scholarlycommons.pacific.edu/globe/vol21/iss1/3.

DeNardis, Laura, and Mark Raymond. "Thinking Clearly About Multistakeholder Internet Governance." Paper presented at 8th National GigaNet: Global Internet Governance Academic Network, Annual Symposium, Bali, Indonesia, October 21, 2013.

Drezner, Daniel. "The Global Governance of the Internet: Bringing the State Back In." *Political Science Quarterly* 119 (2004): 477.

Farrell, Henry, and Abraham Newman. *Underground Empire: How America Weaponized the World Economy*. New York: Henry Holt and Company, 2023.

Fidler, Bradley, and Russ Mundy. *The Creation and Administration of Unique Identifiers, 1967–2017*. Los Angeles: ICANN, 2020. https://www.icann.org/en/system/files/files/creation-administration-unique-identifiers-1967-2017-18nov20-en.pdf.

Flonk, Daniëlle, Markus Jachtenfuchs, and Anke S. Obendiek. "Authority Conflicts in Internet Governance: Liberals vs. Sovereigntists?" *Global Constitutionalism* 9, no. 2 (2020): 364–386.

Floridi, Luciano. "The Fight for Digital Sovereignty: What It Is, and Why It Matters, Especially for the EU." *Philosophy & Technology* 33 (2020): 369–378.

Froomkin, A. Michael. "Almost Free: An Analysis of ICANN's 'Affirmation of Commitments.'" *Journal of Telecommunications and High Technology Law* 9 (2011).

———. "Metaphor Is the Key: Cryptography, the Clipper Chip, and the Constitution." *University of Pennsylvania Law Review* 143 (1994).

———. "Wrong Turn in Cyberspace: Using ICANN to Route around the APA and the Constitution." *Duke Law Journal* 50 (2000): 17.

———. "ICANN 2.0: Meet the New Boss." *Loyola of Los Angeles Law Review* 36 (2002): 1087.

Galloway, Tristan, and He Baogang. "China and Technical Global Internet Governance: Beijing's Approach to Multi-Stakeholder Governance within ICANN, WSIS and the IGF." *China: An International Journal* 12, no. 3 (2014): 72–93.

Glen, Carol M. "Internet Governance: Territorializing Cyberspace?" *Politics & Policy* 42, no. 5 (2014): 635–657.

Gore, Al. "Information Superhighways: The Next Information Revolution." *The Futurist* 25, no. 1 (1991).

Grimm, Dieter. *Sovereignty: The Origin and Future of a Political and Legal Concept.* New York: Columbia University Press, 2015.

Grindal, Karl, Milton Mueller, and Vagisha Srivastava. "Non-governmental Governance of Trust on the Internet: WebPKI as Public Good." Workshop on the Economics of Information Security, 2024.

Grover, Rohan. "The Geopolitics of Digital Rights Activism: Evaluating Civil Society's Role in the Promises of Multistakeholder Internet Governance." *Telecommunications Policy* 46, no. 10 (2022): 102437.

Haggart, Blayne, Natasha Tusikov, and Jan Aart Scholte, eds. *Power and Authority in Internet Governance: Return of the State?* London: Routledge, 2021.

Grabowski, Mark. "Should the U.S. Reclaim Control of the Internet? Evaluating ICANN's Administrative Oversight Since the 2016 Handover." *Nebraska Law Review Bulletin*, August 6, 2018. https://lawreview.unl.edu/Should-the-U.S.-Reclaim-Control-of-the-Internet%3F.

Hardy, Trotter. "The Proper Legal Regime for Cyberspace." *University of Pittsburgh Law Review* 55 (1993).

Hare, Forrest. "Borders in Cyberspace: Can Sovereignty Adapt to the Challenges of Cyber Security?" In *The Virtual Battlefield: Perspectives on Cyber Warfare*, edited by Christian Czosseck and Kenneth Geers, 88–105. Clifton, VA: IOS Press, 2009.

Hill, Richard. *The New International Telecommunications Regulations and the Internet.* Zurich: Springer, 2013.

Hofmann, Jeanette. "Multi-stakeholderism in Internet Governance: Putting a Fiction into Practice." *Journal of Cyber Policy* 1, no. 1 (2016): 29–49.

Hong, Yu, and G. Thomas Goodnight. "How to Think About Cyber Sovereignty: The Case of China." In *China's Globalizing Internet: History, Power, and Governance*, edited by Yu Hong and Eric Harwit, 7–25. London: Routledge, 2022.

Huston, Geoff. "Opinion: ICANN, the ITU, WSIS, and Internet Governance." *The Internet Protocol Journal* 8, no. 1 (2005): 15–28.

Jackson, Robert. "Sovereignty in World Politics: A Glance at the Conceptual and Historical Landscape." *Political Studies* 47, no. 3 (1999): 431–456.

Johnson, Bobbie. *Case Study: Private Platforms.* Stanford, CA: Stanford University Ethics, Technology and Public Policy, 2018. http://ai.stanford.edu/users/sahami/ethicscasestudies/Platforms.pdf.

Johnson, David R., and David Post. "Law and Borders: The Rise of Law in Cyberspace." *Stanford Law Review* 48, no. 5 (1996): 1367–1402.

Jongen, Hortense, and Jan Aart Scholte. "Legitimacy in Multistakeholder Global Governance at ICANN." *Global Governance: A Review of Multilateralism and International Organizations* 27, no. 2 (2021): 298–324.

Klein, Hans. "ICANN and Internet Governance: Leveraging Technical Coordination to Realize Global Public Policy." *The Information Society* 18, no. 3 (2002): 193–207.

———. "Understanding WSIS: An Institutional Analysis of the UN World Summit on the Information Society." *Information Technologies & International Development* 1, no. 3 (2004).

Kleinwächter, Wolfgang. *A New Diplomacy for the 21st Century? Multi-Stakeholder Approach and Bottom-Up Policy Development in the Information Society.* Geneva: United Nations ICT Task Force, 2005.

Knake, Robert. *Internet Governance in an Age of Cyber Insecurity.* Council Special Report #56. New York: Council on Foreign Relations, 2010. https://cdn.cfr.org/sites/default/files/pdf/2010/08/Cybersecurity_CSR56.pdf.

Knight, Jack. *Institutions and Social Conflict.* Cambridge: Cambridge University Press, 1992.

Kolkman, O. "Framework for Describing the IANA." March 2014. https://datatracker.ietf.org/doc/html/draft-iab-iana-framework-02.

Kovacs, Anja, Grace Githaiga, and Joana Varon. *NETmundial: Reflections from Brazil, India and Kenya.* London: Global Partners Digital, 2014. https://www.gp-digital.org/wp-content/uploads/2014/12/Netmundial-Reflections-from-Brazil-India-and-Kenya.pdf.

Krasner, Stephen D. *Sovereignty: Organized Hypocrisy.* Princeton, NJ: Princeton University Press, 1999.

———. "Structural Causes and Regime Consequences: Regimes as Intervening Variables." *International Organization* 36, no. 2 (1982): 185–205.

Kruger, Lennard G. *The Future of Internet Governance: Should the United States Relinquish Its Authority Over ICANN?* Congressional Research Service, September 2016. https://crsreports.congress.gov/product/pdf/R/R44022/24.

Leib, Volker. "ICANN—EU Can't: Internet Governance and Europe's Role in the Formation of the Internet Corporation for Assigned Names and Numbers (ICANN)." *Telematics and Informatics* 19, no. 2 (2002): 159–171.

Lemke, Jayme, and Vlad Tarko, eds. *Elinor Ostrom and the Bloomington School: Building a New Approach to Policy and the Social Sciences.* Montreal: McGill-Queen's Press, 2021.

Litman, Jessica. "The Exclusive Right to Read." *Cardozo Arts & Entertainment Law Journal* 13, no. 1 (1994): 29–54.

Magaziner, Ira C., Ann Grier Cutter, and Len A. Costa. "The Framework for Global Electronic Commerce: A Policy Perspective." *Journal of International Affairs* 51, no. 2 (1998): 527–538.

Mahler, Tobias. *Generic Top-Level Domains: A Study of Transnational Private Regulation.* Cheltenham: Edward Elgar Publishing, 2019.

Malcolm, Jeremy. *Multistakeholder Governance and the Internet Governance Forum.* Perth: Terminus Press, 2008.

Marx, Karl. *A Contribution to the Critique of Political Economy*. Moscow: Progress Publishers, 1977.

Maurer, Tim, and Robert Morgus. *Tipping the Scale: An Analysis of Global Swing States in the Internet Governance Debate*. Centre for International Governance Innovation, Internet Governance Paper No. 7 (May 2014). https://www.cigionline.org/static /documents/gcig_paper_no2.pdf.

Mayer-Schönberger, Viktor, and Malte Ziewitz. "Jefferson Rebuffed: The United States and the Future of Internet Governance." *Columbia Science & Technology Law Review* 8 (2007): 188–228.

McGillivray, Kevin. "Give It Away Now? Renewal of the IANA Functions Contract and Its Role in Internet Governance." *International Journal of Law and Information Technology* 22, no. 1 (2014): 3–26.

Mueller, Milton L. "Against Sovereignty in Cyberspace." *International Studies Review* 22, no. 4 (2020): 779–801.

———. "ICANN Inc.: Accountability and Participation in the Governance of Critical Internet Resources." *Korean Journal of Policy Studies* 24, no. 2 (2009): 91–116.

———. *Networks and States: The Global Politics of Internet Governance*. Cambridge, MA: MIT Press, 2010.

———. *Ruling the Root: Internet Governance and the Taming of Cyberspace*. Cambridge, MA: MIT Press, 2002.

———. *Will the Internet Fragment? Sovereignty, Globalization and Cyberspace*. New York: John Wiley & Sons, 2017.

Mueller, Milton L., and Mawaki Chango. "Disrupting Global Governance: The Internet Whois Service, ICANN, and Privacy." *Journal of Information Technology & Politics* 5, no. 3 (2008): 303–332.

Mueller, Milton L., and Ben Wagner. "Finding a Formula for Brazil: Representation and Legitimacy in Internet Governance." *Internet Policy Observatory* 8 (2014).

Negro, Gianluigi. "A History of Chinese Global Internet Governance and Its Relations with ITU and ICANN." *Chinese Journal of Communication* 13, no. 1 (2020): 104–121.

Nocetti, Julien. "Contest and Conquest: Russia and Global Internet Governance." *International Affairs* 91, no. 1 (2015): 111–130.

North, Douglass. "Institutions." *Journal of Economic Perspectives* 5, no. 1 (1991): 97–112.

Orlova, Alexandra V. "'Digital Sovereignty,' Anonymity and Freedom of Expression: Russia's Fight to Re-Shape Internet Governance." *UC Davis Journal of International Law & Policy* 26, no. 2 (2019): 225–247.

Palfrey, John G. "The End of the Experiment: How ICANN's Foray into Global Internet Democracy Failed." *Harvard Journal of Law & Technology* 17, no. 2 (2004): 409–473.

Palladino, Nicola, and Mauro Santaniello. *Legitimacy, Power, and Inequalities in the Multistakeholder Internet Governance: Analyzing IANA Transition*. Cham, Switzerland: Springer Nature, 2020.

Patrikis, Ernest T., and Stephanie Heller. "The Government's Role in Electronic Commerce." *Annual Review of Banking Law* 18 (1999): 325.

Pednekar-Magal, Vanda, and Peter Shields. "The State and Telecom Surveillance Policy: The Clipper Chip Initiative." *Communication Law and Policy* 8, no. 4 (2003): 429–464.

Perrin, Stephanie. "The Struggle for WHOIS Privacy: Understanding the Standoff Between ICANN and the World's Data Protection Authorities." PhD thesis, University of Toronto Faculty of Information, 2018.

Petillion, Flip, and Jan Janssen. *Competing for the Internet: ICANN Gate–An Analysis and Plea for Judicial Review through Arbitration*. Alphen aan den Rijn, Netherlands: Kluwer Law International BV, 2017.

Post, David G., and Danielle Kehl. "Controlling Internet Infrastructure Part 1: The 'IANA Transition' and Why It Matters for the Future of the Internet." July 27, 2015. https://ssrn.com/abstract=2636417.

———. "Controlling Internet Infrastructure: The 'IANA Transition' and ICANN Accountability, Part II." September 16, 2015. https://ssrn.com/abstract=2671343.

Radu, Roxana. *Negotiating Internet Governance*. Oxford: Oxford University Press, 2019.

Radu, Roxana, and Giovanni De Gregorio. "The New Era of Internet Governance: Technical Fragmentation and Digital Sovereignty Entanglements." In *Hybridity, Conflict, and the Global Politics of Cybersecurity*, edited by Fabio Cristiano and Bibi van den Berg. Lanham, MD: Rowman & Littlefield Publishers, 2023.

Radu, Roxana, Nicolo Zingales, and Enrico Calandro. "Crowdsourcing Ideas as an Emerging Form of Multistakeholder Participation in Internet Governance." *Policy & Internet* 7, no. 3 (2015): 362–382.

Samuelson, Pamela. "The NII Intellectual Property Report." *Communications of the ACM* 37, no. 12 (1994): 21–28.

Sastry, Girish, Lennart Heim, Hadyn Belfield, Markus Anderljung, Miles Brundage, Julian Hazell, et al. "Computing Power and the Governance of Artificial Intelligence." arXiv preprint, February 13, 2024. https://arxiv.org/abs/2402.08797.

Schmitt, Michael N., ed. *Tallinn Manual on the International Law Applicable to Cyber Warfare*. Cambridge: Cambridge University Press, 2013.

Skocpol, Theda. "Bringing the State Back In: Strategies of Analysis in Current Research." In *Bringing the State Back In*, edited by Peter B. Evans, Dietrich Rueschemeyer, and Theda Skocpol, 3–38. Cambridge: Cambridge University Press, 1985.

Schünemann, Wolf J., and Marianne Kneuer. "Do Not Disturb! Studying Discourses of Democratic Sovereignty as Potential Drivers of Internet Fragmentation through Online Control." Presented at ISA Annual Convention, April 6–9, 2021.

Smith, Anthony D. *Nationalism: Theory, Ideology, History*. Hoboken, NJ: John Wiley & Sons, 2013.

Stadnik, Ilona. "Russia: An Independent and Sovereign Internet." In *Power and Authority in Internet Governance: Return of the State*, edited by Blayne Haggart, Natasha Tusikov, and Jan Aart Scholte, 147–167. London: Routledge, 2021.

———. "Sovereign RUnet: What Does It Mean?" *Internet Governance Project*, February 12, 2019. https://www.internetgovernance.org/research/sovereign-runet-what-does -it-mean.

Targowsky, Andrew. *Global Information Infrastructure: The Birth, Vision and Architecture*. Hershey, PA: Idea Group Publishing, 1996.

Thomson, Janice E. "State Sovereignty in International Relations: Bridging the Gap Between Theory and Empirical Research." *International Studies Quarterly* 39, no. 2 (1995): 213–233.

US Intellectual Property Enforcement Coordinator. *2013 Joint Strategic Plan on Intellectual Property Enforcement*. Washington, DC: Executive Office of the President, 2013. https://obamawhitehouse.archives.gov/sites/default/files/omb/IPEC/2013-us -ipec-joint-strategic-plan.pdf.

US National Telecommunications and Information Administration (NTIA). "Statement of Policy on the Management of Internet Names and Addresses." US Department of Commerce, June 5, 1998. http://www.ntia.doc.gov/federal-register-notice /1998/statement-policy-management-internet-names-and-addresses.

von Heinegg, Wolff H. "Legal Implications of Territorial Sovereignty in Cyberspace." In *2012 4th International Conference on Cyber Conflict (CYCON 2012)*, edited by C. Czosseck, R. Ottis, and K. Ziolkowski, 7–19. Talinn: NATO CCD COE Publications, 2012.

Wang, Anqi. "Cyber Sovereignty at Its Boldest: A Chinese Perspective." *Ohio State Technology Law Journal* 16, no. 2 (2020): 395–466.

Weber, Rolf H., and R. Shawn Gunnarson "A Constitutional Solution for Internet Governance." *Columbia Science & Technology Review* 14 (2012).

Weinberg, Jonathan. "Governments, Privatization, and Privatization: ICANN and the GAC." *Michigan Telecommunication & Technology Law Review* 18, no. 1 (2011): 189. https://repository.law.umich.edu/mttlr/vol18/iss1/5.

———. "ICANN and the Problem of Legitimacy." *Duke Law Journal* 50, no. 1 (2000): 187–260.

Werle, Raymund, and Volker Leib. "The Internet Society and Its Struggle for Recognition and Influence." In *Private Organizations in Global Politics*, edited by Karsten Ronit and Volker Schneider, 102–123. London: Routledge, 2013.

Wriston, Walter B. *The Twilight of Sovereignty: How the Information Revolution Is Transforming Our World*. New York: Scribner, 1992.

Yen, Alfred C. "Internet Service Provider Liability for Subscriber Copyright Infringement, Enterprise Liability, and the First Amendment." *Georgetown Law Journal* 88, no. 6 (1999): 1833.

INDEX

Information Policy Series

Edited by Sandra Braman